FABLES OF THE EAST

FABLES OF THE EAST

Selected Tales
1662–1785

Edited by
Ros Ballaster

OXFORD
UNIVERSITY PRESS

OXFORD

UNIVERSITY PRESS

Great Clarendon Street, Oxford OX2 6DP

Oxford University Press is a department of the University of Oxford.
It furthers the University's objective of excellence in research, scholarship,
and education by publishing worldwide in

Oxford New York

Auckland Cape Town Dar es Salaam Hong Kong Karachi
Kuala Lumpur Madrid Melbourne Mexico City Nairobi
New Delhi Shanghai Taipei Toronto

With offices in

Argentina Austria Brazil Chile Czech Republic France Greece
Guatemala Hungary Italy Japan Poland Portugal Singapore
South Korea Switzerland Thailand Turkey Ukraine Vietnam

Oxford is a registered trade mark of Oxford University Press
in the UK and in certain other countries

Published in the United States
by Oxford University Press Inc., New York

© Ros Ballaster 2005

The moral rights of the author have been asserted
Database right Oxford University Press (maker)

First published 2005

British Library Cataloguing in Publication Data

Data available

Library of Congress Cataloging in Publication Data

Fables of the East : selected tales, 1662–1785 / edited by Ros Ballaster.
p. cm.
Includes bibliographical references.
ISBN 0-19-926734-0 (acid-free paper) — ISBN 0-19-926735-9 (pbk. : acid-free paper)
1. Fables, Oriental. 2. Fables. I. Ballaster, Rosalind.
PN981.F33 2005   398.2'095—dc22   2005020146

Typeset by Newgen Imaging Systems (P) Ltd., Chennai, India
Printed in Great Britain
on acid-free paper by
Biddles Ltd., King's Lynn, Norfolk

ISBN 0-19-926734-0 (Hbk.)   978-0-19-926734-7 (Hbk.)
ISBN 0-19-926735-9 (Pbk.)   978-0-19-926735-4 (Pbk.)

1 3 5 7 9 10 8 6 4 2

Contents

v

Contents

TEXTUAL NOTE

Copy-texts are from first editions where possible. Otherwise, I have used later editions as close as possible to the first. Each text is prefaced by an introduction giving the author, date of first publication, and edition used, with relevant context, information about the text and its author and/or translator, and explanation of its significance. The editor's notes concentrate on explaining references to contemporary history and intertextual connections with other writings about oriental cultures.

All texts have been corrected to use speech marks (where often there are none in the original). I have not modernized spelling and punctuation except where it is needed for sense, and usually on the authority of a later edition. Otherwise, I have made no substantive changes to the original texts and hence individual emendations have not been recorded.

Since the critical work that accompanies this anthology, *Fabulous Orients: Fictions of the East in England 1662–1785* (Oxford: Oxford University Press, 2005), provides a full bibliography, I have simply given full references to all works cited in introductions or footnotes. Readers should consult the glossary at the back which offers explanations of oriental terms, general and geographical.

INTRODUCTION

The trope of the Orient in eighteenth-century England is 'backwardness'. To travel to oriental territories, to consume oriental narrative, is to travel 'backward' in time (to retrace ancient history), in space (from the 'new' to the 'old' world), and in identity (from contract and civility to despotism). Accordingly, the kind of story associated with the Orient is the most elementary and ancient form: the fable. Thus, James Beattie commences his 1780 essay, 'On Fable and Romance', with 'General remarks on Ancient and Oriental Prose Fable' as though the two terms were equivalent:

> it may be proper to observe, that the Oriental nations have long been famous for fabulous narrative. The indolence peculiar to the genial climates of Asia, and the luxurious life which the kings and other great men, of those countries, lead in their seraglios, have made them seek for this sort of amusement, and set a high value upon it. When an Eastern prince happens to be idle, as he commonly is, and at a loss for expedients to kill the time, he commands his Grand Visir, or his favourite, to tell him stories. Being ignorant, and consequently credulous; having no passion for moral improvement, and little knowlege of nature; he does not desire, that they should be probable, or of an instructive tendency: it is enough if they be astonishing. And hence it is, no doubt, that those oriental tales are so extravagant. Every thing is carried on by inchantment and prodigy; by fairies, genii, and demons, and wooden horses, which, on turning a peg, fly through the air with inconceivable swiftness.[1]

Beattie goes on to identify Antoine Galland's early eighteenth-century 'translation', known in England as *The Arabian Nights Entertainments*, as the most familiar example of oriental fable, and defends it, despite its incredibility, on the grounds that 'It conveys a pretty

---

[1] James Beattie, 'On Fable and Romance', in *Dissertations, Moral and Critical*, in *The Works of James Beattie*, ed. Roger J. Robinson (London: Routledge/Thoemmes, 1996), 505-74, 508-9.

just idea of the government, and of some of the customs, of those eastern nations' and in the story of 'a barber and his six brothers' there are 'many good strokes of satire and comick description' (510). A paradox emerges. Oriental fable is both ancient and contemporary, both then and now, both there and here, both fantastical and a faithful representation.

And oriental fable is both a fable and not a fable. Samuel Johnson in his 1755 *Dictionary* gives as his first definition of the term that it is 'a feigned story intended to enforce some moral precept'.[2] Yet, Beattie claims that the eastern prince seeks pure entertainment without moral precept. His interest is in the feigning not the moral. And so too, the western reader seeks in his or her reading of the same tales not morality but an acquaintance with the 'real' nature of eastern government and customs or the pleasure of comedy. To complicate the picture even more, Beattie acknowledges that 'whether the tales [of *The Arabian Nights Entertainments*] be really Arabick, or invented by Mons. Galland, I have never been able to learn with certainty' (509). So, western readers' acquaintance with an authentic East may itself be a fable, a feigned story designed by a Frenchman to convey, as Beattie puts it, 'the fashionable forms of Parisian civility' (510).

Fables transport their consumers into other places, other times, other bodies, other species, in order to instruct those consumers about where they are, who they are, and what they are. This anthology explores the different fabulous means by which western writers deployed the Orient for just these 'instructive' ends. It does so following Edward Said's injunction that we recognize that Orientalism has more to do with the Occident than with the Orient; these tales are part of a wider cultural project which creates the object it feigns identifying. Put simply, the Orient is only located geographically as east *of* the West. As Said explains, Orientalism 'not only creates but also maintains; it *is*, rather than expresses, a certain *will* or *intention* to understand, in some cases to control, manipulate, even to incorporate, what is a manifestly different (or alternative and novel) world'.[3]

---

[2] Samuel Johnson, *A Dictionary of the English Language on Cd-Rom the First and Fourth Editions*, ed. Anne McDermott (Cambridge and New York: Cambridge University Press, 1996).

[3] Edward Said, *Orientalism* (London: Routledge & Kegan Paul, 1978), 12.

Introduction

This said, however, Orientalism is not a fixed and unchanging method of creating or maintaining a bifurcated world picture. As John MacKenzie asserts, 'the "oriental obsession" is a continuing and constantly changing phenomenon, repeatedly adapted to the needs of the age and the yearning for innovation'.[4] This anthology addresses a period that has hitherto received little attention from historians of Orientalism, the period after the medieval and early modern conflicts between Islam and Christianity, scholarly exchange (European Renaissance humanist rediscovery of the classics had recourse to Arabic translations from Greek and Roman sources) and trading ventures (the Levant trading company was founded in 1578, the English East India Company in 1600), but before the rise of western imperial power in eastern regions, especially British rule in India. Edward Said sees the Napoleonic invasion of Egypt in 1798 as the 'keynote' of the Orientalist relationship between the Near East and Europe upon which he concentrates.

This anthology and the critical text it accompanies, *Fabulous Orients: Fictions of the East in England 1662–1785* (Oxford: Oxford University Press, 2005), address the period that falls between two significant dates in the history of the British acquisition of its first, most extensive, and most profitable eastern outpost of empire, that of India. In 1662, as part of his marriage settlement with the Portuguese Catherine of Braganza, Charles II acquired Bombay. In 1785, Warren Hastings retired from his position as the first governor-general of India; the appointment of Cornwallis in his place saw a far more predatory and less hybrid form of government in relation to indigenous historical institutions. But the year previously, on 15 January 1784, Hastings's intellectual ally, William Jones, had founded the Asiatick Society of Bengal, which was to continue the work of producing a more rigorous and academic relationship with oriental languages, religions, and history than the previous century had seen. Contact with the great eastern empires (with the exception of China which, after the failure of Lord George Macartney's 1793–4 embassy, becomes marginal to knowledge of the 'East' in Britain) is both wider

---

[4] John MacKenzie, *Orientalism: History, Theory and the Arts* (Manchester: Manchester University Press, 1995), 210.

Introduction

and deeper than hitherto, but also has much more explicit political aims and interests. The piecemeal, sometimes random, contact of the eighteenth century now acquires shape and direction. Enlightenment preoccupations with analogy, shared history, and sameness of self and culture, give way to an increasingly racialized sense of difference. Fictional representations of the East contribute to this shift in attitude with a turn, in the last two decades of the century, to the erotic and exotic fragment and oriental allegory, in place of the popular 'translation' of the sequence of oriental tales and the embedded moral fable of which this anthology provides a number of examples.

I have designed the anthology as a companion volume to the critical text although each can be read independently of the other. Despite its enormous popularity in the eighteenth century, little of the material discussed in *Fabulous Orients* has been reprinted since then. I make few claims for the aesthetic merit of these works, although some (such as the materials by Walpole, Montesquieu, and Wortley Montagu) do have a genuine, if often eccentric, rhetorical charm. Rather, the claims made here are for their cultural significance and especially their unacknowledged contribution to the advancement of prose fiction as the dominant literary mode of the modern period in western parts of the globe. Margaret Anne Doody chastises an ethnocentric tradition dating back (at least) to Ian Watt's 1957 *Rise of the Novel*, which takes a parochial view of the novel as a form that emerges from Protestant and emergent capitalist ideologies in England. She reminds us that 'The history of the Novel is never pure. The stories told by the Novel are not "pure". They are stories of mixture and variety, of boundary-crossing and changing. The Novel itself is not "pure" and never pretends to be.'[5] Doody's work redresses the balance by exploring the literary connection between classical and modern prose fiction; my own turns to the importance of a construct or legacy, if a fabulous one, of oriental fable in the formation of an idea of the novelistic.

One powerful connection between fable and novel is that both are presented as means of giving voice to the powerless. Fables are a form of subaltern discourse, a means of seizing verbal authority. They seek

---

[5] Margaret Anne Doody, *The True Story of the Novel* (London: HarperCollins, 1997), 485.

to teach their addressee (the eastern prince) without his conscious recognition that a didactic act is taking place. They seize control by seizing the imagination. The feigned tale is ostentatiously outlandish, peopled with talking animals, with fairies and djinns, figures who can simultaneously voice challenging or corrective positions and shield their teller from the accusation of subversive intent. Yet, while fables apparently promote action in their design to alter the course of an addressee's (despotic) behaviour, they also draw that addressee into a pleasurable state of inaction, an immersion in story which delays or defers tyrannous action. An anthology such as this cannot do justice to the experience of immersion in a sequence of stories that was clearly so valuable to eighteenth-century readers. Robert Mack's edition of the 'Grub Street' translation of *The Arabian Nights Entertainments* comes close to allowing the interested reader to participate in that experience.[6] But, the compensation in this anthology lies in its ability to provide a sense of the diversity of genre and style within the general designation of the 'oriental tale'. I have included travellers' tales, and real as well as fictional letters, to provide evidence that no encounter with the East is ever 'pure' or free of a network of stories about and from the Orient. Travellers went to eastern territories with stories in their heads and measured what they met there quite self-consciously against those stories. And they rarely found them wanting. Thus, Lady Mary Wortley Montagu can inform her sister in a letter from Istanbul of 10 March 1718 that *The Arabian Nights Entertainments* 'were writ by an Author of this Country and (excepting the Enchantments) are a real representation of the manners here'.[7]

The teller of the oriental fable is seeking to establish narrative credit with a powerful auditor. And this credit is not a matter of profit, but rather survival. The two founding and most familiar voices of the oriental tale-teller in the eighteenth century are those of Scheherazade, the newly married vizier's daughter who tells her sultan husband the *Arabian Nights Entertainments* (1704–17), and Mahmut, the fictional Arabian spy who delivers the six hundred letters *Letters Writ by a*

---

[6] *Arabian Nights Entertainments*, ed. Robert Mack, World's Classics (Oxford: Oxford University Press, 1995).

[7] Lady Mary Wortley Montagu, *The Complete Letters of Lady Mary Wortley Montagu*, ed. Robert Halsband (Oxford: Clarendon Press, 1965), i. 385.

Introduction

Turkish Spy (1687–94). The former text went into nineteen editions by 1798 and the latter into fifteen editions by 1801. The harem woman and the male spy each attempt to build narrative credit with a master or masters to secure their continuing existence. Scheherazade tells her tales before dawn each morning to engage her husband's continuing interest so that he will defer the death-sentence he has vowed to perform each morning after a new wedding night. The paranoid Mahmut, living in disguise as a Moldavian translator in Paris between the years 1637 and 1682, is gathering information about European courts, which he reports back to a number of correspondents at the Ottoman Porte, aware that his survival depends on the quality of that information. He makes explicit parallels between his position and that of the veiled harem woman. To his brother Pestelihali, he writes 'Thou art he, to whom I can unmask. With others I converse (like our Women in *Turkey*) under a Veil.'[8] Mahmut and Scheherazade are engaged in a shared and contradictory enterprise. They rely on their convincing powers of dissimulation (Scheherazade as spinner of tales, Mahmut as master of disguise in Paris) in order to secure their credit with figures of authority who suspect that they may not be loyal (Schahriar's conviction of all women's unchastity, the reports Mahmut receives from the Porte that his integrity is being maligned). They are not only, then, tellers of fables, but figures of fable itself, the strategic invention as a means to a virtuous end.

The fable was not only associated with the Orient because it was identified as a regressive or 'backward' form, but also because the notions of 'imposture' and 'mimicry' had long been attached to oriental persons and cultures. Commentators describe China's superior technology in the creation of 'luxury' goods—porcelain and lacquer—as indicators of a capacity for imitation without inventive originality. European accounts of the life of Muhammad cast him repeatedly as an 'impostor' who passes off a fiction as truth on an oppressed people hungry for leadership. The Qur'an itself is introduced by Alexander Ross in his translation from the French of André de Ryer thus: '*Good Reader, the great* Arabian *Impostor now at last after a thousand years,*

---

[8] Giovanni Paolo Marana, *The Eight Volumes of Letters Writ by a Turkish Spy at Paris*, trans. William Bradshaw, 8 vols. (London, 1707), v, bk. 1, p. 25, Letter 7.

Introduction

is by way of France *arrived in* England, *& his* Alcoran, *or gallimaufry of Errors, (a Brat as deformed as the Parent, and as full of heresies, as his scald head was of scurffe) hath learned to speak* English.'[9] The irony for modern readers lies in our recognition that the key texts which claim to 'voice' the Orient of the period are themselves convincing impostures, the *Letters Writ by a Turkish Spy* the invention of a Francophile Genoese journalist, Giovanni Paolo Marana, and *The Arabian Nights Entertainments* compiled from disparate Arabic sources and radically transformed by the pen of a French scholar and court hanger-on, Antoine Galland. Their dominance as models of oriental narration should also remind us that the English encounter with the East is, until their defeat of the French in the Seven Years War in 1763 and seizure of power in Bengal under Robert Clive, largely mediated through France. Many of the fabulous tales and travellers' accounts that appear in this anthology are translations from the French and this is both representative of the importance of French missionaries (especially Jesuit), scholars (such as Antoine Galland), traders, and professionals (such as the doctor François Bernier) in providing information about the great empires of the East in the eighteenth century *and* a complicating factor in evaluating the British understanding and reception of those territories. Critiques of oriental despotism, absolutism, and religious bigotry in English writings and translations are frequently means of addressing the perceived threat of French absolutism and Catholicism. One Protestant English translator of the French Jesuit account of China by Jean-Baptiste Du Halde seized the opportunity in translating Du Halde's description of Buddhism and Taoism as 'a Heap of Fables and Superstitions' to provide a footnoted commentary criticizing the author for failing to see the parallels with his own Catholicism.[10] Particularly popular in translation were those Anglophile French *philosophes* such as Voltaire and Montesquieu, who used oriental examples, history, and cultures

---

[9] André Du Ryer, *The Alcoran of Mahomet, Translated out of Arabique into French; by the Sieur Du Ryer, Lord of Malezair, and Resident for the King of France, at Alexandria. And Newly Englished, for the Satisfaction of All That Desire to Look into the Turkish Vanities*, trans. Alexander Ross (London, 1649), n.p.

[10] Jean-Baptiste Du Halde, *A Description of the Empire of China and Chinese Tartary, Together with the Kingdoms of Korea, and Tibet*, trans. Emanuel Bowen (London, 1738, 1741), i. 639.

7

Introduction

as a means of promoting deist or atheist and rationalist principles in France.[11] So, too, the letter from the Whig Protestant Lady Mary Wortley Montagu included in this anthology tells the story of a Catholic Spanish lady choosing marriage with her Turkish rapist/ abductor over confinement to a monastery if she return to her family once her ransom is paid.

It would be too simplistic to read all oriental materials as fabulous means of interrogating and criticizing the twin threats to a reformed Britain of Catholicism and European absolutism. As the century progresses, especially, we can discern a genuine enthusiasm and interest in the theologies, practices, social relations, and customs of Persia, China, Ottoman territories, Mughal and Hindu India. But eighteenth-century authors saw no incompatibility between this and the partisan use of analogy or allegory. As in the form of the fable itself the twin purposes of outlining abstract principle and making a political intervention can be served simultaneously rather than one cancelling the other out.

This anthology is organized according to genre in order to illustrate the diverse shapes the oriental tale adopted in the period. However, a further aim is to call attention to the diversity in the ways that different oriental cultures are represented to English readers. Readers of this anthology will be able to identify a contrast between the luxury, excess, and sexuality associated with Islamic Turkey and Persia and Mughal India and the wisdom, restraint, and authority invested in Brahman India and Confucian China.

By far the longest section provides extracts from texts that are described as framed sequences of tales. We open with the most famous example, the frame tales of the *Arabian Nights Entertainments*. For the first time since their original appearance, the frame provided by the translator—Galland's prefatory material—is made available here. This gives a sense of how Galland's text was promoted to a reading public. Dedicated to the daughter of an ambassador with

---

[11] Charles de Secondat Montesquieu, *Persian Letters*, trans. John Ozell (London, 1722) and *The Spirit of Laws*, trans. T. Nugent (London, 1750). François Marie Arouet de Voltaire, *Mahomet the Imposter*, trans. and adapted James Miller and James Hoadly (London, 1744), *The Orphan of China* (London, 1756), and *An essay on universal history: the manners, and spirit of nations, from the reign of Charlemaign to the age of Lewis XIV*, trans. J. Nugent, 4 vols. (Dublin, 1759).

Introduction

whom Galland had served in Istanbul in the early 1680s, the *Arabian Nights Entertainments* is presented as a text under female patronage. Like the teller of the tales, Scheherazade, Galland's dedicatee is established as a mark of learning and culture which can moderate and mediate the power of aristocratic men.

But, Galland's text was not the first sequence of oriental tales to be published in Europe and an alternative tradition associated with the voice of the male sage and wise counsellor to a prince is represented by the inclusion of an animal tale from *The Fables of Pilpay*, first translated into English from a French translation of a Persian source in 1699. A wise and experienced holy man, the imam Horam, is also the teller of the oriental sequence by James Ridley entitled *Tales of the Genii* (1764), and a Hindu hermit tells one of several sequences delivered to the young Indian prince in Alexander Dow's translation of 'Inâyat Allâh Kanbû's *Bahâr-e dâneš* entitled *Tales, Translated from the Inatulla* (1768). If the narrators of these tales are diverse—a harem woman (Galland), a Brahman sage (Pilpay), an imam (Ridley), and a young male courtier (Dow)—the tales they tell concern the familiar theme of the nature and testing of female virtue.

The second section of the anthology turns to what I have termed 'the pseudo-oriental tale' (although there are question marks over the 'authenticity' of the translations of most of the texts taken from framed sequences). Here, the reader will find examples of texts written in conscious imitation of the 'oriental tale' or fictional representations of oriental territories and peoples. Each story concerns the interaction and encounter between East and West, whether through parody of oriental narrative (as in the case of Horace Walpole's hilarious spoof '*Mi Li. A Chinese Fairy Tale*'), or through the claim that oriental narrative can be put to use in western political or philosophical critique (as in the case of Joseph Addison's defence of the fable from a number of the *Spectator*) or through the mythic contrast between occidental rationalism and oriental passion in an inset tale, 'The History of the Christian Eunuch', from Eliza Haywood's novella *Philidore and Placentia*.

The third section provides illustrations of travel and historical writing about eastern territories, two relating to India and one to the Ottoman capital of Istanbul. François Bernier, the sceptical philosopher

9

and doctor, describes a journey taken in 1664 with the court of the Mughal Emperor Aurangzeb from Delhi to Kashmir which both conveys a sense of admiration and awe at the splendour of a court counted the richest in the globe and the personal suffering endured by the author in the final stages of the journey across desert and mountain, prey to both disease and heat. A Jesuit priest, François Catrou, draws on the memoirs of another doctor, the Venetian Niccolo Manucci, to deliver a story which was to gain wide currency in seventeenth- and eighteenth-century oriental tales about the heroic actions of an Indian princess during the Mughal Emperor Akbar's siege of Chitor in 1567–8. Readers will recognize this story from Alexander Dow's 'History of Commladeve' in this anthology and John Dryden also exploited the tale in his play *Aureng-Zebe* (1675), discussed at length in *Fabulous Orients*. Finally, a letter from Lady Mary Wortley Montagu's account of her journey to and residence in Istanbul in the second decade of the eighteenth century with her ambassador husband provides a further example of the enlightened encounter with eastern territories. Lady Mary prepared for publication in the early 1760s, just before her death, a two-volume manuscript drawing on her journals and actual letters written over this period which was published posthumously in 1763 to immediate success and applause. In the letter reprinted here, Lady Mary challenges the commonplace representation of Ottoman culture as repressive to women by contrast with Catholic Europe from her own critical position of Protestant Whiggism.

The letter was an important form for the mediation of the East to the West in this period as the examples of Bernier and Montagu illustrate. The final section of this anthology turns to the popular mode of the fictional letter written in the voice of an oriental informant, a tradition inaugurated by the *Letters Writ by a Turkish Spy* discussed earlier in this introduction. Marana's preface and four letters from the collection are given here. These have been selected to demonstrate the technique of 'reverse ethnography' specific to this kind of epistolary fiction. The oriental informant voice is deployed to provide an enlightened rationalist critique of European political and social mores. However, the four letters also demonstrate the author, Giovanni Paolo Marana's, sophisticated development of Mahmut as a character, driven by anxiety and paranoia about the potential discovery of his mission in Paris and the undermining of his narrative credit with the Ottoman Porte. The tradition of the oriental letter-fiction contributes to the development of the epistolary mode in eighteenth-century Britain in its exploitation of irony. The 'innocent' letter writer can reveal more about himself, as well as the strange culture he occupies, than he intends. Samuel Richardson is only the best-known inheritor of this technique in the eighteenth-century epistolary novel.

Two further examples show the development of the form: Charles Secondat de Montesquieu's provides an exchange of letters between a number of correspondents to and from two intellectually curious male Persian travellers where the *Letters Writ by a Turkish Spy* are exclusively written in the voice of Mahmut; the letters pass between Persia and Paris (and the similarity between the names of the two territories is not lost on the author or reader). Here, as with the *Letters Writ by a Turkish Spy*, I provide the preface and a selection of four letters. The longest returns to the representation of the harem woman and makes even more explicit than Galland the analogical richness of this representation as a means of debating the nature and exercise of political authority. The urbane younger correspondent, Rica, translates for a French court lady a Persian tale about a rebellious harem wife who cleverly defeats a tyrannous husband, a story which foreshadows the rebellion in the harem of his older and more conservative companion-traveller, Usbek, which closes the collection. Rica's letter serves as a further example of a 'reverse ethnography' where a French court lady learns of the comparative and surprising 'freedom' and learning of women in eastern marriage (and hence it can be usefully compared with Lady Mary Wortley Montagu's letter). Finally, two letters are taken from Oliver Goldsmith's periodical essays in the voice of a Chinese informant that were collected as a book under the title *The Citizen of the World* in 1762. Goldsmith has enormous fun with the character of Lien Chi Altangi, the Confucian philosopher and open-minded Chinese traveller in London. The letters given here expose Europeans as ignorant 'collectors' of fragments of Asian culture who fail to recognize the superior civility and philosophical sophistication of Chinese manners. Goldsmith makes the anti-colonial Tory conservative case for scholarly and intellectual—rather than mercantile or missionary—engagement with distant territories.

Introduction

The reader of this anthology will, I hope, be able to make fruitful connections and comparisons between all the selected pieces, as well as identify their influence upon better-known eighteenth-century texts by other authors. But my ambition is that they will also be, as I have been and their contemporary authors and readers were, 'transported', if not by their sometimes cumbersome style, then by their narrative energy. The narrative traffic between East and West in the eighteenth-century world is as lively, complex, and troublesome as the mercantile ventures that so dominated the period. What may surprise is that the model of a simple imperialist appropriation of otherness will not hold as an explanation of the enthusiasm for the oriental fable in eighteenth-century England. Often, eastern territories are represented as a source of wisdom and authority by contrast with a relatively infantile West. If we started with a sense of the 'backwardness' of the oriental fable for eighteenth-century readers, we should conclude with our own 'reverse ethnography' which recognizes that it could also look forward, to the development of the novel as a serious form of cultural engagement with the modern world.

There are parallels to be made between the pre-imperial construction of the 'Orient' in eighteenth-century European narrative and the post-imperial moment we now inhabit. The passion for the oriental fable in the West resurfaces in the traffic between Anglo-American and Indian film in the twenty-first century, in the hybrid fictions of authors such as Salman Rushdie and A. S. Byatt. Salman Rushdie defended his controversial novel *The Satanic Verses* in 1990 in terms that, I suggest, might be applied—despite their all-too-evident failures of empathy and understanding—to the 'fables of the East' represented in this anthology:

The Satanic Verses celebrates hybridity, impurity, intermingling, the transformation that comes of new and unexpected combinations of human beings, cultures, ideas, politics, movies, songs. It rejoices in mongrelization and fears the absolutism of the Pure. *Mélange*, hotchpotch, a bit of this and a bit of that is *how newness enters the world*. . . . *The Satanic Verses* is for change-by-fusion, change-by-conjoining. It is a love-song to our mongrel selves.[12]

---

[12] Salman Rushdie, 'In Good Faith', *Imaginary Homelands* (London: Granta, 1991), 393–414, 394.

1

THE FRAMED
SEQUENCE

From *The Arabian Nights Entertainments*

'translated' by Antoine Galland

Copy-text: vol. 1 of the 4th edition (London, 1713)

Antoine Galland (1646–1715) studied philosophy and classical and oriental languages at the Collège du Plessis in Paris for nine years before becoming secretary to the marquis de Nointel, Louis XIV's ambassador to the Ottoman empire in 1670. He travelled extensively in the Middle East in the mid-1670s and 1680s and on his return to Paris was engaged by Barthélemy d'Herbelot, Professor of Oriental Languages, to assist in preparing the *Bibliothèque Orientale* (published in 1697). In 1702 Galland began translating the tale of 'Sindbad' from an Arabic manuscript. In 1704 he published the first volume of *Mille et Une Nuit*, which drew on tales from a different manuscript. A further six volumes had appeared by 1706, each translated swiftly into English after their publication in French. An eighth volume of 1709 contained some material translated by his fellow orientalist, François Pétis de la Croix. In March 1709 Galland met a Maronite of Aleppo called 'Hanna' who told him oral stories for two months, which provided material for the final four volumes (published between 1711 and 1717). Galland became Professor of Arabic at the Collège Royal in 1709 and died in Paris aged 70 having also translated the Qur'an into French and a number of other oriental texts.

The Framed Sequence

So far, so simple. Muhsin Mahdi explains the complex history of the text in the critical annotations in English which form the third volume of his Arabic edition of Galland's manuscript source, *The Thousand and One Nights* (Leiden: Brill, 1994). All Arabic printings derive from the nineteenth century and it is likely they were influenced by Galland. The primary Arabic four-volume source manuscript used by Galland was compiled in thirteenth- or fourteenth-century Syria, but drew on stories that dated back to the ninth century from ancient (pre-Islamic) Iranian and Indian prototypes. Mahdi compiles his Arabic text from Galland's manuscript source, *Alf Layla wa-Layla* (vols. i and ii of his *Thousand and One Nights*) and Hussain Haddawy translates Mahdi's text into English as *The Arabian Nights* (London: Everyman, 1992). See also, Duncan Black McDonald, 'A Bibliographical and Literary Study of the First Appearance of the Arabian Nights in Europe', *Library Quarterly* 2 (1932): 387–420.

I give here Galland's prefatory material to indicate the way in which he framed his text for consumption by a European readership, calling attention to its politeness and insisting that the tales provide an insight into the lives of contemporary oriental cultures despite his own extensive knowledge of the varied histories, languages, religions, and mores of those territories. The influence of Galland's 'translation' in the English oriental tale cannot be overestimated. It was hugely popular, running into many editions throughout the eighteenth century and referred to, imitated, parodied by writers on both sides of the channel. It has subsequently enjoyed lively critical attention. See especially: Robert Irwin, *The Arabian Nights: A Companion* (London: Allen Lane, 1994); and Peter Caracciolo (ed.), *The Arabian Nights in English Literature: Studies in the Reception of the Thousand and One Nights into British Culture* (Basingstoke: Macmillan, 1988).

From The Arabian Nights Entertainments

The Epistle Dedicatory, to the Right Honourable the Lady Marchioness *d'O*, Lady of Honour to the Dutchess of *Burgundy*.

MADAM,

The great Kindness I receiv'd from M. de Guilleragues,[1] *your illustrious Father, during my Abode at* Constantinople, *some Years ago, are too fresh in my Mind, for me to neglect any Opportunity of Publishing what I owe to his Memory. Were he still alive for the Welfare of* France, *and my particular Advantage, I would take the Liberty to Dedicate this Work to him; not only as my Benefactor, but as a Person most capable of judging what is Fine, and inspiring others with the like Sentiments. Every one remembers the wonderful Exactness of his Judgment, the meanest of his Thoughts had something in them that was Shining; and his lowest Expressions, were always Exact and Nice, which made every one admire him: For never had any Man so much Wit and so much Solidity. I have seen him at a time when he was so much taken up with the Affairs of his Master, that no body could expect any thing from him, but what related to his Ministry, and his profound Capacity to manage the most knotty Negotiations; yet all the Weight of his Employment diminish'd nothing of his inimitable Pleasantness, which charm'd his Friends, and was agreeable even to those barbarous Nations with whom that Great Man did treat. After the Loss of him, which to me is irreparable, I could not address my self to any other Person than your self, Madam, since you alone can supply the Want of him to me; therefore it is that I take the Boldness to beg of you the same Protection for this Book, that you was pleas'd to grant to the* French *Translation of the Seven* Arabian *Stories that I had the Honour to present you.*[2]

You may perhaps wonder, Madam, that I have not since that Time presented them to you in Print; but the reason of it is, that when I was about putting them in the Press, I was inform'd that those Seven Stories

[1] Gabriel-Joseph de Lavergne de Guilleragues, was the ambassador to the Sublime Porte whom Galland accompanied on his appointment in September 1679. His daughter, the dedicatee of the first volume of the *Nights*, was a distinguished lady-in-waiting to the duchesse de Borgogne, wife of Louis, duc de Bourgogne, dauphin de France.

[2] The seven voyages of Sindbad the Sailor which Galland translated from a separate manuscript he obtained in Istanbul before he acquired the *Alf Layla wa Layla* manuscript. He published the Sindbad tales in later volumes of *The Arabian Nights Entertainments*.

17

were taken out of a prodigious Collection of Stories of the like sort, entituled, One Thousand and One Nights. *This Discovery oblig'd me to suspend the Printing of them, and to use my Endeavours to get that Collection; I was forced to send for it from* Syria, *and I have translated into* French *this First Volume, being One of the Four that were sent me. These Stories will certainly divert you, Madam, much more than those you have already seen. They are new to you, and more in Number: You will also perceive, with pleasure, the ingenious Design of this anonymous* Arabian, *who has given us these Stories after the manner of his Country, Fabulous indeed, but very diverting.*

I beg, Madam, your Acceptance of this small Present, which I have the Honour to make you, it is a publick Testimony of my Acknowledgment of the profound Respect, with which I am, and shall for ever be,

Madam,
   Your most humble and
     most obedient Servant,
     GALLAND

PREFACE

There's no occasion to prepossess the Reader with an Opinion of the Merit and Beauty of the following Work. There needs no more than to read it to satisfy any Man that hitherto nothing so Fine of this Nature, has appear'd in any Language.

What can be more ingenious, than to compose such a prodigious Quantity of pleasant Stories, whose Variety is surprizing, and whose Connexion is so wonderful? We know not the Name of the Author of so great a Work; but probably it is not all done by one Hand; for how can we suppose that one Man alone, could have Invention enough to make so many fine Things?

If Stories of this sort be pleasant and diverting, because of the Wonders they usually contain; these have certainly the Advantage above all that have yet been publish'd, because they are full of surprizing Events, which engage our Attention, and shew how much the *Arabians* surpass other Nations in Composures of this sort.

From The Arabian Nights Entertainments

They must also be pleasing, because of the Account they give of the Customs and Manners of the Eastern Nations, and of the Ceremonies of their Religion, as well Pagan as Mahometan, which are better describ'd here, than in any Author that has wrote of 'em, or in the Relations of Travellers. All the Eastern Nations, Persians, Tartars, and Indians, are here distinguish'd, and appear such as they are, from the Sovereign to the meanest Subject; so that without the Fatigue of going to see those People in their respective Countries, the Reader has here the Pleasure to see them act, and hear them speak. Care has been taken to preserve their Characters, and to keep their Sense; nor have we varied from the Text, but when Modesty obliged us to it. The Translator flatters himself, that those who understand *Arabick*, and will be at the pains to compare the Original with the Translation, must agree, that he has shew'd the *Arabians* to the *French*, with all the Circumspection that the Niceness of the *French* Tongue, and of the Time requires; and if those who read these Stories, have but any Inclination to profit by the Examples of Virtue and Vice, which they will here find exhibited, they may reap an advantage by it, that is not to be reap'd in other Stories, which are more proper to corrupt than to reform our Manners.

Arabian Nights *Entertainments*

The Chronicles of the *Sassanians*,[3] the Ancient Kings of *Persia*, who extended their Empire into the *Indies*, over all the Islands thereunto belonging, a great way beyond the *Ganges*, and as far as *China*, acquaint us, that there was formerly a King of that Potent Family, the most Excellent Prince of his Time: He was as much belov'd by his Subjects, for his Wisdom and Prudence, as he was dreaded by his Neighbours, because of his Valour, and his War-like and well Disciplin'd Troops. He had two Sons; the eldest *Schahriar*, the worthy

---

[3] Sassanians: the Sassanid dynasty ruled across what is now Iran and Iraq and parts of central Asia from about 226 until the Arabian conquest in 641. Its capital was at Ctesiphon, in central Iraq. In other words, this is a pre-Islamic dynasty, although many of the *Nights* tales refer to a later period under the Abbasid caliphate (*c.*749–1258) and the reign of Harun al-Raschid in particular (786–900).

Heir of his Father, and endow'd with all his Virtues. The youngest *Schahzenan*, was likewise a Prince of incomparable Merit. After a long and glorious Reign, this King died, and *Schahriar* mounted his Throne. *Schahzenan* being excluded from all Share of the Government, by the Laws of the Empire, and oblig'd to live a private Life, was so far from envying the Happiness of his Brother, that he made it his whole Business to please him, and effected it without much difficulty. *Schahriar*, who had naturally a great Affection for that Prince, was so charm'd with his Complaisance, that out of an Excess of Friendship, he would needs divide his Dominions with him, and gave him the Kingdom of *Great Tartary*; *Schahzenan* went immediately and took possession of it, and fix'd the Seat of his Government at *Samarcande*, the Metropolis of the Country.

After they had been separated Ten Years, *Schahriar* having a passionate Desire to see his Brother, resolved to send an Ambassador to invite him to his Court. He made choice of his Prime Visier for the Embassy, sent him to *Tartary* with a Retinue answerable to his Dignity, and he made all possible haste to *Samarcande*. When he came near the City, *Schahzenan* had notice of it, and went to meet him with the principal Lords of his Court, who, to put the more Honour on the Sultan's Minister, appeared in Magnificent Apparel. The King of *Tartary* receiv'd the Ambassador with the greatest Demonstrations of Joy, and immediately asked him concerning the Welfare of the Sultan his Brother. The Visier having acquainted him that he was in Health, gave him an Account of his Embassy. *Schahzenan* was so much affected with it, that he answered thus: '*Sage Visier, the Sultan, my Brother does me too much Honour; He could propose nothing in the World so acceptable; I long as passionately to see him, as he does to see me. Time has been no more able to diminish my Friendship than his. My Kingdom is in Peace, and I desire no more but Ten Days to get my self ready to go with you. So that there's no Necessity of your entering the City for so short a time: I pray you to pitch your Tents here, and I will order Provisions in abundance for your self, and your Company.*' The Visier did accordingly, and as soon as the King returned, he sent him a prodigious Quantity of Provisions of all sorts, with Presents of great Value.

In the mean while *Schahzenan* made ready for his Journey, took Orders about his most important Affairs, appointed a Council to govern in his Absence, and named a Minister, of whose Wisdom he had sufficient Experience, and in whom he had an entire Confidence, to be their President. At the end of Ten Days his Equipage being ready, he took his Leave of the Queen his Wife, and went out of Town in the Evening with his Retinue, pitch'd his Royal Pavilion near the Vizier's Tent, and discours'd with that Ambassador till Midnight. But willing once more to embrace the Queen, whom he lov'd entirely, he return'd alone to his Palace, and went straight to her Majesty's Apartment, who not expecting his Return, had taken one of the meanest Officers of the Household to her Bed, where they lay both fast a-sleep, having been in Bed a considerable while.

The King entered without any noise, and pleas'd himself to think how he should surprize his Wife, who he thought lov'd him as entirely as he did her: But how strange was his Surprise, when by the Light of the Flambeaus which burn all Night in the Apartments of those Eastern Princes,[4] he saw a Man in her Arms! He stood unmovable for a time, not knowing how to believe his own Eyes: but finding it was not to be doubted; 'How,' says he to himself, 'I am scarce out of my Palace, and but just under the Walls of *Samercande*, and dare they put such an Outrage upon me! Ah! perfidious Wretches, your Crime shall not go unpunish'd. As King I am to punish Wickedness committed in my Dominions; and as an enrag'd Husband, I must sacrifice you to my just Resentment.' In a word, the unfortunate Prince, giving way to his Rage, drew his Cimeter, and approaching the Bed, kill'd them both with one blow, turn'd their sleep into Death: And afterwards taking them up, threw them out at a Window into the Ditch that surrounded the Palace.

Having avenged himself thus, he went out of Town privately, as he came into it; and returning to his Pavilion, without saying one word of what had happen'd, he ordered the Tents to be struck, and to make ready for his Journey. This was speedily done, and before Day he began his March, with Kettle Drums and other Instruments of Musick, that fill'd every one with Joy, except the King, who was so much troubled at the disloyalty of his Wife, that he was seiz'd with

---

[4] This comment reveals Galland's editorial/authorial presence. He here signposts the idea that the text is a means of informing western readers about the manners and customs of the East, but breaks the illusion of a 'translation' from an authentic eastern source.

extreme Melancholy, which prey'd upon him during his whole Journey.

When he drew near the Capital of the *Indies*, the Sultan *Schahriar*, and all his Court came out to meet him: The Princes were overjoy'd to see one another, and alighting, after mutual Embraces, and other marks of Affection and Respect, they mounted again, and entered the City, with the Acclamations of vast Multitudes of People. The Sultan conducted his Brother to the Palace he had provided for him, which had a Communication with his own, by means of a Garden, and which was so much the more Magnificent, that it was set apart as a Banqueting House for publick Entertainments and other Diversions of the Court, and the Splendor of it had been lately augmented by new Furniture.

Schahriar immediately left the King of *Tartary*, that he might give him time to Bath himself, and to change his Apparel. And as soon as he had done, he came to him again, and they sat down together upon a *Sofa* or *Alcove*. The Courtiers kept at a distance out of Respect, and those two Princes entertain'd one another suitably to their Friendship, their Nearness of Blood, and the long separation that had been betwixt 'em. The time of Supper being come, they eat together, after which they renewed their Conversation, which continued till *Schahriar* perceiving that it was very late, left his Brother to his Rest.

The unfortunate *Schahzenan* went to Bed; and tho the Conversation of his Brother had suspended his Grief for some time, it return'd upon him with more violence; so that instead of taking his necessary Rest, he tormented himself with cruel Reflections: All the Circumstances of his Wife's Disloyalty represented themselves afresh to his Imagination, in so lively a manner, that he was like one besides himself. In a word, not being able to sleep, he got up, and giving himself over to afflicting thoughts, they made such an Impression upon his Countenance, that the Sultan could not but take notice of it; and said thus to himself, 'What can be the matter with the King of *Tartary*, that he is so melancholy? Has he any cause to complain of his Reception? No surely, I have receiv'd him as a Brother whom I love, so that I can charge my self with no Omission in that respect. Perhaps it grieves him to be at such a distance from his Dominions, or from the Queen, his Wife: Alas! if that be the matter, I must forthwith

From The Arabian Nights Entertainments

give him the Presents I design'd for him, that he may return to *Samarcande* when he pleases.' Actually next Day *Schahriar* sent him Part of those Presents, being the greatest Rarities, and the richest Things that the *Indies* could afford. At the same time he endeavour'd to divert his Brother every Day by new Objects of Pleasure, and the finest Treats, which instead of giving the King of *Tartary* any Ease, did only increase his Sorrow.

One Day *Schahriar* having appointed a great Hunting-Match, about two days Journey from his Capitol, in a Place that abounded with Deer; *Schahzenan* pray'd him to excuse him, for his Health would not allow him to bear him Company. The Sultan, unwilling to put any Constraint upon him, left him at his Liberty, and went a Hunting with his Nobles. The King of *Tartary* being thus left alone, shut himself up in his Apartment, and sat down at a Window, that look'd into the Garden. That delicious Place, and the sweet Harmony of an infinite number of Birds, which chose it for a Place of Retreat, must certainly have diverted him, had he been capable of taking pleasure in any thing; but being perpetually tormented with the fatal Remembrance of his Queen's infamous Conduct, his Eyes were not so often fix'd upon the Garden, as lifted up to Heav'n to bewail his Misfortune.

Whilst he was thus swallow'd up with Grief, an Object presented itself to his view, which quickly turn'd all his Thoughts another way. A secret Gate of the Sultan's Palace opened all of a sudden, and there came out of it 20 Women, in the midst of whom march'd the Sultaness, who was easily distinguish'd from the rest, by her Majestick Air. This Princess thinking that the King of *Tartary* was gone a hunting with his Brother the Sultan, came up with her Retinue near the Windows of his Apartment, for the Prince had plac'd himself so, that he could see all that pass'd in the Garden, without being perceiv'd himself. He observ'd that the Persons who accompanied the Sultaness, threw off their Veils, and long Robes, that they might be at more freedom; but was wonderfully surpriz'd when he saw ten of 'em to be Blacks,[5] and that each of 'em took his Mistress. The Sultaness, on her part, was not

---

[5] The eunuchs who served in the harem in the Ottoman and Persian court were always of African descent. See Paul Rycaut, *The Present State of the Ottoman Empire* (London, 1668): 'The Black Eunuchs are ordained for the service of the Women in the *Seraglio*; as

long without her Gallant. She clapp'd her Hands and called '*Masoud, Masoud*'; and immediately a Black came down from a *Tree*, and run to her in all haste.

Modesty will not allow, nor is it necessary to relate what pass'd betwixt the Blacks and the Ladies. It's sufficient to say, that *Schahzenan* saw enough to convince him, that his Brother had as much cause to complain as himself. This amorous Company continued together till Midnight, and having bath'd all together in a great Pond, which was one of the chief Ornaments of the Garden, they dress'd themselves, and re-entered the Palace by the secret Door, all except *Masoud*, who climb'd up his Tree, and got over the Garden-Wall the same way as he came in.[6]

All this having passed in the King of *Tartary's* sight, it gave him occasion to make a multitude of Reflections. 'How little reason had I', says he, 'to think that no body was so unfortunate as my self? It is certainly the unavoidable Fate of all Husbands, since the Sultan my Brother, who is Sovereign of so many Dominions, and the greatest Prince of the Earth, could not escape it. The Case being so, what a Fool am I to kill my self with Grief! I'll throw it off, and the Remembrance of a Misfortune so common, shall never after disturb my Quiet.' So that from that moment he forbore afflicting himself; Being unwilling to sup, till he saw the whole Scene that was acted under his Windows, he called then for his Supper, eat with a better Appetite than he had done at any time after his coming from *Samercande*, and listened with pleasure to the agreeable Consort of Vocal and Instrumental Musick, that was appointed to entertain him while at Table.

He continued after this to be of a very good Humour; and when he knew that the Sultan was returning, he went to meet him, and paid

---

the White are to the attendance of the Grand Signior, it not seeming a sufficient remedy by wholly dismembring them, to take the Women off from their inclinations to them, as retaining some relation still to the Masculine Sex, but to create an abhorrency in them; they are not only castrated, but Black, chosen with the worst features that are to be found among the most hard-favoured of that *African* race' (37). However, sexual relations could and did still take place between eunuchs (who were castrated most commonly through removal or crushing of the testicles) and harem women (see Alev Lytle Croutier, *Harem: the World Behind the Veil* (London: Abbeville Press, 1989), 135).

[6] The implication is that Masoud is not, like the other 'blacks', a eunuch who serves in the harem. Thus, there is a risk that he may be fathering illegitimate children with the Sultaness.

him his Complements, with a great deal of Gaiety. *Schahriar* at first took no notice of this great Alteration; but expostulated with him modestly, why he wou'd not bear him Company at Hunting the Stag; and without giving him time to reply, entertain'd him with the great Number of Deer, and other Game, that he had kill'd, and what Pleasure he had had in the Sport. *Schahzenan* heard him with Attention, gave answers to every thing, and being rid of that Melancholy, which formerly over-clouded his Wit, he said a thousand agreeable and pleasant things to the Sultan.

Schahriar, who expected to have found him in the same Condition as he left him, was overjoy'd to see him so chearful; and spoke to him thus: 'Dear Brother, I return Thanks to Heav'n for the happy Change it has made in you during my Absence, I am extremely rejoyc'd at it; but I have a Request to make to you, and conjure you not to deny me.' 'I can refuse you nothing,' replies the King of *Tartary*, 'you may command *Schahzenan* as you please, Pray speak, I am impatient till I know what it is you desire of me.' 'Ever since you came to my Court,' replies *Schahriar*, 'I found you swallow'd up in a deep Melancholy, and I did in vain attempt to remove it by Diversions of all sorts. I imagin'd it might be occasion'd by reason of your Distance from your Dominions, or that Love might have a great share in it; and that the Queen of *Samercande*, who, no doubt is an accomplish'd Beauty, might be the Cause of it. I don't know if I be mistaken, but I must own, that this was the particular Reason why I would not importune you upon the Subject, for fear of making you uneasy. But without my being able to contribute any thing towards it, I find now upon my return, that you are in the best Humour that can be, and that your Mind is entirely delivered from that black Vapour which disturb'd it. Pray do me the favour to tell me, why you were so melancholy, and how you came to be rid of it.'

Upon this the King of *Tartary* continued for some time as if he had been in a Dream, and contriving what he should answer, but at last reply'd as follows; 'You are my Sultan and Master, but excuse me, I beseech you, from answering your Question.' 'No, dear Brother,' said the Sultan, 'you must answer, I will take no denial.' *Schahzenan* not being able to withstand those pressing Instances, answer'd; 'Well then, Brother, I will satisfie you, since you command me'; and having told him the Story of the Queen of *Samercande*'s Treachery, 'This', says he, 'was the Cause of Grief; pray judge, whether I had not reason enough to give my self up to it.'

'O! My Brother,' says the Sultan, in a Tone which shew'd that he had the same Sentiments of the matter with the King of *Tartary*: 'What a horrible Story do you tell me! How impatient was I, till I heard it out! I commend you for punishing the Traitors, who put such an Outrage upon you. No body can blame you for that Action; It was just, and for my part, had the Case been mine, I should scarce have been so moderate as you. I should not have satisfy'd my self with the Life of one Woman, I verily think I should have sacrificed 1000 to my Fury. I cease now to wonder at your Melancholy. The Cause of it was too sensible, and too mortifying, not to make you yield to it. Oh Heaven! what a strange Adventure! Not I believe the like on't ever befell any Man, but your self. But in short, I must bless God, who has comforted you: and since I doubt not but your Consolation is well grounded; be so good as to let me know what it is, and conceal nothing from me.' *Schahzenan* was not so easily prevailed upon in this point, as he had been in the other, because of his Brother's Concern in it. But being obliged to yield to his pressing Instances, answer'd, 'I must obey you then, since your Command is absolute; yet am afraid that my Obedience will occasion your Trouble to be greater than ever mine was. But you must blame your self for it, since you force me to reveal a thing, which I should otherwise have buried in Eternal Oblivion.' 'What you say', answers *Schahriar*, 'serves only to increase my Curiosity. Make haste to discover the Secret, whatever it be.' The King of *Tartary* being no longer able to refuse, gave him the Particulars of all that he had seen of the Blacks in disguise, of the lewd Passion of the Sultaness and her Ladies; and to be sure he did not forget *Masoud*. 'After having been Witness to those infamous Actions,' says he, 'I believed all Women to be naturally that way inclined; and that they could not resist those violent Desires. Being of this Opinion, it seemed to me to be an unaccountable Weakness in Men, to make themselves uneasy at their Infidelity. This Reflection brought many others along with it, and, in short, I thought it the best thing I could do, to make my self easie. It cost me some Pains indeed, but at last I effected it, and if you'll take my Advice, you shall follow my Example.'

From The Arabian Nights Entertainments

Tho the Advice was good, the Sultan could not take it, but fell into a Rage. 'What!' says he, 'is the Sultaness of the *Indies* capable of Prostituting her self in so base a manner! No, Brother, I can't believe what you say, except I saw it with my Eyes; yours must needs have deceiv'd you; the matter is so important, that I must be satisfied of it my self.' 'Dear Brother,' answers *Schahzenan*, 'that you may without much difficulty. Appoint another Hunting match, and when we are out of Town with your Court and mine, we will stop under our Pavilions, and at night let you and I return alone to my Appartment; I am certain that next day you will see what I saw.' The Sultan approv'd the Stratagem, immediately appointed a new Hunting Match: And that same day the Pavilions were set up at the Place appointed.[7]

Next Day the two Princes set out with all their Retinue, they arriv'd at the Place of Encampment, and staid there till Night. Then *Schahriar* call'd his Grand Vizier, and without acquainting him with his Design, commanded him to stay in his Place during his Absence, and to suffer no Person to go out of the Camp upon any account whatever. As soon as he had given this Order, the King of *Grand Tartary* and he took Horse, pass'd thro' the Camp *incognito*, return'd to the City, and went to *Schahzenan*'s Apartment. They had scarce plac'd themselves at the same Window where the King of *Tartary* had seen the disguised Blacks act their Scene, but the secret Gate open'd, the Sultaness and her Ladies entered the Garden with the Blacks, and she having call'd upon *Masoud*, the Sultan saw more than enough to convince him plainly of his Dishonour and Misfortune.

'O Heavens,' cry'd he, 'What Indignity! What Horror! Can the Wife of a Sovereign, such as I am, be capable of such an infamous Action? After this, let no Prince boast of his being perfectly happy. Alas! my Brother,' continues he, (embracing the King of *Tartary*) 'let's both renounce the World, Honesty is banish'd out of it; if it flatter us the one Day, it betrays us the next; let us abandon our Dominions and Grandeur; let's go into foreign Countries, where we may lead an obscure Life, and conceal our Misfortune.' *Schahzenan* did not at all approve of this Resolution, but did not think fit to

---

[7] On this practice of sending ahead an entire encampment to be joined by the Mughal emperor and his party in 17th-c. India, see François Bernier, 'A Voyage to Kachemire' in Part 3.

contradict *Schahriar* in the Heat of his Passion. 'Dear Brother,' says he, 'your Will shall be mine, I am ready to follow you whither you please; but promise me that you will return, if we can meet with any one that is more Unhappy than our selves.' 'I agree to it,' says the *Sultan*, 'but doubt much whether we shall.' 'I am not of your Mind in this,' replies the King of *Tartary* 'I fansie our Journey will be but short.' Having said thus, they went secretly out of the Palace by another Way than they came. They travell'd as long as 'twas Day; and lay the first Night under the Trees, and getting up about Break of Day, they went on till they came to a fine Meadow upon the Bank of the Sea, in which Meadow there were Tufts of great Trees at some distance from one another. They sat down under those Trees, to rest and refresh themselves, and the chief Subject of their Conversation, was the Lewdness of their Wives.

They had not sat long till they heard a frightful Noise, and a terrible Cry from the Sea, which fill'd them with Fear; then the Sea opening, there rose up a Thing like a great black Column, which reach'd almost to the Clouds. This redoubled their Fear, made them rise speedily, and climb up into the Tree to hide themselves. They had scarce got up, till looking to the Place from whence the Noise came, and where the Sea opened, they observed that the black Cloud was advanced, winding about towards the Shoar, cleaving the Water before it. They could not at first think what it should be, but in a little time they found, That it was one of those malignant *Genies*,[8] that are mortal Enemies to Mankind, and always doing them Mischief. He was black, frightful, had the Shape of a Giant of a prodigious Stature, and carried on his Head a great Glass-box, shut with four Locks of fine Steel. He entered the Meadow with his Burden, which he laid down just at the Foot of the Tree where the two Princes were, who looked upon themselves to be dead Men. Mean while, the *Genie* sat down by his Box, and opening it with four Keys that he had at his Girdle, there came out a Lady Magnificently Apparelled, of a Majestick Stature, and a compleat Beauty. The Monster made her sit down by him, and

---

[8] The Arabic term 'jinn' is the collective name of a class of spirits (some good, some evil) supposed to interfere powerfully in human affairs (*OED*). Genies are made of the element of fire rather than earth and the category includes giants according to Galland's entry in the *Bibliothèque Orientale* (Paris, 1697). Genies can have relations with humans.

eying her with an amorous Look: 'Lady' (says he) 'nay, most Accomplished of all Ladies, who are admired for their Beauty, my charming Mistress, whom I carried off on your Wedding-Day, and have loved so constantly ever since, let me sleep a few Moments by you, for I found my self so very sleepy, that I came to this Place to take a little Rest.' Having spoke thus, he laid down his huge Head upon the Lady's Knees, and stretching out his Legs, which reach'd as far as the Sea, he fell asleep presently, and snor'd so, that he made the Banks to echo again.

The Lady happening at the same time to look up to the Tree, saw the two Princes, and made a Sign to them with her Hand to come down without making any Noise. Their Fear was extraordinary, when they found themselves discovered, and they prayed the Lady by other Signs to excuse them; but she, after having laid the Monster's Head softly down, rose up, and spoke to them with a low but quick Voice, to come down to her; she would take no Denial. They made Signs to her, that they were afraid of the *Genie*, and would fain have been excused. Upon which she ordered them to come down, and if they did not make haste, threatened to awake the Giant, and bid him kill them.

These Words did so much intimidate the Princes, that they began to come down with all possible Precautions, lest they should awake the *Genie*. When they came down, the Lady took 'em by the Hand, and going a little farther with them under the Trees, made a very urgent Proposal to them. At first they rejected it, but she oblig'd them to accept it by new Threats. Having obtained what she desir'd, she perceiv'd that each of 'em had a Ring on his Finger, which she demanded of 'em. As soon as she receiv'd them, she went and took a Box out of the Bundle, where her Toilet was, pull'd out a String of other Rings of all sorts, which she shew'd them, and ask'd them if they knew what these Jewels meant. 'No,' say they, 'we hope you will be pleas'd to tell us.' 'These are', replies she, 'the Rings of all the Men to whom I have granted my Favour. There are full Fourscore and Eighteen of 'em, which I keep as Tokens to remember them, and I ask'd yours for the same Reason, to make up my Hundred. So that', continues she, 'I have had a Hundred Gallants already, notwith-standing the Vigilance of this Wicked *Genie*, that never leaves me.

He is much the nearer for locking me up in this Glass-Box, and hiding me in the Bottom of the Sea: I find a way to cheat him for all his Care. You may see by this, that when a Woman has form'd a Project, there's no Husband or Gallant that can hinder her putting it in execution. Men had better not put their Wives under such Restraint, if they have a mind they should be Chaste.' Having spoke thus to them, she put their Rings upon the same String with the rest, and sitting her down by the Monster, as before, laid his Head again upon her Lap, and made a Sign for the Princes to be gone.

They return'd immediately by the same way they came, and when they were out of Sight of the Lady and the *Genie, Schahriar* said to *Schahzenan*; 'Well, Brother, what do you think of this Adventure? Has not the *Genie* a very faithful Mistress? And don't you agree that there's no Wickedness equal to that of Women?' 'Yes, Brother,' answers the King of *Great Tartary*; 'and you must also agree, that the Monster is more unfortunate, and has more Reason to complain, than we. Therefore, since we have found what we sought for, let's return to our Dominions, and let not this hinder us to marry again. For my part, I know a Method by which I think I shall keep inviolable the Faith that any Wife shall plight to me. I will say no more of it at present, but you will hear of it in a little Time, and I am sure you will follow my Example.' The Sultan agreed with his Brother, and continuing their Journey, they arrived in the Camp the third Night after they left it.

The News of the Sultan's return being spread, the Courtiers came betimes in the Morning before his Pavilion to wait on him. He order'd them to enter, receiv'd them with a more pleasant Air than formerly, and gave each of them a Gratification.[9] After which, he told 'em he would go no further, order'd them to take Horse, and return'd speedily to his Palace.

As soon as ever he arriv'd, he run to the Sultaness's Apartment, commanded her to be bound before him, and deliver'd her to the Grand Visier, with an Order to strangle her, which was accordingly executed by that Minister, without enquiring into her Crime. The enraged Prince did not stop here, he cut off the Heads of all the Sultanesses Ladies with his own Hand. After this rigorous

---

[9] Gratification: a gratuity (*OED*).

Punishment, being perswaded that no Woman was Chaste, he resolv'd, in order to prevent the Disloyalty of such as he should afterwards marry, to wed one every Night, and have her strangled next Morning. Having impos'd this cruel Law upon himself, he swore that he would observe it immediately after the Departure of the King of *Tartary*, who speedily took leave of him, and being loaden with Magnificent Presents, set forwards on his Journey.

Schahzenan being gone, *Schahriar* ordered his Grand Visier to bring him the Daughter of one of his Generals. The Visier obey'd; the Sultan lay with her, and putting her next Morning in his Hands again, in order to be strangled, commanded him to get him another next Night. Whatever Reluctancy the Visier had to put such Orders in Execution, as he ow'd blind Obedience to the Sultan his Master, he was forced to submit. He brought him then the Daughter of a Sub-altern, whom he also cut off next Day. After her he brought a Citizen's Daughter; and, in a word, there was every Day a Maid married and a Wife murdered.

The Rumour of this unparallel'd Barbarity, occasion'd a general consternation in the City, where there was nothing but Crying and Lamentation. Here a Father in Tears, and unconsolable for the Loss of his Daughter, and there tender Mothers dreading lest theirs should have the same Fate, making the Air to resound beforehand with their Groans. So that instead of the Commendations and Blessings which the Sultan had hitherto receiv'd from his Subjects, their Mouths were now fill'd with Imprecations against him.

The Grand Visier, who, as has been already said, was the Executioner of this horrid Injustice against his will, had two Daughters, the eldest call'd *Scheherazade*, and the youngest *Dinarzade*: the latter was a Lady of very great Merit; but the Elder had Courage, Wit, and Penetration infinitely above her Sex; she had read abundance, and had such a prodigious Memory, that she never forgot any thing. She had successfully applied herself to *Philosophy, Physick, History*, and the Liberal Arts; and for Verse exceeded the best Poets of her Time: Besides this, she was a perfect Beauty, and all her fine Qualifications were crown'd by solid Virtue.

The Visier passionately loved a Daughter so worthy of his tender Affection; and one Day, as they were discoursing together, she says to him, 'Father, I have one Favour to beg of you, and most humbly pray you to grant it me.' 'I will not refuse it,' answers he, 'provided it be just and reasonable.' 'For the Justice of it,' says she, 'there can be no Question, and you may judge of it by the Motive which obliges me to demand it of you. I have a Design to stop the Course of that Barbarity which the Sultan exercises upon the Families of the City. I would dispel those unjust Fears which so many Mothers have of losing their Daughters in such a fatal manner.' 'Your Design, Daughter', replies the Visier, 'is very commendable; but the Disease you would remedy, to me seems incurable; how do you pretend to affect it?' 'Father,' says *Scheherazade*, 'since by your means the Sultan makes every Day a new Marriage, I conjure you by the tender Affection you bear to me, to procure me the Honour of his Bed.' The Visier could not hear this without Horror. 'O Heaven!' replies he in a Passion, 'Have you lost your Senses, Daughter, that you make such a dangerous Request to me? You know the Sultan has sworn by his Soul, that he will never lie above one Night with the same Woman, and to order her to be kill'd next Morning, and would you that I should propose you to him? Pray consider well to what your indiscreet Zeal will expose you?' 'Yes, dear Father,' replies this Vertuous Daughter, 'I know the Risk I run; but that does not frighten me. If I perish, my Death will be Glorious; and if I succeed, I shall do my Country an important Piece of Service.' 'No, no,' says the Visier, 'whatever you can represent to engage me, to let you throw your self into that horrible Danger, don't you think that ever I will agree to it. When the Sultan shall order me to strike my Poniard into your Heart, alas! I must obey him, and what a dismal Imployment is that for a Father? Ah! if you don't fear Death, yet at least be afraid of occasioning me the mortal Grief of seeing my Hand stain'd with your Blood.' 'Once more, Father,' says *Scheherazade*, 'grant me the Favour I beg.' 'Your Stubborness', replies the Visier, 'will make me angry; why will you run Headlong to your Ruin? They that don't foresee the End of a dangerous Enterprize, can never bring it to a happy Issue. I am afraid the same thing will happen to you, that happen'd to the Ass, which was well, and could not keep himself so.' 'What Misfortune befel the Ass?' replies *Scheherazade*. 'I'll tell it you,' says the Visier, 'if you'll hear me.'

From The Arabian Nights Entertainments

FABLE

'*The Ass, the Ox, and the Labourer*'

'A very rich Merchant had several Country Houses, where he had abundance of Cattle of all sorts. He went with his Wife and Family to one of those Estates, in order to improve it himself. He had the Gift of understanding the Language of Beasts, but with this Condition, that he should intepret it to no Body on pain of Death, and this hinder'd him to communicate to others what he learn'd by the means of this Gift.

'He had in the same Stall, an Ox and an Ass, and one day as he sat near them, and diverted himself to see his Children play about him, he heard the Ox say to the Ass, *Sprightly*: "O how happy do I think you, when I consider the Ease you enjoy, and the little Labour that's requir'd of you. You are carefully rubb'd down and wash'd, you have well dresst Corn, and fresh clean Water. Your greatest Business is to carry the Merchant our Master, when he has any little Journey to make, and were it not for that you would be perfectly Idle. I am treated in a quite different manner, and my Condition is as Unfortunate, as yours is Pleasant. It's scarce Day-light when I am fasten'd to a Plow, and there they make me work till Night to till up the Ground; which fatigues me so, that sometimes my strength fails me. Besides, the Labourer, who is always behind me, beats me continually. By drawing the Plow, my Tail is all flea'd,[10] and in short, after having laboured from Morning till Night, when I am brought in, they give me nothing to eat but sorry dry Beans, not so much as cleans'd from Sand, or other things as pernicious; and to heighten my misery, when I have fill'd my Belly with such ordinary Stuff, I am forced to lie all Night in my own Dung: so that you see I have reason to envy your Lott."

'The Ass did not interrupt the Ox, till he had said all that he had a mind to say; but when he had made an end, he answer'd, "They that call you a foolish Beast, don't lye, you are too simple, you let them carry you whither they please, and shew no manner of Resolution. In the mean time, what Advantage do you reap by all the Indignities you suffer? You kill your self for the Ease, Pleasure and Profit of those that

---

[10] flea'd: flayed.

give you no thanks for so doing. But they would not treat you so, if you had as much Courage as Strength.

' "When they come to fasten you to the Stall, why don't you make Resistance? why don't you strike them with your Horns, and shew that you are angry, by striking your Foot against the Ground? And in short, why don't you frighten them by bellowing aloud? Nature has furnish'd you with means to procure you Respect, but you don't make use of them. They bring you sorry Beans, and bad Straw; eat none of 'em, only smell to 'em and leave 'em. If you follow the advice I give you, you will quickly find a change, for which you will thank me." The Ox took the Asses Advice in very good part, and own'd he was very much oblig'd to him for it. "Dear *Sprightly*," adds he, "I will not fail to do all that you have said, and you shall see how I shall acquit my self." They held their peace after this Discourse, of which the Merchant heard every word.

'Next Morning betimes, the Labourer comes to take the Ox: He fasten'd him to the Plow, and carried him to his ordinary Work. The Ox who had not forgot the Asses Counsel, was very troublesome and untowardly all that day, and in the Evening, when the Labourer brought him back to the Stall, and began to fasten him to it, the malicious Beast, instead of presenting his Horns willingly as he us'd to do, was restive, and went backward, bellowing; and then made at the Labourer, as if he would have push'd him with his Horns: In a word, he did all that the Ass advis'd him to. Next Day the Labourer came as usual, to take the Ox to his Labour; but finding the Stall full of Beans, the Straw that he put in it the Night before not touch'd, and the Ox lying on the Ground with his Legs stretch'd out, and panting in a strange manner, he believ'd him to be sick, pity'd him, and thinking that it was not proper to carry him to Work, went immediately and acquainted the Merchant with it.

'Who perceiving that the Ox had follow'd all the mischievous Advices of the Ass whom he thought fit to punish for it, he ordered the Labourer to go and put the Ass in the Ox's place, and to be sure to work him hard. The Labourer did so, the Ass was forced to draw the Plow all that Day, which fatigued him so much the more, that he was not accustom'd to that sort of Labour; besides, he had been so soundly beat, that he could scarce stand when he came back.

'Mean while the Ox was mightily pleas'd, he eat up all that was in his Stall, and rested himself the whole Day. He was glad at the Heart that he had follow'd the Ass's Advice, blessed him a thousand times for it, and did not fail to complement him upon it, when he saw him come back. The Ass answer'd not one Word, so vex'd was he to be so ill treated; but says within himself, "it's by my own Imprudence I have brought this misfortune upon my self. I liv'd happily, every thing smil'd upon me. I had all that I could wish, it's my own fault, that I am brought to this miserable condition; and if I can't contrive some way to get out of it, I am certainly undone;" and as he spoke thus, his Strength was so much exhausted, that he fell down at his Stall, as if he had been half dead.'

Here the Grand Visier address'd himself to *Scheherazade*, and said: 'Daughter, you do just like the Ass, you will expose your self to Destruction by your false Prudence. Take my Advice, be easy, and don't take such Measures as will hasten your Death.' 'Father,' replies *Scheherazade*, 'the Example you bring me, is not capable of making me change my Resolution, I will never cease Importuning you until you present me to the Sultan to be his Bride.' The Visier perceiving that she insisted in her Demand, replied, 'Alas then! since you will continue obstinate, I shall be obliged to treat you in the same manner as the Merchant I named just now treated his Wife a little time after. The Merchant understanding that the Ass was in a lamentable Condition, was curious to know what passed betwixt him and the Ox; therefore, after Supper he went out by Moon-light, and sat down by them, his Wife bearing him Company. When he arriv'd, he heard the Ass say to the Ox, "Comerade, tell me, I pray you, what you intend to do to Morrow when the Labourer brings you Meat?" "What will I do?" says the Ox, "I will continue to do as you taught me. I will go off from him, and threaten him with my Horns, as I did Yesterday, I will feign my self to be sick, and just ready to die." "Beware of that," replies the Ass, "it will ruin you; for as I came Home this Evening, I heard the Merchant our Master say something that makes me tremble for you." "Alas, what did you hear?" says the Ox; "as you love me hide nothing from me, my dear *Sprightly*." "Our Master", replied the Ass, "had these sad Expressions to the Labourer; 'Since the Ox does not eat, and is not able to work, I would have him kill'd to morrow, and we will give his Flesh as an Alms to the Poor for God's sake; as for his Skin, that will be of use to us, and I would have you give it the Currier[11] to dress, therefore don't fail, but send for the Butcher.' This is what I had to tell you," says the Ass. "The Concern I have for your Preservation, and my Friendship for you oblig'd me to let you know it, and to give you new Advice. As soon as they bring you your Bran and Straw, rise up and eat heartily. Our Master will by this think that you are cur'd, and no doubt will recall his Orders for killing you; whereas if you do otherwise, you are certainly gone."

'This Discourse had the effect which the Ass design'd. The Ox was strangely troubled at it and bellow'd out for Fear. The Merchant, who heard the Discourse very attentively, fell into such a Fit of Laughter, that his Wife was surpriz'd at it, and said, "Pray Husband tell me what you laugh at so heartily, that I may laugh with you." "Wife," says he, "you must content your self with hearing me laugh." "No," replies she, "I will know the Reason." "I cannot give you that Satisfaction," answers he, "but only that I laugh at what our Ass just now said to our Ox. The rest is a Secret, which I am not allow'd to reveal." "And what hinders you from revealing the Secret?" says she. "If I tell it you," answers he, "it will cost me my Life." "You only jeer me," cry'd his Wife; "what you tell me now cannot be true. If you don't satisfie me presently what you laugh at, and tell me what the Ox and Ass said to one another, I swear by Heaven that you and I shall never bed together again."

'Having spoke thus, she went into the House in a great Fret, and setting her self in a Corner, cried there all Night. Her Husband lay alone, and finding next Morning that she continued in the same Humour, told her, she was a very foolish Woman to afflict her self in that manner, the thing was not worth so much; and that it did concern her as little to know the matter, as it concern'd him much to keep it secret: "Therefore I conjure you to think no more of it." "I shall still think so much of it", says she, "as never to forbear Weeping till you have satisfy'd my Curiosity." "But I tell you very seriously", replied he, "that it will cost me my Life, if I yield to your Indiscretion." "Let

---

[11] Currier: 'one whose trade is the dressing and colouring of leather after it is tanned' (*OED*).

what will happen," says she, "I do insist upon it." "I perceive", says the Merchant, "that 'tis impossible to bring you to Reason, and since I foresee that you will occasion your own Death by your Obstinacy, I will call in your Children, that they may see you before you die." Accordingly he call'd for 'em, and sent for her Father and Mother, and other Relations. When they were come and heard the Reason of their being call'd for, they did all they could to convince her that she was in the wrong, but to no purpose: She told 'em she would rather die than yield that Point to her Husband. Her Father and Mother spoke to her by her self, and told her that what she desired to know was of no Importance to her, but they could gain nothing upon her, either by their Authority or Intreaties. When her Children saw that nothing would prevail to bring her out of that sullen Temper, they wept bitterly. The Merchant himself was like a Man out of his Senses, and was almost ready to risk his own Life, to save that of his Wife, whom he lov'd dearly.

'Now, my Daughter,' says the Visier to *Scheherazade*, 'this Merchant had Fifty Hens, and a Cock, with a Dog, that gave good heed to all that pass'd, and while the Merchant was sat down, as I said, and considering what he had best to do, he sees his Dog run toward the Cock, as he was treading a Hen,[12] and heard him speak to him thus; "Cock," says he, "I am sure Heaven will not let you live long, are you not asham'd to do that thing to Day?" The Cock standing on Tiptoe, answers the Dog fiercely, "And why", says he, "should I not do it to Day as well as other Days?" "If you don't know," replies the Dog, "then I tell you, that this Day our Master is in great Perplexity. His Wife would have him reveal a Secret which is of such a Nature, that it will cost him his Life if he doth it. Things are come to that pass, that it is to be fear'd he will scarcely have Resolution enough to resist his Wife's Obstinacy, for he loves her, and is affected with the Tears that she continually sheds, and perhaps it may cost him his Life. We are all alarmed at it, and you only insult our Melancholy, and have the Impudence to divert your self with your Hens."

'The Cock answer'd the Dog's Reproof thus: "What, has our Master so little Sense? He has but one Wife, and can't govern her; and

---

[12] treading: 'the action of the male bird in coition' (*OED*).

tho I have Fifty I make 'em all do what I please. Let him make use of his Reason, he will speedily find a Way to rid himself of his Trouble": "Ho," says the Dog, "what would you have him do?" "Let him go into the Room where his Wife is," says the Cock, "lock the Door, and take a good Stick and thrash her well, and I'll answer for it, that will bring her to her right Wits, and make her forbear to ask him any more what he ought not to tell her." The Merchant had no sooner heard what the Cock said, but he took up a good Stick, went to his Wife, whom he found still a crying, and shutting the Door, belabour'd her so soundly, that she cried out, *"It is enough, Husband, it is enough, let me alone, and I will never ask the Question more."* Upon this, perceiving that she repented of her impertinent Curiosity, he forbore drubbing her, and opening the Door, her Friends came in, were glad to find her cur'd of her Obstinacy, and complemented her Husband upon this happy Expedient to bring his Wife to Reason. Daughter', adds the Grand Visier, 'you deserve to be treated as the Merchant treated his Wife.'

'Father', replies *Scheherazade*, 'I beg you would not take it ill that I persist in my Opinion. I am nothing moved by the Story of that Woman. I can tell you abundance of others, to perswade you that you ought not to oppose my Design. Besides, Pardon me for declaring to you, that your opposing me would be in vain; for if your Paternal Affection should hinder you to grant my Request, I would go and offer my self to the Sultan.' In short, the Father being overcome by the Resolution of his Daughter, yielded to her Importunity, and tho' he was very much griev'd that he could not divert her from such a fatal Resolution, he went that Minute to acquaint the Sultan, that next Night he would bring him *Scheherazade*.

The Sultan was much surpriz'd at the Sacrifice which the Grand Visier made to him. 'How could you resolve upon it', says he, 'to bring me your own Daughter?' 'Sir,' answers the Visier, 'it's her own Offer. The sad Destiny that attends it could not scare her; she prefers the Honour of being your Majesty's Wife one Night, to her Life.' 'But don't mistake your self, Visier,' says the Sultan, 'to Morrow, when I put *Scheherazade* into your Hands, I expect you should take away her Life; and if you fail, I swear, that you your self shall die.' 'Sir,' rejoins the Visier, 'my Heart without doubt will be full of Grief to execute your Commands; but it is to no purpose for Nature to murmur;

tho' I be her Father, I will answer for the Fidelity of my Hand to obey your Order.' *Schahriar* accepted his Minister's Offer, and told him he might bring his Daughter when he pleas'd.

The Grand Visier went with the News to *Scheherazade*, who receiv'd it with as much Joy, as if it had been the most agreeable thing in the World; she thank'd her Father for having obliged her in so sensible a manner, and perceiving that he was overwhelmed with Grief, she told him, in order to his Consolation, that she hop'd he would never repent his having married her to the Sultan; but that, on the contrary, he should have cause to rejoice in it all his Days.

All her Business was to put her self in a Condition to appear before the Sultan, but before she went, she took her Sister *Dinarzade* apart, and says to her, 'My dear Sister, I have need of your Help in a Matter of very great Importance, and must pray you not to deny it me. My Father is going to carry me to the Sultan to be his Wife, don't let this frighten you, but hear me with Patience. As soon as I am come to the Sultan, I will pray him to allow you to lie in the Bride-Chamber, that I may enjoy your Company this one Night more. If I obtain that Favour, as I hope to do, remember to awake me to Morrow, an Hour before Day, and to address me in these or some such Words: *"My Sister, if you be not asleep, I pray you that till Day-break, which will be very speedily, you would tell me one of the fine Stories of which you have read so many."* Immediately I will tell you one; and I hope by this means to deliver the City from the Consternation they are under at present.' *Dinarzade* answer'd, That she would obey with pleasure, what she requir'd of her.

The time of going to Bed being come, the Grand Visier conducted *Scheherazade* to the Palace, and retir'd, after having introduc'd her into the Sultan's Apartment. As soon as the Sultan was left alone with her, he order'd her to uncover her Face, and found it so beautiful, that he was perfectly charm'd with her; and perceiving her to be in Tears, ask'd her the reason. 'Sir,' answer'd *Scheherazade*, 'I have a Sister, who Loves me tenderly, as I do her; and I could wish that she might be allow'd to be all Night in this Chamber, that I might see her, and bid her once more adieu. Will you be pleas'd to allow me the Comfort of giving her this last Testimony of my Friendship?' *Schahriar* having consented to it, *Dinarzade* was sent for, who came with all possible

Diligence. The Sultan went to Bed with *Scheherazade*, upon an *Alcove* rais'd very high, according to the Custom of the Monarchs of the East, and *Dinarzade* lay in a Bed that was prepared for her, near the Foot of the *Alcove*.

An Hour before Day, *Dinarzade* being awake, fail'd not to do as her Sister order'd her. 'My dear Sister,' cries she, 'if you be not asleep, I pray, until Day-break, which will be in a very little time, that you will tell me one of those pleasant Stories you have read; Alas! this may perhaps be the last time that ever I shall have that satisfaction.'

Scheherazade, instead of answering her Sister, address'd her self to her Sultan, thus; 'Sir, will your Majesty be pleas'd to allow me to give my Sister this satisfaction?' 'With all my Heart,' answers the Sultan. Then *Scheherazade* bid her sister listen, and afterwards addressing her self to *Schahriar*, began thus.

THE FIRST NIGHT

'The Merchant and the Genie'

'SIR,

There was formerly a Merchant, who had a great Estate in Lands, Goods, and Money. He had abundance of Deputies, Factors, and Slaves. He was oblig'd from time to time, to take Journeys, and talk with his Correspondents; and one day being under a necessity of going a long Journey, about an Affair of Importance, he took Horse, and put a Portmanteau behind him, with some Bisket and Dates, because he had a great Desert to pass over, where he could have no manner of Provisions. He arriv'd without any accident at the end of his Journey; and having dispatch'd his Affairs, took Horse again, in order to return Home.

'The 4th Day of his Journey, he was so much incommoded by the heat of the Sun, and the Reflexion of that Heat from the Earth, that he turn'd out of the Road, to refresh himself under some Trees, that he saw in the Country. There he found at the Root of a great Walnut-Tree, a Fountain of very clear running Water, and alighting, tied his Horse to a Branch of a Tree, and sitting down by the Fountain, took some Bisket and Dates out of his Portmanteau, and as he eat his Dates, threw the Shells about on both sides of him. When he had done eating, being a good Mussulman, he wash'd his Hands, his Face, and his Feet, and said his Prayers.[13] He had not made an end, but was still on his Knees, when he saw a *Genie* appear, all white with Age, and of a monstrous Bulk: who advancing towards him with a Scimitar in his Hand, spoke to him in a terrible Voice, thus: "Rise up, that I may kill thee with this Scimitar, as you have kill'd my Son"; and accompanied those Words, with a frightful Cry. The Merchant being as much frightened at the hideous Shape of the Monster, as at those threatening Words, answer'd him trembling, "Alas! my good Lord, of what Crime can I be guilty towards you, that you should take away my Life?" "I will", replies the *Genie*, "kill thee, as thou hast kill'd my Son." "O Heaven!" says the Merchant, "how should I kill your Son, I did not know him, nor ever saw him." "Did not you sit down when you came hither," replies the *Genie*, "did not you take Dates out of your Portmanteau, and as you eat 'em, did not you throw the shells about on both sides?" "I did all that you say," answers the Merchant, "I cannot deny it." "If it be so," replied the *Genie*, "I tell thee, that thou hast kill'd my Son; and the Way was thus: When you threw your Nutshells about, my Son was passing by, and you threw one of 'em into his Eye, which kill'd him; therefore I must kill thee." "Ah! my Lord, Pardon me!" cry'd the Merchant. "No Pardon," answers the *Genie*, "no Mercy: Is it not just, to kill him that has kill'd another?" "I agree to it," says the Merchant; "but certainly I never kill'd your Son; and if I have, it was unknown to me, and I did it innocently; therefore I beg you to pardon me, and to suffer me to live." "No, no," says the *Genie*, persisting in his Resolution, "I must kill thee, since thou hast kill'd my Son"; and then taking the Merchant by the Arm, threw him with his Face upon the Ground, and lifted up his Scimiter, to cut off his Head.

'The Merchant all in Tears, protested he was innocent, bewail'd his Wife and Children, and spoke to the *Genie* in the most moving Expressions that could be uttered. The *Genie*, with his Scimiter still lifted up, had so much Patience, as to hear the Wretch make an end of

---

[13] Salat, the daily ritual prayer enjoined upon all Muslims as one of the five Pillars of Islam. Prayer is preceded by ablution.

his Lamentations, but would not relent. "All this whining", says the Monster, "is to no purpose, tho' you should shed Tears of Blood, that shall not hinder me to kill thee, as thou kill'dst my Son." "Why!" replied the Merchant, "can nothing prevail with you? will you absolutely take away the Life of a poor Innocent?" "Yes," replied the *Genie*, "I am resolved upon it." ' As she had spoke those Words, perceiving it was Day, and knowing that the Sultan rose betimes in the Morning to say his Prayers, and hold his Council, *Scheherazade* held her peace. 'Lord! Sister,' says *Dinarzade*, 'what a wonderful Story is this?' 'The remainder of it', says *Scheherazade*, 'is more surprising, and you will be of my mind, if the Sultan will let me live this Day, and permit me to tell it you next Night.' *Schahriar*, who had listened to *Scheherazade* with Pleasure, says to himself, 'I will stay till to Morrow, for I can at any time put her to death, when she has made an end of the Story': So having resolved not to take away *Scheherazade*'s Life that Day, he rose and went to his Prayers, and then call'd his Council.

All this while the Grand Visier was terrible uneasy. Instead of sleeping, he spent the Night in Sighs and Groans, bewailing the Lot of his Daughter, of whom he believ'd that he himself should be the Executioner. And as, in this melancholy Prospect, he was afraid of seeing the Sultan, he was agreeably surpriz'd, when he saw the Prince enter the Council-Chamber without giving him the fatal Orders he expected.

The Sultan, according to his Custom, spent the Day in regulating his Affairs; and when Night came, he went to bed with *Scheherazade*. Next Morning before Day, *Dinarzade* fail'd not to address her self to her Sister, thus: 'My dear Sister, if you be not asleep, I pray you till Day-break, which must be in a very little time, to go on with the Story you began last Night.' The Sultan, without staying till *Scheherazade* ask'd him leave, bid her make an end of the Story of the *Genie* and the Merchant, 'for I long to hear the Issue of it'; upon which *Scheherazade* spoke, and continued the Story as follows.

'The Fable of the Mouse, that was Changed into a Little Girl'

from *The Fables of Pilpay* (1699)

Bidpai, translated by Joseph Harris from the
French translation of Gilbert Gaulmin and David Sahid
Les Fables de Pilpay (1698)

Copy text: 1st edition (London, 1699)

European translators were not slow to see the relation
between a tradition of indigenous 'Indian' writing, the
nītiśāstra, a treatise on government, and the western tradition
of the *speculum principis*, or mirror for princes. One of the
earliest collection of oriental fables to appear in English were
those associated with the Hindu sage and fabulist known as
Bidpai, or Pilpay. Pilpay is representative of a tradition of
oriental tale-telling in Europe which presents models of
wisdom and rational order in oriental cultures for the West
to emulate, a tradition particularly associated with the animal
fable. The figure of the 'sage' teller is central to this tradition
and is imitated in examples in this anthology from James
Ridley and Oliver Goldsmith.

The earliest translation of the Pilpay tales had appeared in 1570. It was a translation by Sir Thomas North of an Italian 1552 translation of an Arabic version (*c.*750, Ibn al-Muqaffa's *Kalilah wa Dimnah*) of the sixth-century translation into Syriac of the Pahlavi (old Persian) translation. In 1696, Antoine Galland suggested to his publisher, Claude Barbin, that he produce a translation from a sixteenth-century translation from the Arabic into Ottoman Turkish, *Humayan Namah*, but problems with the library holding the copy resulted in the release instead of a translation by Gilbert Gaulmin and David Sahid from the first four chapters of a Persian translation of *Kalilah wa Dimnah*, the *Anwar-e Sohayli*, under the title *Les Fables de Pilpay* (1698).

It was this French text which formed the source for Joseph Harris's close English translation in 1699, which he dedicated to the duke of Gloucester, Queen Anne's heir. Harris produced a corrected and enlarged version of the same text in 1747; his changes consisted of the addition of one fable ('The Countryman and Several Rats') not found in his French source, and the addition of explanatory footnotes. Harris's footnotes confirm a tendency throughout the corrected and enlarged text to foreground the oriental nature of the tales and their context (for example the term 'monk' in the 1699 version is habitually changed to that of 'dervise' in the 1747 version). In 1724, Galland's translation from the Ottoman Turkish was published posthumously under the title *Les Contes et Fables Indiennes*, having been completed by Thomas-Simon Gueullette (a lawyer-turned-writer who wrote and published a number of oriental tales in imitation of Galland). This collection contained one new fable 'Les Singes, l'Oiseau et le voyageur' from the Ottoman source and excluded two tales from the *Fables de Pilpay*. Galland/Gueullette's text does not appear to have been translated into English.

Pilpay tells the fables in the collection to the Indian king, Dabschelim, to teach him how to govern well and generously while remaining always suspicious of his apparent allies. The name Pilpay is explained in Harris as meaning 'friendly physician'. The introduction to Galland's translation of the Ottoman version asserts that 'Bid' and 'pai' means 'Philosophe Charitable' (p. vi) and should be preferred to the etymology of the name Pilpai/Pilpay from the Persian term for elephant feet and applied by Persians at the Mughal court to native Indians whose unclad feet were thought to resemble those of elephants.

The collection is a complicated frame narrative. The outer frame involves a wise vizier telling his Chinese monarch about the influence of the Hindu sage Pilpay upon his Indian king Dabschelim. Dabschelim goes in search of a treasure only to discover that the treasure is in fact Pilpay's wisdom. Pilpay's stories are grouped in four chapters each containing several fables, often enboxed with other fables, which demonstrate four morals: that we ought to avoid the insinuations of flatterers and back-biters (twenty-six tales in Harris's 1747 translation and twenty-five in the 1699 translation); that the wicked come to an ill end (ten tales); how we ought to make choice of friends and what advantage may be reaped from their conversation (eight tales); and that we ought always to distrust our enemies, and be perfectly informed of what passes among them (twelve tales).

The logic for this grouping is generated by a 'frame' story of the machinations of the fox Damna to gain ascendancy in the kingdom of the lion. Damna discovers that the lion-king will not leave his palace because he is frightened by the bellowing of an ox in a nearby meadow and persuades the ox to come to court and bow before the king; the ox, much to Damna's frustration, is rapidly exalted to the position of the king's favourite and Damna plots to plant doubts in the lion's mind as to the ox's loyalty resulting in a fight in which the ox is killed. A series of stories between Damna and his wife, Kalilah, between Damna and the lion, and between Damna and the ox, debate the role of deceit in government and whether it brings about good or evil ends. At the beginning of the next chapter, Dabschelim asks Pilpay to reveal to him how the fox's deceit came to light and Pilpay tells him that the lion appoints a leopard minister to investigate Damna; the leopard, with the help of the lion's mother, discovers his perfidy. The leopard and the lion's mother seek to bring about disclosure from the fox's own mouth rather than accusing him outright and this results in a series of tales in which Damna proves his eloquence only to have his deceit revealed by the leopard giving witness of conversations overheard between Damna and his wife. The fox is sentenced to be starved to death between four walls.

The last two chapters revert to direct narration of a series of fables by Pilpay to Dabschelim, the first proving the value of friendship and alliance between different beasts and the second the importance of distrusting one's enemies and being well informed about their doings. A frame story of war between the ravens and the owls and the victory of the ravens through the use of a spy in the owl court holds this theme together. The extract here comes from these closing stories. Here, the raven spy in the owl court, Carchenas, has arrived with horrible self-inflicted injuries at the owl's court claiming he has been expelled from the raven company, and against the advice of the courtiers, the king owl has taken pity on him.

For the complicated genealogy of the fables associated with Pilpay/Bidpai, see *The Fables of Bidpai: the Earliest English Version of the Fables of Bidpai, 'the Morall Philosophie of Doni' by Sir Thomas North*, ed. Joseph Jacobs (London, 1888).

As for *Carchenas*, he behav'd himself so well, that in a little time he won the Love of all the Court. The King of the Owls confided in him, and began to do nothing without first consulting him. One day *Carchenas* addressing himself to the King: 'Sir,' said he, 'the King of the Ravens has abus'd me so unjustly, that I shall never dye satisfy'd, till I have first gratify'd my Revenge. I have been a long time rummaging my Brains for the Means: But I have bethought my self, that I never can compass it safely nor handsomly, so long as I wear the shape of a Raven. I have heard Men of Learning and Experience say, that he who has been ill us'd by a Tyrant, if he makes any wish, he must put himself into the Fire; for that while he continues there all his wishes will be heard. For which reason I beseech your Majesty that I may be thrown into the Fire, to the end that in the middle of the Flames, I may beg of God to change me into an Owl. Perhaps Heaven will hear my Prayer, and then I shall be able to revenge my self upon my Enemy.'

The chief Minister that had spoken against *Carchenas* was then in the Assembly, and hearing this luscious[1] Speech, 'O Traytour,' cry'd he, 'whither tends all this superfluous Language? Now art thou weaving mischief, as sure as God is in Heaven. Sir,' added he, turning to the King, 'you may caress this wicked Fellow as long as you please, he will never change his Nature. The Mouse was metamorphos'd into a Maid, and yet she could not forbear wishing to have a Rat for her Husband.' 'You love to tell Fables,' said the King to him in Raillery; 'and I will hear this Fable of yours for once; but I will not promise you to be a Pin the better for it.'

'The Fable of the Mouse, that was Chang'd into a Little Girl'

'A Person of Quality walking one Day by the side of a Fountain, saw a Mouse fall at his Feet from the Bill of a Raven who had held it a little too carelessly. The Gentleman out of pity took it up and carry'd it home; but fearing lest it should cause any disorder, he pray'd the Gods to change it into a Maid. Which was presently done; so that instead of a Mouse, of a sudden he saw a very pretty Girl, which he Bred up. Some Years after the good Man seeing her big enough to be Marry'd, "chuse out", said he to her, "in all the whole extent of Nature, what Being pleases thee best, and I will make him thy Husband." "I would", said the Virgin, "have a Husband so strong, that he should never be vanquish'd." "That must needs be the Sun," reply'd the old Gentleman: And therefore the next Morning, said he to the Sun, "my Daughter desires an invincible Husband, will you Marry her?" "Alas," answer'd the Sun, "yonder Cloud enfeebles my Beams; address your self to that." Then the good Man made his Compliment to the Cloud. "Alas," said the Cloud, "the Wind drives me as it pleases." The old Gentleman nothing discourag'd, desir'd the Wind to Marry his Daughter. But the Wind laying before him, that his strength was stopt by such a Mountain, he address'd himself to the Mountain. "Oh! Sir," said the Mountain, "the Rat is stronger than I; for he pierces me in every side,

---

[1] luscious: 'sweet, and highly pleasing to the eye, ear, or mind' (*OED*).

and eats into my very Bowels"; whereupon the old Gentleman went at length to the Rat, who consented to Marry his Daughter, saying withal that he had been a long time seeking out for a Wife. So the old Gentleman returning home, ask'd his Daughter whether she would Marry a Rat. Now he expected that she would have abhorr'd the Thoughts of such a Marriage; but he was amaz'd to see her out of Patience to be united to a Rat. Thereupon the old Man went to his Prayers again, and desir'd the Gods that they would turn his Daughter into a Mouse as she was before, which they did accordingly.'

But the King of the Owls attributing all these Remonstrances to his chief Minister's Jealousie of the Raven, took little notice of 'em. In the mean time *Carchenas* observ'd the comings in and goings out of the Owls, and when he had perfectly inform'd himself of every thing, he left 'em and return'd to the Ravens. And he gave the King his Master an Account of every thing that had past, and then, 'Sir,' said he, 'now is the time for us to be reveng'd of our Enemies. In a Mountain that I know, there is a Cave where all the Owls meet every day, and this Mountain is environ'd with a Wood. Your Majesty needs no more but to command your Army to carry a great Quantity of that Wood, to the Mouth of the Cave. I will be ready at hand to kindle the Wood, and then all the Ravens shall flutter round about, to blow the Fire into a flame. By which means such Owls as shall adventure out, will be burnt in the flames, and such as stay within shall be smother'd.'

The King approv'd the Raven's Counsel, and ordering his whole Army to set forward, they did as *Carchenas* had contrived it, and by that means destroy'd all the Owls. By this example you see that sometimes submission to an Enemy is requisite for the eluding of their wicked Designs.[2]

---

[2] This is the voice of Pilpay who narrates these tales directly to his king, Dabschelim, in the closing sections of the collection.

'The History of Commladeve'

from *Tales, from the Inatulla of Delhi* (1768)

'Inâyat Allâh Kanbû, 'translated' by Alexander Dow

Copy-text: vol. i of the 1st edition (London, 1768)

The Inatulla of Delhi is 'Inâyat Allâh Kanbû, a seventeenth-century Persian officer in the Mughal service who became a devout Sufi. The 'Tales' are the *Bahâr-e dâneš*, a romance about Prince Jahandarsah and Princess Bahravar Banu, told to the narrator by a young Brahman in Hindi and subsequently rendered in Persian. Two English translations by East India Company men, Alexander Dow and Jonathan Scott, appeared in 1768 and 1799 respectively (the latter under the title *Bahar-Danush; or, Garden of Knowledge* with an introduction and notes that were very critical of the freedom of Dow's translation). In my opinion Dow's is the more interesting version, first because it indicates the tensions among British men serving in India over Robert Clive's rapacious economic policy and second because Dow altered his source to accord with more familiar structures and tropes of the oriental tale: for example, he replaces the young male Brahman narrator of the outer frame with a young and seductive female narrator on the model of Scheherazade (see ' "Dreams of Men Awake": India', in Ros Ballaster, *Fabulous Orients*).

49

Dow (d. 1779) was a Scottish soldier who rose through the ranks to be recommended to the East India Company at Calcutta. He entered as an ensign in the Bengal infantry in 1760 and was promoted to lieutenant in 1763, and captain in 1764. On leave in England in 1768, he published the *Tales* as well as a translation from Muhammad Kâsim Hindû Shâh Firishtah entitled *The History of Hindostan* with the prefix, 'Dissertation concerning the customs, manners, language, religion and philosophy of the Hindoos'. An oriental play called *Zingis* was performed and printed in 1769 and Dow returned to India to be promoted to lieutenant-colonel. In 1772 he published a continuation of Firishtah's *History* which covered the period to the death of Aurangzeb with two dissertations: 'On the Origin and Nature of Despotism in Hindostan' and 'An Enquiry into the State of Bengal'. In 1774 he returned again to England to the unsuccessful production of another oriental tragedy called *Sethona*. He died in India in 1779. A correspondent of the Scottish Enlightenment philosopher David Hume, Dow reveals in all his writings a critical agonistic vein (largely prompted by his hostility to Robert Clive) which implies that the British can learn from the Muslim and Hindu cultures they encounter, as well as take advantage of that knowledge to increase their profit and influence in the region.

Dow was proficient in Persian and expresses a frustrated desire to learn Sanskrit as well as about the Hindu religion from the tight-lipped 'pundits' that were his instructors. The introduction to the *Tales* draws attention to the metaphorical excess and flowery rhetoric of oriental writers and his own text imitates this idea extensively, producing a style that is profoundly laboured for modern readers and clearly grated on some of his contemporary readers since an entry in George Erskine Baker's *Biographica Dramatica* (London, 1782) describes him as 'utterly unqualified for the production of learning or of fancy, either in prose or metre' (ii. 336).

The tales told in the sequence are directed towards instructing the young Indian Prince Jehandar who falls hopelessly in love with the description (and later portrait) of a princess of China (here called Gulzara). That description is provided in this extract by his close friend, who has transmigrated into the body of a parrot after he has been mauled to death by a tiger. The parrot has also overheard the story of Commladeve confided to Gulzara. Commladeve is an Indian princess who has been sold into slavery by Jehandar's jealous mistress, Mherpirwir, and the parrot delivers his story in the presence of the latter. The rest of the two volumes consist of tales told by courtiers about female infidelity to persuade Jehandar against his apparently hopeless pursuit of Gulzara, followed by a series of tales told to him by a Brahman sage in the mould of Pilpay (see introduction to *The Fables of Pilpay*), which provide him with models of male courage and leadership and finally make it possible for him to win his love.

Neither the parrot-narrator nor the story of Commladeve, as Dow's rival translator, Scott, points out, is found in Dow's source text. There are parallels between the story of Commladeve and that of the Rani Padmani and Akbar's siege of Chitor in 1567 in François Catrou's *General History of the Mogol Empire* (1709) also reproduced in this anthology (Part 3). Dow had himself told this story in his 'History of Akbar' in his *History of Hindostan* translated from Firishtah (ii. 253–5) but this, in line with his Persian source, was a purely political account of the conflict with no sexual motive ascribed to Akbar. Jonathan Scott speculates that the tale was fabricated from a novel called *Pudmawut*, containing the adventures of a Raja and Rannee of Chitore. Commladeve's tale combines fairy tale or fable with the historical reality of Mughal expansion. The invention of the parrot-narrator gives Dow the opportunity to develop in fictional form his understanding of Hindu theories of transmigration which he had outlined in his 'Dissertation' prefixed to the first volume of his translation from Firishtah. Dow provides footnotes to his text explaining the Persian terms he is using which are provided here as footnotes by letter. My editorial comments are given as footnotes by number.

The Framed Sequence
Chapter III. History of the PARROT[1]

'Magnanimous protector of the world; it is not secret to your enlightened mind, that there are three great principles in nature; intellect, life, and matter. The first producing all the mental faculties; the second, vital motion; and the third, the five elements, earth, water, fire, air, and akash,[a] of which all bodies are composed, animate and inanimate; by a certain plasticity in the atoms, impressed by the Intelligent Principle.

'Now when the vital principle assumes to itself a body of fire, air and akash, it becomes what we call spirit or soul, and is endued with perception and the activity of thought in its motions. The atoms of which all animals are formed, are contained in the grosser elements of earth and water; souls are afterwards associated with them for the purposes of generation, and various creatures are produced according to the species to which they are respectively annexed. But as these bodies are subject to a dissolution called death, the soul returns to its former state; and if it has inhabited a body endued with rational faculties, it becomes accountable for its actions, and is destined to heaven or hell, for a certain time, in proportion to its merits or crimes; but if its crimes are not in the extreme, it is destined to animate another creature of an inferior degree, till in the course of providence it again inspires the body of a man; if then its actions are perfectly virtuous, it is absorbed in the divine essence, divested of all body, where it remains to all eternity, unconscious both of pleasure and pain.[2]

---

[1] Dow may have come across Diyâ al-Dîn Nakhshabî's *Tales of a Parrot* first published in 1792 in translation from a Persian manuscript by B. Gerrans which he says is 'intitled Tooti namêh'. An English and Persian parallel text was published in Calcutta and then in London in 1801 from a 17th-c. abridgement by Muhammed Khudavand of Nakhshabi's revision of this collection of Indic tales.

[a] A pure element or aether, according to the brahmin philosophy.

[2] In his 'Dissertation concerning . . . the Hindoos', Dow explains reanimation in similar terms, though reference to a dialogue between 'Brimha' (Brahma) and his son, Narud (whom Dow describes as 'reason') in which Brimha explains the tripartite principle of creation—Brimha, Bishen (Vishnu), and Shibah (Siva)—and the reanimation of the soul in other bodies as a punishment for evil (those who are good, he says, are immediately reabsorbed into the divine essence). Dow concludes that 'the Brahmins, contrary to the ideas formed of them in the west, invariably believe in the unity, eternity, omniscience and omnipotence of God, that the polytheism of which they have been accused is no more than a symbolical worship of the divine attributes' (Firishtah, *History of Hindostan*, i, p. lvvii).

'The History of Commladeve'

'In this manner the soul of your faithful slave[3] was, after death, associated with the body of a parrot;[4] and having passed through the course of regeneration, was pleased with its happy state, but soon found that all creatures on earth are surrounded with the thorns of care, and gnawed by the caustic of sorrow.

'When my little wings were fledged, and endued with sufficient strength to bear me in safety through the air, with a flock of my chattering companions, I strayed among the fields and the gardens, revelling among the sugar plantations, and devouring the most delicious blossoms, rocked in the cradle of spring.

'When the season of love approached, I made love to a virgin bride, whose wings were tipped with gold, and her head crowned with sapphire. Her coyness was conquered by assiduity, and at last she consented to resign the treasure of her charms to my passion.

'With mutual toil, and intuitive dexterity, we built our commodious habitation in the hollow of a mango tree, that the fruit, which was then in blossom, might subsist our young. But no sooner was our happiness almost compleat, by the view of a beautiful progeny, than a hideous snake, twining his scaly length around the trunk of the tree, wound himself up; and directed to the nest by their cries, devoured them one by one, in sight of their fluttering parents.

'My consort was inconsolable for her offspring, and for some days sat moping like an owl, over the ruins of the palace of pleasure, while I endeavoured in vain to soothe her woes, redoubling my own distress by sympathizing with her sorrows. But the muddy torrent of grief, at length, by degrees, subsided; and the landscape of pleasure was again reflected in the mirror of joy.

[3] The prince's dearest friend, Jewan Sadit, killed by a tiger through the conspiracy of Budbucht the evil courtier who is jealous of the favourite. Jonathan Scott notes that Dow probably took this story from the account he translated from Firishtah of the Emperor Jehangir's (reigned 1605–27) attempts to assassinate Shere Askun, husband of Mher-ul-Nissa's (later Nourmahal) in order to leave her free to marry him. Jehangir tricks Shere Askun into volunteering to wrestle a tiger unarmed, and the brave warrior, despite being terribly wounded, survives, only to be assassinated by the Omrahs of the Suba of Bengal when he attempts to retreat from Delhi with his wife to their estate in Burdwan some six months later (ii. 24–30).

[4] Jonathan Scott's more faithful 1799 translation has the Prince Jehaundar encounter a conceited young man with a parrot when he is out hunting. The parrot tells Jehaundar he is the heir apparent to the crown and ring of these regions and gives him a ruby worth a kingdom.

53

'Having smoothed our ruffled plumes, and expanded the wings of swiftness, we flew to a distant land, where we alighted in a paradisal garden adjoining to a royal mansion, gorgeous as the palaces of light on the rosy plains of evening. We afterwards found that the place was called Chanbalich, the imperial residence of the puissant emperor of Chathay.[b]

'Enchanted with the beauties of the place, in comparison of which the choicest flowers of poetic description appear like weeds in the garden of spring, we fixed on a mulberry tree for the construction of a second abode; and having completed it with taste and elegance, we drank joy from the bursting grape, and eat sweetness from the rosy nectarine.

'But alas! one morning as the chaste partner of my life was hopping among the nursery of seeds, she was caught in the glossy neck in the treacherous snare of the gardener.

'Anxious at her unusual delay, I began to beat the wings of enquiry, and found her struggling, and even almost expiring, in this indissoluble chain of captivity.

'A long time I endeavoured, with my little bill, to untie the fatal noose, but found it a fruitless labor; so perching on a neighbouring tree, I bewailed my captivated mate, wringing my soul with sorrow.

'I had not remained long in this cruel situation, when I heard the brazen door of the royal zennana[c] opened towards the garden; and lo! a company of beautiful damsels issued forth, playing heavenly strains upon a variety of instruments of music.

'But in beauty, grace, and majesty, conspicuous above the rest, shone the royal virgin Gulzara[d] like Zohara[e] on the rosy fields of morn, when she rises with her sparkling attendants from bathing in the eastern deep.

'No dew-drop glistening in the ray of morning, could display half the brightness of her eyes; nor could the softness of the rose of Damask compare with the fragrant blossoms of her cheeks. Her arched eye-brows were bows to kill, but her heart was tender, and her hands soft, to withdraw the weapon from the wound. From her red

[b] China.   [c] The seraglio.   [d] The flower-garden.
[e] The morning star, or Venus.

lips distilled balsamic sweets, and her panting breasts displayed a paradise of joy. The breezes from her ebon hair, stole precious essence to perfume the meads, where the beauteous nirgis,[f] in sweet languor, reclines his head, turning, in expectation of her approach, its never-closing eyes. Nor do the meads rejoice alone in her presence, the sprightly lark, borne on the wings of pleasure, mistakes the opening of her eyes for the morning.

'But words can no more paint her beauties, than the brightest colours in the treasury of nature can paint the meridian ray.

'What insupportable pangs did I feel, when I perceived one of her attending nymphs running towards the companion of my distress, and seizing the screaming captive with the rude hand of violence; but her adorable mistress perceiving her, ran towards the place, and having checked the maid for the rudeness of her manner, stretched forth the delicate hand of compassion, and with all the tenderness of pity disengaged her from the cruel snare, stroking her glittering wings.

'I felt some comfort at this gracious reception, but the loss of my lovely partner for ever recurred to my distracted mind; determined at once rather to perish in company with my consort than to pine in the dark desart of solitude, I flapped the wings of love, and perched upon the alabaster hand of Gulzara, which held my captivated love.

'Frightened at my intrusion she started back, but soon perceiving the cause, I beheld the transparent pearls trickling from the full roses of spring,[g] while the silver tongue of harmony pronounced these words of favor.

' "Go, happy couple, go, enjoy your constant loves; go feast without fear on the most delicious fruits of my garden. Let me never be the cause of grief, nor, like the proud tyrant man, pervert the laws of nature. Ah! why was I born a princess to be thus immured in these cold walls where love is denied access, and beauty perisheth like a flower in the desart!"

'So saying she released my companion, when we flew on the wings of ecstasy to our little nest, chattering expressions of gratitude. But we had not remained long in our joyful habitation, when we beheld the divine princess advancing towards the foot of the tree, where with one

---

[f] A kind of flower, probably the Narcissus.   [g] Her cheeks.

of her fair confidants she reclined on a mossy bank; while the other nymphs, by her command, retired to a respectful distance, whispering the breath of envy.

'Bending the ear of attention, my mind soon mounted to the zenith of the astonishment, at the curious conversation which ensued.'

Here the parrot, ruffling up his plumes, made a short pause, on which the prince, whose curiosity was excited, desired him to proceed with his narration. But the lady,[5] whose bosom, during the narrative, had often swelled with envy, while her cheeks glowed with shame, darting a scornful eye at the parrot, then leering upon the prince, thus addressed him:

'Sacred repository of wisdom, permit not the vain tales of this lying prattler to find belief in the auditory of your mind; but as it seems to please the prince, he may amuse us with his imaginary adventures, which are divested of the shadow of truth.'

The prince checked her presumption with a frown, and the parrot, obedient to his command, unlocked the fountain of eloquence to call forth the flowers of imagination on the cultivated garden of the mind.

Chapter IV. 'The History of COMMLADEVE'[h]

'The silver-robed daughter of beauty, with a smile benign as the evening ray, obliquely glancing through a flower in spring, thus questioned her lovely companion.

' "It must be so, my dear Commladeve; the peculiar dignity which I have always observed in your actions, assures me that you were not bred to servility, nor inured to the chains of bondage: do therefore satisfy my curiosity in this point, permitting the seal of secrecy to be melted by the generous warmth of my friendship."

'Commladeve with a sigh, thus replied.—"Fair queen of perfections, it were surely the height of ingratitude in the obsequious slave of your presence, to keep any thing, under the veil of secrecy, concealed from your bountiful eyes. But you will be pleased to remember, that

---

[5] Mherpirwir, the prince's favourite mistress. Her name, Dow informs us, means 'nourisher of love'.

[h] This, in the Shanscrit language, means fair as the lotus or water-flower.

not my own vanity, but your royal commands, obliged me to a recital of my adventures."—With that she wiped a bright tear that stood in the corner of her eye, and thus, with melodious voice, charmed the ear of attention.

' "If a long pearl-string of ancestry should be deemed fortunate for the possessor, few could with greater propriety be ostentatious of fortune's favors than I; but this is so far from contributing one drop to the measure of my happiness, that it has become a source of bitterness in the troubled fountain of my fate.

' "My progenitors from time immemorial, were rajas of the fertile kingdom of Chitor,[i] which they ruled by the scepter of justice and the love of their subjects, more than by the sword of power. But at length the spear of Islamism[j] pierced the peaceful shades of our retirement, so that our innocent plains streamed with blood and gleamed with hostile arms.

' "I was then in my thirteenth year, and had, four years before, been betrothed to Ammarsein, heir to the potent kingdom of Tilling,[k] but had never seen him, but once, at the pompous celebration of our nuptials. After the destructive flames of war had for some time been blown from side to side before the contending gales of victory, notwithstanding our rajaputs[l] did justice to loyalty and their native valor, yet, from the superior skill and number of the enemy, the house of our prosperity was consumed, and my father, who had resolved to perish with his country, was found wounded in the field, and carried prisoner in triumph to Delhi.

' "I had previously been sent off with my mother to a small fortress situated upon a steep mountain, in the middle of an impervious wood. I escaped the rude hands of captivity; but alas! we had no prospect to soothe our eyes, except the smoking ruins of our desolated kingdom.

' "Unfortunate for my father, as the little beauty, wit, and other accomplishments, which I was then said to have possessed, were exaggerated by the voice of fame. It reached, at length, the ears of the vizier; he became desirous to gratify his passion, with the unblown rose of my virginity: he therefore began to solicit my father with fair

---

[i] One of the antient kingdoms of Hindostan, now a province of the Decan.
[j] Mahommedans. [k] Now called Golconda, or Tillingana.
[l] The fighting tribe of Hindoos.

promises of liberty, restoration, and royal favor;[6] but he would not consent to grace the cabinet of prostituted love with this jewel of paternal affection. But at the same time unwilling to rouze the resentment of the vizier by a downright refusal, he endeavoured to temporize, by evasions, till other objects should engage his mind.

' "But at length, the patience of the vizier was exhausted, and the insidious fawning of the lion changed to menaces of rage. My unfortunate father was thrown into a dungeon, where his ears were only gratified by the music of his own chains, and his tongue only moistened by the tears of his aged eyes.

' "Here he conversed but with his own miseries, whilst death, his most wished-for companion was thrust back at the threshold of his abode. What could he do? The power of human fortitude was vanquished, and nature shrank at a constancy of woe. So having consented to write an order for my delivery, he was freed from the weight of his chains, and indulged with the extent of a garden, where a guard of Abyssinian slaves surrounded him, with a wall of iron.

' "The bearer of this order being bribed with a ring, carried at the same time a private letter to my mother, informing her of the cruelty of his situation, and begging some method might be contrived to convey him a relieving potion,[m] which was now the only possible hope of preserving the skirts of his honor unstained, and the laws of his gods inviolated.

' "Unfortunately this letter, wrote with the gall of sorrow, conveyed that deadly poison to my dear mother, which my father had requested at her hand; and in the dreadful moment when life stood quivering at the cold door of the house of clay, she thrust the letter into my hand, and, with a smile, to encourage the example, resigned her soul to heaven.

' "The current of my blood ran back, the face of my condition was darkened, and the owl of affliction began to scream in the hollow of my ears. But I soon recovered from this transitory death, and a glimpse of reviving hope shot through the dark dungeon of my despair.

---

[6] Dow changes this figure from the Mughal sultan in his source to that of a vizier.
[m] Poison.

' "I immediately gave orders for my retinue to be prepared, in compliance with my father's command; but, instead of my maids of honor, I gave private instructions that twenty of the bravest warriors of the court should be cloathed in complete armour, and attend me in covered doolys[n] to the imperial court of Delhi.

' "The joyful vizier being informed of my approach by a messenger, by whom I requested the favor of first paying a visit to my father, it was granted me without hesitation. Accordingly, when the doolys were carried within my father's apartments, and all the bearers and servants had retired, I threw myself at his feet, and clasping his trembling knees, informed him of the desparate scheme I had undertaken for his deliverance.

' "There was no time for hesitation, he embraced me tenderly, and seizing a sword and shield, which I had prepared for him, while I waved another sabre in my own hand, he commanded me to follow under the shadow of his protection.

' "So placing himself at the head of his brave warriors, he fell upon the guards in the passage, carrying death before him to the gate, where we mounted the Arabian coursers of my retinue, so that by favor of the night and the crowd we escaped the precincts of the city, and were far advanced on our journey before day.

' "Now the vizier, like a hungry panther when robbed by the tiger of his prey, gnashed the sharp teeth of resentment, and, having dispatched a party of horse in pursuit, we observed them in a cloud of dust, the very moment we had alighted in a grove, to unbrace the strained sinews of toil.

' "I was immediately remounted, and commanded with one trusty servant to fly; and, however desirous I was to abide the event, my father was not to be disobeyed.

' "I soon perceived the bloody work of death commenced between unequal numbers, and looking forward beheld another body of cavalry on full gallop on the road toward me. I concluded myself now in the jaws of inevitable ruin, so drawing a poignard, I raised the hand of resolution against my own existence; when I heard a well-known

[n] Covered chairs, in which women are carried on men's shoulders.

voice crying, 'Stop! stop! your rash hand, illustrious princess, and in us behold your loyal servants!'

' "I immediately perceived him to be the faithful dewan° of my father, in company with my young lord Ammarsein, who being informed of my bold undertaking, had advanced to secure our retreat.

' "The joyful prince threw himself on the ground to salute me; but beckoning, I exclaimed; 'my father! my father!' He apprehended my meaning, bounded into his saddle; commanded three horsemen to attend me, and with the rest of his troop, on fiery hoof, flew to the scene of action; where I was afterwards informed my father, with five of wounded friends, remaining of his train, like wood-men in the meridian hour, scarce raised the arms of languor. But this seasonable relief soon veiled the face of danger; for the prince, like a young lion in his first attempt, exulted in his might, and strewed the field with slaughter.

' "While my heart burnt on the embers of anxiety, I observed six horsemen advancing on the wings of speed. I fluttered with expectation, like a lark when the dawn proclaims the glad tidings of the morning.

' "But alas! what was my disappointment and terror, when my attendants were smote with the sword, my weapons wrested from my hands? I remember no more; for I was carried off insensible of existence, and on my recovery found myself lying in a covered pal-langky,[7] travelling I knew not wither, and guarded by a company of horsemen.

' "Now all the horrors of my fate crowded at once upon my mind. I conceived myself in the hands of a cruel enemy, whom I considered as the murderer of my father, of my mother, of my husband, of my friends, and the intended murderer of my own virtue.

' "I was, in short, carried to Delhi, dragged into a magnificent zennana, and by the abominable hands of eunuchs, laid upon a bed of state.[8]

' "I had not long remained here to ruminate on my miseries, when I beheld an old tottering wretch enter the apartment, with a long black

---

° Steward.   [7] pallangky: palanquin.

[8] A Hindu maid would consider eunuchs an 'abomination' where in Islamic courts they were high-status servants.

beard dyed with antimony, a staff in his withered hand, and his hollow eyes like candles in the socket, expiring in the last flames of desire; he advanced, and thus addressed me:

' " 'Let thy griefs be dispelled, O fair light of my eyes! I come to worship the rising sun of thy beauties, and enfold thee in the arms of love.'

' " 'Art thou that monster', said I, 'who, dead to humanity as to pleasure, riseth, like a ghost from the grave, to devour the flesh of the living, and suck blood from the veins of the innocent? Go, spectre! go, direct thy adoration to heaven, and infold with those withered arms the altar of thy offended God.'

' "Wounded by the dart of reproach, for a moment, he hesitated between patience and anger; but, at length, his meagre jaws grinned a horrid smile, and he staggered forward to embrace me; when, with all the force of horror and resentment, I threw him at full length on the floor.

' "He arose uttering exclamations of rage, and with a fierce countenance retiring, told me, that since my folly had rejected his lenity, it must experience the effects of his power.

' "As he left me no time for reply, I threw myself down on the bed of affliction, fluttering like a bird in a snare, dreading the hands of the fowler;[9] but my attention was soon drawn from my condition, by the appearance of an antiquated daughter of Time, whose breasts hung withered and low, and whose flaming eyes were like festering wounds. Her long prominent nose, seemed a hook to suspend her lower jaw, and a crooked gash between, devouring her own lips, extended from ear to ear.

' "Bent, like a beggar on crutches, she limped towards me; and, with the squeaking voice of a squirrel, thus presented her deceitful address.

' " 'Fair princess, whose beauties brighten my aged eyes, and recall the past joys of my youth, let me approach the eyes of discernment with the jewels of wisdom, and drop into the ear of attention the salutary balm of advice.

---

[9] fowler: 'one who hunts wild birds' (*OED*).

' " 'How much is your fortune to be envied, sweet princess, who, as yet, in the morning of life, hast risen, with superior lustre, to the zenith of terrestrial bliss! What do I say? Here paradise itself smiles around. Here love has taken up his abode. Here the treasures of Karoon[P] are accumulated for you: variety to please the sight; music to charm the ear; and a thousand maidens, cloathed in gold, obsequious to the turn of your eye. What more is to be enjoyed, or what more is to be desired? Let therefore the curtain of virgin modesty be withdrawn, and the light of pleasure shine freely into the perfumed apartment of love.'

' "Thus the vile sorceress continued her strain of temptation, till rage fermenting in my bosom, burst forth in a torrent of abuse. When the hag perceived her wheedling arts were vain, she tottered out muttering revenge, and presently returned with a band of base eunuchs, who seized me by her command, bound me up to one of the pillars, and began to raise their whips over me, and threaten me with the terror of the scourge; but my spirits being expended in the struggle, my eyes were overshadowed with darkness, the current of my blood stood still, and for some time I remained without motion, the pale companion of the dead.

' "When I recovered from this state of mortality, I found myself unbound on a coach, surrounded by a number of beautiful females, pressing my limbs with their tender hands, and others besprinkling my face with water made of artificial snow, while the mother of prostitution was sitting squat on the cart on the carpet, like the trunk of an aged tree.

' "When she perceived me recover, she withdrew, telling me she hoped her next visit would find me more sensible of my own folly, and thankful for her intended favors.

' "I now addressed myself to the ladies around, acknowledged their humanity, at the same time informing them that their care for my recovery had to me proved the greatest misfortune, for that death was the only friend from whom I now hoped relief, and that a grave was the only bed in which I wished to repose.

' "I perceived this declaration drew sympathizing tears into the bright eyes of one of this fair assembly, which prepossessed me so

---

[P] A person, who according to the Mahommedans, was possessed of immense wealth.

much in her favor, that I courteously requested the others would retire, and leave me to recover my fatigue, giving, at the same time, a private hint to the lady who I intended should remain.

' "When they had all taken leave, I took hold of this favorite lady's hand, when I perceived I had lost a ruby of inestimable value, from the ring-finger of my own, which gave me some concern, as it had been the nuptial gift of my lord Ammarsein; but I took no further notice at that time of this least of my misfortunes.

' "When I had seated the lady by me, I told her I was well assured, that the breast which possessed so much humanity, harboured no guile: that therefore I had chosen her for the repository of my confidence, and the companion of my distress. She returned me thanks for my favorable opinion, which she hoped, by her behaviour to deserve; and assured me whatever I had to communicate, should remain under the seal of secrecy, locked up in the treasury of her heart.

' "Without further ceremony, I began to unfold the black book of my destiny, which we blotted together with our tears; and, when I had finished the mournful tale, she hastily arose, and desired me to compose myself a little; then embracing me tenderly, told me she was going, at the risque of her life, to effect my immediate deliverance. With this she instantly ran out of the room.

' "I was somewhat astonished at this abrupt behaviour, but soon found that my friend was true to her word. Being intimate with Mherpirwir, the favorite mistress of the illustrious prince Jehandar, she hastened to pay her a visit, and, relating the particulars of my story, it was communicated to the sultan." '

The prince here interrupting the parrot, told him he remembered the whole, but was impatient to know by what means she had travelled to the court of Cathay. The parrot resumed his narrative, but first begged that the lady, who now began to discover strong emotions of anxiety, might retire.

The lady, unable to suppress her passion, flew like a fury to the bird, and would have instantly deprived him of his head, had not the prince seized her hands, and commanded her, instantly, to leave the room: she obeyed in a flood of tears, to the no small astonishment of the sultan. The poor parrot recovering from his fright, proceeded thus:

' "The generous prince", continued the fair Commladeve, "was no sooner informed of these deeds of darkness, than he commanded the attendance of the vizier; and having pierced his heart with the lances of reproach, told him his life must now answer for an immediate delivery of the captive maid.

' "The vizier having exhausted all his long practiced arts of flattery and deceits, finding the prince unshaken in his purpose, trembled for the impending blow, and was constrained to give orders for my delivery.

' "Accordingly the chojaserai[q] was dispatched with a guard and a close litter, with orders to convey me to the prince's zennana,[r] whose respect and complaisance permitted him not to alarm me with the light foot of curiosity.

' "Here I found my faithful friend, who durst nor return to her habitation: she introduced me to the courtly Mherpirwir, by whom I was engaged to a repetition of all she had heard before, and, having supped together on the most exquisite rarities of the season, I was conducted into a magnificent apartment to feast on the sweets of repose.

' "Here sleep, the twin brother of death, in spite of fear, distress, and anxiety, visited my aching eyes; and next morning, when the king of stars[10] pierced through the casements of my solitude, I found myself, like the traveller of the desert, who had, accidentally, met with a fountain to quench his burning thirst.

' "A number of female slaves immediately attended to attire me; and in a few hours, I was conducted by the chief eunuch, to the antichamber of the great durbar,[s] where he directed me to a rent in the purdo,[t] to be a witness of what passed in the hall. Here I beheld the young sultan seated in majesty on a gorgeous throne, which was exquisitely formed in the shape of an expanded peacock,[11] feathered

---

[q] Master of the household; generally the chief eunuch.
[r] Women's apartment, or seraglio.
[s] The audience chamber.
[10] King of stars: the sun.
[t] A curtain or skreen.
[11] The reference is to the famous 'peacock' throne built for the Mughal Emperor Shah Jahan in the early 17th c. The throne was backed by gilded, enamelled, jewel-encrusted representations of two open peacocks' tails. The Iranian conqueror Nader Shan seized it

with precious jewels, bright as the variegated bow, with the golden-mooned train, like a canopy of fire projecting over his sacred head: a gilded book in his left hand, and a studded scepter in his right: while a thousand omrahs, in glittering brocade, with their hands joined obsequiously before, formed an extensive avenue according to their rank, from the foot of his awful tribunal."

'Here she was interrupted by the adorable Gulzara, who requested a particular description of your majesty's person; which, with the boldest strokes of the pencil of rhetoric, she attempted; and, to all appearance, raised such emotions in her panting breast, as might prove unfavourable, to her future repose. When the fair Commladeve had endeavoured to gratify her curiosity on this head, she thus proceeded on the flowery paths of narration.

' "I now beheld the vizier conducted by chobdars,ᵘ towards the throne, bowing his face three times to the ground, while they proclaimed health to the king of the world!—When his accusation was read aloud, he humbled his furrowed forehead to the dust; and, uncovering his bald head, made a confession of guilt in tears, but begged, that in consideration of his past services, he might be permitted to grasp the skirts of mercy, and that the expiring flame of his life might be left to the extinguishing hand of nature. To which the prince made this reply: though mercy was the attribute of heaven itself, yet we give birth to a thousand crimes by forgiving one. Thus, at last, the weed of wickedness becomes so luxuriant in the soil of life, that the hand of toil is never able to root it out.

' "When I heard these words, I trembled for the irrevocable decree, and, compassionating the unfortunate wretch, begged the choja would make intercession for his life in my behalf, and acquaint the prince, that hearing my father and husband were still alive, I had nothing to demand of the vizier but a ruby ring which I held in particular estimation, and which was stolen from my finger, as I imagined, by some of the eunuchs of his zennana.

when he captured Delhi in 1739 so Dow would not have seen the actual object. It is, however, described by numerous European visitors to the Mughal court, including Mannuci and Bernier (see Part 3, 'Travels and History').

ᵘ Mace-bearers.

' "The prince, though with seeming reluctance, remitted the severity of his intentions, but threw him from the height of his office, with these remarkable words:

' " 'When the pillars of the state are rotten, the fabric must fall to the ground; we therefore lighten thy weak shoulders of the weight of government, and permit thee to walk to thy grave in peace, and let God be the judge of thy sins.'

' "He then commanded the ring to be restored; for which purpose all the eunuchs who were present, were called, and strictly questioned concerning the theft, but they stood obstinately to their innocence, and insinuated, that as the old woman was present, she ought equally with them to be suspected of the crime.

' "The old sorceress was accordingly sent for, but vehemently denied the charge; upon which the vizier and omrahs proposed the torture to draw confession from the accused, but the prince objected to this method, saying;

' " 'There is nothing concealed from the eyes of those whom God has chosen to be the judges of his people, why therefore should the innocent suffer with the guilty, and his ministers be charged with injustice? Let therefore the accused be carried into separate apartments, till we have consulted the Genius of Truth.'

' "As soon as they were carried off, the prince ordered a small quantity of hing[v] to be brought, and having rubbed it on the cover of the book which he held in his hand, he desired it might be placed on a table in the adjoining chamber. He then ordered back the prisoners, one by one and commanded them to walk into the chamber, and there, with their right hand on the book, to swear to their innocence before God; when, if they were guilty of the fact, the power of their arm would inevitably be taken away; but if guiltless, they should receive no hurt.

' "At this I observed some of the courtiers turning the sneer of contempt, while others, with open mouths, devoured the air of astonishment; and I must confess, I myself had no favorable opinion of this method of trial. But when I saw the first eunuch returning, and heard the prince commanding one of the omrahs to examine whether his hand was tainted with the smell, I began to see through this artifice,

[v] A kind of drug.

and admired the sagacity of the scheme. In short, all the eunuchs upon examination, were discharged, but when the old woman came to the trial, her conscience accused her of guilt; and fearing the wrath of heaven, she returned without touching the book; for upon the strictest examination, her hand was found perfectly untainted with the odor.

' "She immediately confessed her crime, and implored forgiveness, but she was decreed to be scourged out of the city, while the whole court resounded with acclamations of praise of the prince's wisdom.

' "Thus I recovered my ring, and retired greatly delighted with the sultan's behaviour, which my heart, unexperienced in guile, soon disclosed to the piercing eye of Mherpirwir. She flamed with jealous rage, till she found means to effect my destruction.

' "However fair the externals of my present condition now appeared, nothing could in fact be more delusive. It was not sufficient to be conscious that the veil of my chastity was as snow, since the rigorous tenets of our religion rendered me polluted in the eyes of my family and friends, and an abomination to the arms of my husband.^w What could I do? My heart in spite of reason and honor rebelled against my own repose, and a delirious imagination presented me, night and day, with the enchanting idea of the illustrious sultan, insomuch that I thought of liberty no more, and trembled for the hour of my departure.

' "I was now informed that the generous prince had reinstated my father in his dominions, and had ordered a magnificent retinue, with honor, to attend me to his court. The news was like thunder to my ear, and, tossed by a whirlwind of passion, I ran to the chojaseray, conjuring him to inform the prince, that as I was now excommunicated from the society of my friends for ever, I requested permission to remain under the royal shade of his bounty, and pass the future days of my life in some solitary corner of obscurity.

' "The prince was astonished at my request, but immediately gave orders for an appointment of slaves, and all other necessaries suitable to the dignity of my birth. This having reached the ears of Mherpirwir, she was stung by the scorpion of jealousy more and more, till she

---

^w By the Hindoo religion, all persons who associate with another sect, in any manner whatever, are polluted and excommunicated.

quickly accomplished my ruin. That very night I was seized by a band of ruffians, in disguise, and carried by a Mogul merchant[12] to the court of Chathay, through a variety of dangers and distresses, and sold as a slave to the incomparable Gulzara." '

Here the prince arose, striding thrice across the apartment with hasty step, while the lightning of a storm of rage darted from under his cloudy brow; but sitting down, he commanded his attention while the parrot continued his tale.

'The adorable Gulzara, here wiping the sweet tear of compassion, like the benign dew of heaven which stands glistening in the morning ray, with a voice that could charm to innocence the serpent in the hand of danger, thus her lovely companion addressed:

' "O Commladeve! why do you afflict my ear with that odious word *slave*? You must be sensible, my friend, that I never considered you in that light. Are we not all free by nature; and surely accursed are they who inhumanely impose chains of bondage on their fellow creatures? O Commladeve, methinks I could love the prince, but Gulzara would die before she could betray you. What a wretch must that lady be, who could thus make so light a sacrifice of innocence! Surely were such a magnanimous prince acquainted with the baseness of her mind, an assemblage of all the beauties of our sex could not draw him within the circle of her charms. Were I disposed to that infection of envy, my heart would sicken at her happiness in his love. But why should we envy the happiness of others, when it only diminishes our own!

' "You must have heard that my royal father, Alta Chan, has destined me, at a proper age, to the arms of Tuli Chan, fourth son of the most puissant monarch Chingez Chan,[x] the conqueror of the world; who, from being a captain in the service of Onick Chan, king of Mogulistan, shaded with his victorious standards the crimsoned face of the extended earth, and reduced the power of a thousand kings within the grasp of his potent hand.[13]

---

[12] A reference to the silk road, the major trade and travel route between Asia, the Middle East and Europe in ancient and medieval times which passed through Samarkand.

[x] Zengis Chan, the Great.

[13] The nomadic leader Genghis Khan (1162?–1227) conquered a huge empire that stretched through Asia from the Yellow Sea to the Black Sea, overrunning northern China from 1208 to 1215. Tamerlane, founder of the Indian Mughal empire, was also descended

' "But the young lion Tuli Chan, like his father, delighteth in nothing but in rapine and blood. Bred up in the fields of slaughter, his soul is shut up to humanity; he places his boast in depopulating kingdoms, and glories in his own might; with him love is but the lust of a savage, and beauty but the play-thing of the hour. What happiness can I expect with such a man? Ah, were he the magnanimous Jehandar!" 'So saying, she arose erect, while her jet-black hair rolled behind, like the deep stream round the marble rock, as it falls from the hills of Sewalic. Then, seizing the arm of Commladeve, they walked into the zennana, like the daughters of light,[y] when they retire into the gilded apartments of Paradise.'

Fired with the description of this fair idol of perfection, and the idea of rivalling so great a prince, the sultan gave the reins of reason into the hand of imagination, and ran headlong into the wilderness of love.

Like Mudgeno[z] he frequented the silent shades, talked with the trees, and reasoned with the floods, sat lonely with sorrow, and passed the night in tears.[14] Insnared like a bird in Gulzara's flowing hair, he incessantly besought heaven to end his wretched existence, or permit the united streams of their life to flow through the regions of joy. Let not the manner of his love surprise us; love assaults the ears as well as he assails the eyes; for the image of beautiful objects in description, pass over polished minds, fair as the reality over polished glass; the only difference is, that the last retains no impression, but the first on the table of memory leaves the objects deeply engraved.

---

from Genghis Khan. Genghis Khan's Mongol empire was partitioned between his sons on his death in 1227. Genghis Khan is represented in plays such as Voltaire's *Orphan of China* (translated in 1756) as a warrior king impervious to sentiment, whether of love or family. Gulzara's father is a Chinese prince whose dominion is subject to the Mongol dynasty. The contrast between a gentle and civilized Chinese civilization and a warrior Mongol or Tartar invader was a common one in 18th-c. European writings about the Orient, also familiar from Voltaire's play.

[y] The Houries, or the women promised by Mohammed to his followers in Paradise.

[z] Famed in a fine poem for his love for Leilli.

[14] The story of Layli and Madjnun dates back to the 7th c. in Arabic writing and was adopted widely in Persian literature from the 12th c. with a version by the poet Nezami in his collection known as the *Khamsa*. The poet-hero's name means madman and there are close parallels between his besotted pursuit of Layli (whose father rejects Madjnun's father's overtures for their marriage thinking the hero is a madman, just as in this tale Gulzara's father rejects those of Jehandar's). Like Madjnun, Jehandar departs for the wilderness to live a miserable life where a hermit tries to console him.

The prince now neglected to hear the sequel of the parrot's adventures; but some days after, he commanded him to repeat the whole, and asked him a thousand questions concerning the fair bride of his imagination. This only inflamed him the more, when the parrot thus concluded his tale to the ruin of the conceited Mherpirwir.

'In this peaceful habitation, with my beloved mate, I enjoyed for some time a life of uninterrupted pleasure, and we were often fed by the fair hand of this guardian angel of Eden. At length misfortune found out our retreat in a cat's rapacious form, when my mate was devoured in protecting her helpless young, and they too perished in the same unrelenting claws, which left your slave to sorrow.

'The scene of my former joys became odious to my eyes, and I wandered on the wings of distraction, till one day, gnawed by the worm of hunger, I alighted on a fig-tree, in a garden, when I found myself entangled in a net;[aa] there was I caught by the boy you beheld, and had the happiness soon after of recognizing my generous prince, and of reciting my adventures.

'Now in your bosom I seek protection from the rage of that bubble of pride, who, with a handful of beauty, would exalt herself as the criterion of perfection, and the fairest of the daughters of men. Does she think the fertility of the fancy of nature could be expended in one poor piece? or all the beauties of the garden of creation comprehended in a single flower?

'Under this extensive star-built arch of heaven, how many noble exhibitions of the divine hand, strokes of transcendant beauty, and beings that each other excel in the infinite scale of perfection; and were this gilded insect of vanity to unfold her wings in the presence of the divine Gulzara, her spark would be lost in the blaze, like the fire-fly in the ray of the morning.'

[aa] Nets used to preserve fruit from the birds, and save it in its fall.

'The Adventures of Urad'

from *The Tales of the Genii: or, the delightful lessons of Horam, the Son of Asmar* (1764)

James Ridley

Copy-text: vol. i of the 1st edition (London, 1764)

James Ridley (1736–65) was the Oxford-educated son of a doctor who had held a fellowship of New College, Oxford, before he took orders. He obtained a chaplaincy in the East India Company's service but gave up the post to become chaplain to a marching regiment. On his return because of ill health in 1762 from France where his regiment was serving in the Seven Years War, he took up his father's living in Exeter, and died only three years later. His *Tales of the Genii* purport to be written by Charles Morrell, an English ambassador at Bombay, but are in fact invented by Ridley. In the tradition of the oriental tale devised to instruct a prince, Ridley dedicated the work to George, prince of Wales. The work had gone into seven editions by 1861 and was translated into French and German. Ridley had already published two novels—*The History of James Lovegrove, Esquire* (1761) and *The Schemer, or Universal Satirist, by that Great Philosopher Helter van Scelter* (1763)—before this his most successful work appeared in print.

The Framed Sequence

'Charles Morell' first encounters the *Tales of the Genii* in a Persian manuscript but loses his copy only to meet the author himself, a wise imam called Horam, at Fort St George in Madras. Horam claims to have composed the tales when he was instructor to Osmir, the vicious son of the Mughal emperor, Aurangzeb (reigned 1658–1707). In the tales, two children, Patna and Coulor, are spirited to a council of twenty-eight genii on golden thrones by a female genie, where they listen to their tales of how they have imparted 'instructive lessons' to mortals. The chief genie, the silver-haired Iracagem, oversees the proceedings. There are nine tales in the collection, set in locations Persian, Turkish, and Indian, all of which concern the attempts of mortals—with the aid or hindrance of genii—to discern moral truth behind the veil of disguise. The Protestant churchman Ridley concludes the tale by claiming that the age of genii and Islamic supernatural authority has been overtaken by the Christian faith, based on the fleshly truth of Jesus. In so doing, he is also asserting the British succession to Mughal rule in India and heralding what he saw as a new era of virtuous Christian government. However, the imam Horam, an admirer of the new science and especially Isaac Newton, has plenty of sharp comments about European covetousness in the Orient which suggests that Ridley was also arguing, in the years following the British defeat of the French in the territory, for a Protestant Christian—rather than mercantile—mission in India.

Like Alexander Dow, Ridley imitates what he takes to be a 'Persian' manner of writing—metaphorical, ornate, and repetitive. However, in the story given below he also domesticates the oriental tale, presenting his heroine Urad as an oriental version of Samuel Richardson's Pamela, her virtue constantly beleaguered and relying on a robust faith and religious instruction of virtue to protect her. The supernatural elements are a mere cover, like Ridley's use of the oriental tale to deliver Christian revelation.

'The Adventures of Urad; or, the Fair Wanderer. Tale the Fifth'

... after the Assembly were seated, the sage *Iracagem* arose and said, 'The Lessons of my Brethren Yesterday were first designed to inculcate a regular Search after Happiness, which Religion alone can teach us. . . . Obedience to *Alla* will make all Things easy to us. . . . To trust therefore in him, to love him, to exalt him, to obey, and to give him Praise, is the chief End and Creation of Man.

'But as mutual Weakness requires mutual Support, so the great *Alla* has given to his Children, the Laws and the Duties of social Morality, which twill be best explained to their tender Minds by Example, fraught with the Blessings of Instruction. Therefore, O Sister,' said the sage *Iracagem* to her, whose throne was placed by *Hassarack*'s, 'let this favored Assembly partake of your entertaining Advice.'

The *Genius*[1] immediately arose, and began the Adventures of *Urad*; or the Fair Wanderer.

'On the Banks of the River *Tigris*, far above where it washes the lofty City of the faithful,[2] lived *Nouri* in poverty and widowhood, whose employment it was to tend the Worm, who clothes the richest and the fairest with its beautiful Web.[3] Her Husband, who was a Guard to the Caravans of the Merchants, lost his Life in an Engagement with the wild *Arabs*,[4] and left the poor Woman no other means of subsisting herself, or her infant Daughter *Urad*, but by her Labors among the Silk-worms, which were little more than sufficient to support Nature, although her Labors began ere the Sun-beams played

---

[1] A Genius is a Genie, see n. 8 'Arabian Nights Entertainments'.

[2] The Tigris is a river in Turkey and Iraq. The 'city of the faithful' is Baghdad which was founded in 762 as the capital of the Abbasid dynasty of Shi'ite Islam. The tale is situated on a disputed border between Persia and Turkey.

[3] Nouri is engaged in the production of silk. Persia became a centre of silk trade between East and West under the Parthians (247 BC–AD 224). Production of silk involves the care of the domesticated silkworm from the egg stage through completion of the cocoon and the production of mulberry trees that provide leaves upon which the worms feed. The silkworm caterpillar builds its cocoon by producing and surrounding itself with a long, continuous fibre, or filament. This filament is unwound in a single strand and then several strands are woven together to produce silk yarn.

[4] The Bedouin, nomadic Arabic-speaking peoples of the Middle Eastern deserts.

on the Waters of the *Tigris*, and ended not till the Stars were reflected from its Surface.

'Such was the business of the disconsolate *Nouri*, when the voluptuous *Almurah*[5] was proclaimed Sultan throughout his extensive Dominions; nor was it long before his Subjects felt the power of their Sultan; for *Almurah* resolving to inclose a large Tract of Land for Hunting and Sporting, commanded the Inhabitants of fourteen hundred Villages to be expelled from the Limits of his intended Inclosure.

'A piteous Train of helpless and ruined Families, were in one day driven from their Country and Livelihood, and obliged to seek for Shelter amidst the Forests, the Caves, and Deserts, which surround the more uncultivated Banks of the *Tigris*.

'Many passed by the cottage of *Nouri*, the Widow, among whom she distributed what little Remains of Provision she had saved from the Earnings of her Labors the Day before; and her little Stock being exhausted, she had nothing but Wishes and Prayers left for the rest.

'It happened among the numerous Throngs that travelled by her Cottage, that a young Man came with wearied Steps, bearing on his Shoulders an old and feeble Woman, whom sitting down on the ground before the door of *Nouri*, he besought her to give him a Drop of water, to wash the Sand and the Dust from his parched Mouth.

'*Nouri* having already distributed the Contents of her Pitcher, hastened to the River to fill it, for the wearied young Man; and as she went, she begged a Morsel of Provisions from a Neighbour, whose Cottage stood on a Rock which overlooked the Flood.

'With this, and her Pitcher filled with Water, she returned, and found the feeble old Woman on the ground, but the young Man was not with her.

---

[5] One of the Ottoman sultans of the early modern period named Murat, but there is not enough information within the text to establish which. The nearest contemporary Murat to the reign of Aurangzeb in which Horam is ostensibly composing his tales is Murat IV (ruled 1623–40). On his accession Murat IV was ruthless in enforcing discipline and eliminating the weakness of the Ottoman state which was then in a state of political and financial anarchy. This would fit with Horam's 'biography' in that he is raised in Persia until enslaved by a Turkish Bashaw and sold to an English merchant. He acquires his freedom only on his master's death and, after a brief sojourn in England, takes up employment with Aurangzeb. He would therefore have been a young man living in Persia during the Ottoman reign of Murat IV.

' "Where," said *Nouri*, "O afflicted Stranger, is the pious young Man, that dutifully bore the Burden of Age on his Shoulders?" "Alas," answered the Stranger, "my Son has brought me hither from the Tyranny of *Almurah*, and leaves me to perish in the Deserts of the *Tigris*: no sooner were you gone for the Water than a Crowd of young Damsels came this way, and led my cruel Son from his perishing Mother: but, courteous Stranger," said she to *Nouri*, "give me of that Water to drink, that my Life fail not within me, for Thirst, and Hunger, and Trouble, are hastening to put an end to the unhappy *Houadir*."

'The tender and benevolent *Nouri* invited *Houadir* into the Cottage, and there placed her on a Straw-bed, and gave her the Provisions and a Cup of Water to drink.

'*Houadir* being somewhat refreshed by the Care of *Nouri*, acquainted her with the cruel Decree of *Almurah*, who had turned her Son out of his little Patrimony, where by the Labor of his Hands, he had for many Years supported her, and that till that Day she had ever found him a most dutiful and obedient Son; and concluded with a Wish, that he would shortly return to his poor helpless Parent.

'*Nouri* did all she could to comfort the wretched *Houadir*, and having persuaded her to rest a while on the Bed, returned to the Labors of the Day.

'When her Work was finished, *Nouri* with the Wages of the Day purchased some Provisions, and brought them Home to feed herself and the little *Urad*, whose Portion of Food, as well as her own, had been distributed to the unhappy Wanderers.

'As *Nouri* was giving a small Morsel to *Urad*, *Houadir* awaked, and begged that *Nouri* would be so kind as to spare her a Bit of Provision.

'Immediately before *Nouri* could rise, the little *Urad* ran nimbly to the Bed, and offered her Supper to the afflicted *Houadir*, who received it with great Pleasure from her Hands, being assured her Mother would not let *Urad* be a Loser by her Benevolence.

'*Houadir* continued several Days with the Widow *Nouri*, expecting the Return of her Son, till giving over all Hopes of seeing him, and observing that she was burdensome to the charitable Widow, she one evening, after the Labors of the Day, thus addressed her hospitable Friend.

' "I perceive, benevolent *Nouri*, that my Son has forsaken me, and that I do but rob you and your poor Infant of the scanty Provision, which you, by your hourly Toil, are earning: wherefore, listen to my Proposal, and judge whether I offer you a suitable Return: there are many parts of your Business, that, old as I am, I can help you in, as the winding your Silk, and feeding your Worms. Employ me, therefore, in such Business in the Day as you think me capable of performing; and at Night, while your necessary Cares busy you about the House, give me Leave (as I see your Labor allows you no spare Time) to instruct the innocent *Urad* how to behave herself, when your Death shall leave her unsheltered from the Storms and Deceits of a troubled World."

'*Nouri* listened with Pleasure to the Words of *Houadir*.

' "Yes", said she, "benevolent Stranger, you well advise me how to portion my poor Infant *Urad*, whom I could neither provide for by my Industry, nor instruct, without losing the daily Bread I earn for her: I perceive a little is sufficient for your Support; nay, I know not how, I seem to have greater Plenty since you have been with me than before; wherefore it be owing to the Blessing of Heaven on you, I know not."

' "Far be it from me", said *Houadir*, "to see my generous Benefactor deceived; but the thinness of Inhabitants, occasioned by the Tyranny of *Almurah*, is the Cause that your Provisions are more plentiful; but yet I insist upon bearing my Part in the Burden of the Day, and *Urad* shall share my Evening's Labor."

'From this time *Houadir* commenced an useful Member in the Family of *Nouri*, and *Urad* was daily instructed by the good old Stranger in the Pleasures and Benefits of a virtuous, and the Horrors and Curses of an evil Life.

'Little *Urad* was greatly rejoiced at the Lessons of *Houadir*, and was never better pleased than when she was listening to the mild and pleasing Instructions of her affable Mistress.

'It was the Custom of *Houadir*, whenever she taught *Urad* any new Rule or Caution, to give her a Pepper-corn, requiring of her, as often as she looked at them, to remember the Lessons which she learnt at the Time she received them.

'In this Manner *Urad* continued to be instructed, greatly improving, as well in Virtue and Religion, as in Comeliness and Beauty, till she was near Woman's Estate, so that *Nouri* could scarce believe she was the Mother of a Daughter so amiable and graceful in Person and Manners. Neither was *Urad* unskilled in the Labors of the Family, or the Silk-worm; for *Nouri* growing old and sickly, she almost constantly by her Industry supported the whole Cottage.

'One Evening as *Houadir* was lecturing her attentive pupil, *Nouri*, who lay sick on the straw-bed, called *Urad* to her.

' "My dear Daughter," said *Nouri*, "I feel, alas, more for you than myself; while *Houadir* lives, you will have indeed a better Instructor, than your poor Mother was capable of being unto you; but what will my innocent Lamb, my lovely *Urad* do, when she is left alone, the helpless Prey of Craft, or Lust, or Power? Consider, my dear Child, that *Alla* would not send you into the World to be necessarily and unavoidably wicked: Therefore always depend upon the Assistance of the holy Prophet when you do right, and let no Circumstance of Life, nor any Persuasion, ever bias you to live otherwise, than according to the chaste and virtuous Precepts of the religious *Houadir*. May *Alla*, and the Prophet of the Faithful, ever bless and preserve the Innocence and Chastity of my dutiful and affectionate *Urad*!"

'The widow *Nouri* spoke not again, her Breath for ever fled from its Confinement, and her Body was delivered to the Waters of the *Tigris*.

'The inconsolable *Urad* had now her most difficult Lesson to learn from the patient *Houadir*, nor did she think it scarcely dutiful to moderate the Violence of her Grief.

' "Sorrows," said *Houadir*, "O duteous *Urad*, which arise from Sin, or evil Actions, cannot be assuaged without Contrition or Amendment of Life; there the Soul is deservedly afflicted, and must feel before it can be cured; such Sorrows may my amiable Pupil never experience! But the Afflictions of Mortality, are alike the Portions of Piety or Iniquity; it is necessary that we should be taught to part with the desirable Things of this Life by Degrees, and that by the Frequency of such Losses, our Affections should be loosened from their earthly Attachments. While you continue good, be not dejected, O my obedient *Urad*; and remember, it is one Part of Virtue to bear, with Patience and Resignation, the unalterable Decrees of Heaven; not but what I esteem your Sorrow, which arises from Gratitude, Duty, and Affection; I do not teach my Pupil to part with her dearest Friends without Reluctance, or wish her to be unconcerned at the Loss of those, who by a marvellous Love, have sheltered her from all those Storms which must have in a Moment overwhelmed helpless Innocence. Only remember that your Tears be the Tears of Resignation, and that your Sighs confess an Heart humbly yielding to his Will, who ordereth all Things according to his infinite Knowledge and Goodness."

' "O pious *Houadir*," replied *Urad*, "just are thy Precepts; 'twas *Alla* that created my best of Parents, and *Alla* is pleased to take her from me; far be it from me, though an infinite Sufferer to dispute his Will; the Loss indeed wounds me sorely, yet will I endeavour to bear the blow with Patience and Resignation!"

'*Houadir* still continued her kind Lessons and Instructions, and *Urad*, with a decent Solemnity, attended both her Labors and her Teacher, who was so pleased with the Fruits which she saw springing forth from the seeds of Virtue that she had sown in the Breast of her Pupil, that she now began to leave her more to herself, and exhorted her to set apart some Portion of each day to pray to her Prophet, and frequent Meditation and Recollection of the Rules she had given her, that so her Mind might never be suffered to grow forgetful of the Truths she had treasured up; "For", said the provident *Houadir*, "when it shall please the Prophet to snatch me also from you, my dear *Urad* will then have only the Pepper-corns to assist her."

' "And how, my kind Governess," said *Urad*, "will those Corns assist me?"

' "They will," answered *Houadir*, "each of them, if you remember the Precepts I gave you with them, but not otherwise, be serviceable in the Times of your Necessities."

'*Urad*, with great Reluctance, from that Time, was obliged to go without her Evening Lectures, which Loss affected her much; for she knew no greater Pleasure in Life, than hanging over *Houadir*'s persuasive Tongue, and hearing, with fixed Attention, the sweet Doctrines of Prudence, Chastity, and Virtue.

'As *Urad*, according to her usual Custom (after having spent some few early Hours at her Employment) advanced towards the Bed to call her kind Instructor, whose Infirmities would not permit her to rise betimes, she perceived that *Houadir* was risen from her Bed.

'The young Virgin was amazed at the Novelty of her Instructor's Behaviour, especially as she seldom moved without Assistance, and hastened into a little Inclosure to look after her; but not finding *Houadir* there, she went to the neighbouring Cottages, none of whom could give any account of the good old Matron; nevertheless the anxious *Urad* continued her search, looking all around the Woods and Forest, and often peeping over the Rocks of the *Tigris*, as fearful that some Accident might have befallen her. In this fruitless Labor the poor Virgin fatigued herself, till the Sun, as tired of her Toils, refused any longer to assist her Search, when returning to her lonely Cot, she spent the Night in Tears and Lamentations.

'The helpless *Urad* gave herself up entirely to Grief; and the Remembrance of her affectionate Mother, added a double Portion of Sorrows to her Heart; she neglected to open her lonely Cottage, and went not forth to the Labors of the Silk-worm; but Day after Day, with little or no Nourishment, she continued weeping the Loss of *Houadir*, her mild Instructor, and *Nouri*, her affectionate Mother.

'The neighbouring Cottagers observing, that *Urad* came no longer to the Silk-works, and that her Dwelling was daily shut up, after some Time knocked at her Cottage, and demanded if *Urad*, the Daughter of *Nouri*, was living.

'*Urad* seeing the Concourse of people, came weeping and trembling toward the Door, and asked them the cause of their coming.

' "O *Urad*", said her neighbours, "we saw you, not long ago, seeking your Friend *Houadir*, and we feared, that you also were missing, as you have neither appeared among us, nor attended your daily Labors among the Worms, who feed and provide for us by their subtle Spinning."

' "O, my friends," answered *Urad*, "suffer a wretched Maid to deplore the Loss of her dearest Friends; *Nouri*, from whose Breasts I sucked my natural Life, is now a Prey to the Vultures on the Banks of the *Tigris*; and *Houadir*, from whom I derive my better Life, is passed away from me like a Vision in the Night."

'Her rustick Acquaintance laughed at these sorrows of the Virgin *Urad*.

' "Alas," said one, "is *Urad* grieved, that now she has to work for one, instead of three?"

' "Nay", cried another, "I wish my old Folks were as well bestowed."

' "And I", said a third, "were our House rid of the old-fashioned Lumber that fills it at present, my superannuated Father and Mother, would soon bring a healthy young Swain to supply their places with Love and Affection."

' "Aye, true," answered two or three more, "we must look out a clever young Fellow for *Urad*: Who shall she have?"

' "O if that be all," said a crooked old Maid, who was famous for Match-making, "I will send *Darandu* to comfort her before Night, and, if I mistake not, he very well knows his Business."

' "Well, pretty *Urad*," cried they all, "*Darandu* will soon be here, he is fishing on the *Tigris*; and it is but just, that the River which has robbed you of one Comfort, should give you better."

'At this Speech, the rest laughed very heartily, and they all ran away, crying out, "O she will do very well when *Darandu* approaches."

'*Urad*, though she could despise the trifling of her Country Neighbours, yet felt an Oppression on her Heart at the name of *Darandu*, who was a Youth of incomparable Beauty, and added to the Charms of his person an engaging Air, which was far above the reach of the rest of the Country Swains, who lived on those remote Banks of the *Tigris*. "But, O *Houadir*, O *Nouri*," said the afflicted Virgin to herself, "never shall *Urad* seek in the Arms of a Lover, to forget the Bounties and Precepts of so kind a Mistress and so indulgent a Parent."

'These Reflections hurried the wretched *Urad* into her usual sorrowful Train of Thoughts, and she spent the rest of the Day in Tears and Weeping, calling for ever on *Nouri* and *Houadir*, and wishing that the Prophet would permit her to follow them out of a World, where she foresaw neither Comfort nor Peace.

'In the Midst of these melancholy Meditations, she was disturbed by a knocking at the Door; *Urad* arose with trembling, and asked, who was there?

' "It is one", answered a Voice, in the softest Tone, "who seeketh Comfort and cannot find it; who desires Peace, and it is far from him."

' "Alas", answered *Urad*, "few are the comforts of this Cottage, and Peace is a Stranger to this mournful Roof; depart, O Traveller, whosoever thou art, and suffer the disconsolate *Urad* to indulge in Sorrows, greater than those from which you wish to be relieved."

' "Alas", answered the Voice without, "the Griefs of the beautiful *Urad* are my Griefs; and the Sorrows which afflict her, rend the Soul of the wretched *Darandu!*"

' "Whatever may be the Motive for this charitable Visit, *Darandu*," answered *Urad*, "let me beseech you to depart; for ill does it become a forlorn Virgin, to admit the Conversation of the Youths that surround her: leave me, therefore, O Swain, ere Want of Decency make you appear odious in the Sight of the Virgins who inhabit the rocky Banks of the rapid *Tigris*."

' "To convince the lovely *Urad*", answered *Darandu*, "that I come to sooth her Cares, and condole with her in her Losses (which I heard but this Evening) I now will quit this dear Spot, which contains the Treasure of my heart, as however terrible the parting is to me, I rest satisfied that it pleases the fair Conqueror of my Heart, whose peace to *Darandu* is more precious than the Pomegranate in the sultry noon, or the silver scales of ten thousand Fishes, inclosed in the nets of my faithful comrades."

'*Darandu* then left the Door of the Cottage, and *Urad* reclined on the Bed, till Sleep finished her Toils, and for a Time released her from the severe Afflictions of her unguarded Situation.

'Early in the Morning the fair *Urad* arose, and directed her Steps to the Rocks of the *Tigris*, either invited thither by the melancholy Reflections which her departed Mother occasioned, or willing to take a nearer and more unobserved View of the gentle *Darandu*.

'*Darandu*, who was just about to launch his Vessel into the River, perceived the beauteous Mourner on the Rocks, but he was too well versed in Love Affairs to take any Notice of her; he rather turned from *Urad*, and endeavoured, by his Behaviour, to persuade her, that he had not observed her, for it was enough for him to know that he was not indifferent to her.

'*Urad*, though she hardly knew the Cause of her Morning Walk, yet continued on the Rocks till *Darandu* had taken in the Nets, and with his Companions was steering up the Stream, in quest of the Fishes of the *Tigris*.

'She then returned to her Cottage more irresolute in her Thoughts, but less than ever inclined to the Labors of her Profession.

'At the Return of the Evening, she was anxious lest *Darandu* should renew his Visit; an Anxiety, which though it arose from Fear, was yet near allied to Hope; now was she less solicitous about Provisions, as all her little Stock was entirely exhausted, and she had no other Prospect before her than to return to her Labors, which her Sorrows had rendered irksome and disagreeable to her.

'While she was meditating on these Things, she heard a knocking at the Door, which flutter'd her little less than the Fears of Hunger, or the Sorrows of her lonely Life.

'For some Time she had not courage to answer, till the knocking being repeated, she faintly asked, who was at the Door?

' "It is *Lahnar*," answered a female, "*Lahnar*, your Neighbour, seeks to give *Urad* Comfort, and to condole with the distressed Mourner of a Mother and a Friend."

' "*Lahnar*", answered *Urad*, "is then a Friend to the afflicted, and kindly seeks to alleviate the Sorrows of the wretched *Urad*."

'She then opened the door, and *Lahnar* entered with a Basket on her Head.

' "Kind *Lahnar*," said the fair Mourner, "leave your Burthen at the Door, and enter in this Cottage of Affliction. Alas! alas! there once sat *Nouri*, my ever affectionate Mother, and there *Houadir*, my kind Counsellor and Director, but now are their Seats vacant, and Sorrow and Grief are the only Companions of the miserable *Urad*!"

' "Your Losses are certainly great", answered *Lahnar*, "but you must endeavour to bear them with Patience, especially as they are the common Changes and Alterations of Life; your good mother *Nouri* lived to a great Age, and *Houadir*, tho' a kind Friend, may yet be succeeded by one as amiable; but what I am most alarmed at, O *Urad*, is your Manner of Life; we no longer see you busied among the Leaves of the Mulberries, or gathering the bags of Silk, or preparing them for the Wheels; you purchase no Provisions among us, you seek no Comfort in Society, you live like the Mole, buried under the Earth, who neither sees nor is seen."

' "My Sorrows indeed hitherto", replied *Urad*, "have prevented my Labor, but To morrow I shall again rise to my wonted Employment."

' "But even To-night," said *Lahnar*, "let my Friend take some little Nourishment, that she may rise refreshed, for Fasting will deject you as well as Grief; and suffer me to partake with you, and see in this Basket I have brought my Provisions, some boiled Rice, and a few Fish, which my kind brother *Darandu* brought me this Evening from the river *Tigris*."

' "Excuse me, kind *Lahnar*," answered *Urad*, "but I must refuse your Offer; Grief has driven away Appetite, to aught but itself, far from me, and I am not solicitous to take Provisions which I cannot use."

' "At least", replied *Lahnar*, "permit me to sit beside you, and eat of what is here before us."

'Upon which, without other Excuses, *Lahnar* emptied her Basket, and set a Bowl of Rice and Fish before *Urad*, and began to feed heartily on that which she brought for herself.

'*Urad* was tempted by Hunger, and the example of *Lahnar* to begin, but she was anxious about tasting the Fish of *Darandu*, wherefore she first attempted the boiled Rice, but her Appetite was most inclined to the Fish, of which she at last ate very heartily, when she recollected, that as she had partaken with *Lahnar*, it was equal whatever Part she accepted.

'*Lahnar*, having finished her Meal, and advised *Urad* to think of some Methods of social Life, took her Leave, and left the unsettled Virgin to meditate on her strange Visitor.

'*Urad*, though confused, could not help expressing some Pleasure at this Visit, for such is the Blessing of Society, that it will always give Comfort to those, who have been disused to its sweet Effects.

'But *Urad*, though pleased with the Friendship of *Lahnar*, yet was confounded, when some few Minutes after she perceived her again returning.

' "What", said *Urad*, "brings back *Lahnar* to the Sorrows of this Cottage?"

' "*Urad*", said *Lahnar*, "I will rest with my Friend To-night, for the Shades of Night cast Horrors around, and I dare not disturb my Father's Cottage by my late Approach."

'As they prepared for their homely Bed, *Urad* turning round, beheld *Lahnar*'s Breast uncovered, and saw, by the Appearance, it was no Female she was preparing to receive into her Bed. She immediately shrieked out, and *Darandu*, the fictitious *Lahnar*, leaped eagerly forward, and caught her in his Arms.

' "O delicious *Urad*," said he, "I die, I die without you; your Tears, your Calls are vain, the Cottage is lonely, and no Traveller walks by Night to meet the wild Beasts of the Forest; therefore let us take our Fill of Love, for *Darandu* will not otherwise be satisfied."

'*Urad*, full of Trembling, Confusion, Horror, and Despair, raved in his Arms, but could not get free. He still pressed her close, and endeavoured to pull her toward the Bed, when she recollecting her lost Friend *Houadir*, felt for a Pepper-corn, and let it fall to the Ground.

'A violent rapping was in a Moment heard at the Cottage, at which *Urad* redoubled her Outcries, and *Darandu*, with Shame and Confusion, quitted his Mistress, and looked trembling toward the Door.

'*Urad* ran forward and opened the Door, when the Son of *Houadir* entered, and asked *Urad* the Reason of her Cries.

' "O thou blessed angel," said *Urad*, "but for you, that wicked Wretch, disguised in his Sister's Cloaths, had ruined the too credulous *Urad*."

'But *Darandu* was fled, as Guilt is ever fearful, mean, and base.

' "Now, *Urad*," said the Son of *Houadir*, "before you close your Doors upon another Man, let me resume my former Features."

'Upon which *Urad* looked, and beheld her old Friend *Houadir*.

'At the sight of *Houadir*, *Urad* was equally astonished and abashed.

' "Why blushes *Urad*?" said *Houadir*, "and her Blushes are the Blushes of Guilt."

' "How, O *Genius*," said *Urad*, "for such I perceive thou art, how is *Urad* guilty? I invited not *Darandu* hither, I wished not for him."

' "Take Care", answered *Houadir*, "what you say; if you wished not for him, you hardly wished him away; and but for your Imprudence he had not attacked you.

' "Consider, how have your Days been employed since I left you? Have you continued to watch the Labors of the Silk-worm? Have you repeated the Lessons I gave you? Or has the Time of *Urad* been consumed in Idleness and Disobedience? Has she shaken off her Dependence on *Mahomet*, and indulged the unavailing Sorrows of her Heart?"

' "Alas," answered the fair *Urad*, "repeat no more, my ever-honored *Houadir*; I have indeed been guilty, under the Mask of Love and Affection, and I now plainly see the Force of your first Rule, that Idleness is the Beginning of all Evil and Vice. Yes, my dearest *Houadir*, had I attended to your Instructions, I had given no Handle to *Darandu*'s wicked intentions; but yet methinks some Sorrows were allowable for the Loss of such a Mother and such a Friend."

' "Sorrows", answered *Houadir*, "proceed from the Heart, and totally indulged, soon require a Change and Vicissitude in our Minds; wherefore in the Midst of your Griefs, your Feet involuntarily wandered after *Darandu*, and your Soul softened by the idle Sighs was the more easily impressed by the Deceits of his Tongue.

' "But this remember, O *Urad*, for I must, I find, repeat an old Instruction to you, that of all Things in the World nothing should so much engage a Woman's Attention as the Avenues which lead to her Heart. Such are the Wiles, the Deceits of Men, that they are rarely to be trusted with the most advanced Post; give them but Footing, though that Footing be innocent, and they will work Night and Day till their Wishes are accomplished.

' "Trust not, therefore, to yourself alone, nor suffer your Heart to plead in their Favour, lest it become as much your Enemy as the tempter Man.

' "Place your Security in Flight, and avoid every evil, every idle, every gay Desire, lest it lead you into Danger; for hard it is to turn the Head and Looks backward, when a beautiful or agreeable Object is before you. Remember my Instructions, O *Urad*, make a prudent Use of your Pepper-corns, and leave this Place, which holds a Man sensible to your Softness, and resolute in his own dark and subtle Intention."

'*Urad* was about to thank *Houadir*, but the *Genius* was fled, and the Eye-lids of the Morning were opening in the East.

'*Urad* in a little Wallet packed up her small Stock of Necessaries, and full of Terror and full of Uncertainty, struck into the Forest, and without Reflection took the widest Path that offered.

'And first it was her Care to repeat over deliberately the Lessons of *Houadir*. She then travelled slowly forward, often looking, and fearing to behold the wicked *Darandu* at her Heels.

'After walking through the Forest for the greater Part of the Day, she came to a deep Descent, on each side overshadowed with lofty Trees; this she walked down, and came to a small Spot of Ground, surrounded by Hills, Woods, and Rocks. Here she found a Spring of Water, and sat down on the Grass to refresh herself after the Travels of the Day.

'As her Meal was almost at an End, she heard various Voices issuing from the Woods, on the Hills opposite to that which she came down.

'Her little Heart beat quick at this Alarm, and *Urad* recollecting the Advice of *Houadir*, began to repeat the Lessons of her Instructor, and ere long she perceived through the Trees, several Men coming down the Hill, who at Sight of *Urad* gave a loud Halloo, and ran forward, each being eager who should first seize the Prize.

'*Urad* trembling and sighing at her Danger, forgot not to drop one of her Pepper-corns, and immediately she found herself changed into a Pismire, and with great Pleasure she looked for a Hole in the Ground, and crept into it.

'The Robbers coming down to the Bottom of the Vale, were surprized to find their Prize eloped, but they divided into separate Bodies, resolved to hunt till Night, and then appointed that little Vale as the place of Rendezvous.

'*Urad* perceiving that they were gone, wished herself into her original Form; but, alas, her Wish was not granted, and the once beautiful *Urad* still continued an ugly Pismire.

'Late at Night the Robbers returned, and the Moon shining bright, reflected a gloomy Horror upon their despairing Faces; *Urad* shuddered at the Sight of them, though so well concealed, and dared hardly peep out of her Hole, so difficult it is to forget our former Fears.

'The Gang resolved to spend the rest of the Night in that Place, and therefore unloaded their Wallets, and spread their Wine and Provisions on the Banks of the Spring, grumbling and cursing each other all the Time for their unfortunate Search.

' "I would to *Alla*", says one, "I had taken hold of her, and I would soon have kissed her into a good Humor."

' "You ugly wretch," said another, "she would have died at the Thoughts of you: But if I had caught her—"

' "Yes," said a third, "with those bloody Hands that have butchered two Maidens already To-day."

' "Aye," returned he, "and she should have suffered the same Sauce."[6]

' "Well," answered the Captain of the Gang, "if I had secured her, she should have gone fairly round among you all."

'*Urad* heard this with the utmost Horror and Indignation, and praised continually the gracious *Alla*, who had rescued her from such inhuman Wretches.

'While they, with singing and drinking, spent the greatest Part of the Night, and wishing that their Comrades, in the other Part of the Forest had been with them, at length falling into Drunkenness and Sleep, they left the World to Silence and Peace.

'*Urad* finding them fast asleep, crawled out of her Hole, and going to the first, she stung him in each Eye, and thus she went round to them all.

'The Poison of the little Pismire working in their Eyes, in a short Time occasioned them to wake in the utmost Tortures; and perceiving they were blind, and feeling the Pain, they each supposed his Neighbour had blinded him, in order to get away with the Booty; this so enraged them, that feeling about, they fell upon one another, and in a short Time almost the whole Gang was demolished.

'*Urad* beheld with Astonishment the Effect of her Stings, at a Wish resumed her pristine Form, saying at the same Time to herself "I now perceive, that Providence is able, by the most insignificant Means, to work in the greatest Purposes."

'Continuing her Journey through the Forest, she was terribly afraid of meeting with the second Band of Robbers, and therefore she directed her Steps with the greatest Caution and Circumspection.

'As she walked forward, and cast her Eyes all around, and stopped at every motion of the Wind, she saw the Son of *Houadir* coming to meet her in the Path in which she was travelling.

'At this Sight *Urad* ran towards him, and with Joy begged her old Governess would unmask herself, and entertain her with Instruction and Persuasion.

[6] To serve with the same sauce: to subject to the same kind of usage (*OED*).

' "No, my dear child", answered the Son of *Houadir*, "that I cannot do at present, the Time is not as yet come. I will first, as you have been tried, lead you to the Palace of the *Genii* of the Forest, and present your unspotted Innocence before them; for O my sweet *Urad*, my heavenly Pupil," said he, kissing, and taking her in his Arms, "your Virtue is tried, I have found you worthy of the Lessons which I gave you. I foresaw Evils might befall you, and therefore I took Pity on your Innocence, and lived with *Nouri*, your Mother, that I might train up my beloved *Urad* in the Paths of Virtue; and now your trial is passed, *Urad* shall enjoy the Happiness of a *Genii*."

'*Urad*, tho' somewhat confounded at *Houadir*'s Embrace under the Appearance of a Man, yet with great Humility thanked her Benefactor. And the Son of *Houadir* turning to the left, led *Urad* into a little bye Path so concealed, that few, if any, might ever find its Beginning.

'After a long Walk through various Turnings and intricate Windings, they came to a small mean Cottage, where the Son of *Houadir* leading the Way, *Urad* followed.

'The Son of *Houadir* striking Fire with his Stick, a bright Flame arose from the Center of the Floor, in which he cast divers Herbs, and repeating some Inchantments, the back Side of the Cottage opened, and presented to the view of *Urad* a beautiful Dome, where she saw sitting round a table a numerous Assembly of gay Persons of both Sexes.

'The Son of *Houadir* leading in *Urad*, said, "This, my dear Pupil, is the Assembly of the *Genii* of the Forest" and presenting her to the Company, "Behold," said he, "the beautiful and well tried *Urad*; but here you may cast off your Reserve, fair Maid, and indulge in the innocent Pleasures of the *Genii* of the Forest."

'The Son of *Houadir* then led her to the Table, and seated her on the same Sofa with himself.

'The Remainder of the Day was spent in Mirth and Pleasure, nor did the Female *Genii* refuse the gay Advances of their Partners.

'*Urad* having never beheld any Thing splendid or magnificent, was greatly delighted at the gay Company and beautiful Saloon, nor did she seem to receive the Caresses of the Son of *Houadir* so reluctantly as before.

'The Adventures of Urad'

'At Night *Urad* was shown a glorious Apartment to rest in, and the Son of *Houadir* attended her.

' "My dear *Houadir*" said *Urad*, "when shall I behold your proper shape, when shall I see you as my tutelary *Genius*?"[7]

' "That", answered the Son of *Houadir*, "I shall be in every Shape, but call neither one nor the other my *proper* Shape, for to a *Genius* all Shapes are assumed; neither is this my proper Shape, nor the Wrinkles of an old Woman; but to confess the Truth, O beautiful *Urad*, from the first Moment of your Birth, I resolved to make you my Bride, and therefore did I so patiently watch your growing Years, and instructed you in the Fear of Vice and Love of Virtue. Come therefore, O beautiful Virgin, and let me, in those precious Arms, reap the Fruit of my long Labor and Toil."

'*Urad*, astonished at the Words of the Son of *Houadir*, knew not what Answer to make; but the natural Timidity of her Sex, and the Strangeness of the Proposal, filled her with strange Apprehensions; however, she begged at least that the *Genius* would for a Time leave her to herself, that the Blushes of her Cheeks might be covered in Solitude.

' "No, my lovely *Urad*", answered the Son of *Houadir*, "never, never, will thy faithful *Genius* leave thee, till thou hast blessed me with the Possession of what I hold dearer than even my spiritual Nature."

' "Why then", said *Urad*, "didst thou bestow so many Pepper-corns upon me, as they now will become useless?"

' "Not useless," said the Son of *Houadir*, "they are indeed little Preservatives against Danger, but I have the Seeds of some Melons, which will not only rescue you, but always preserve you from Harm. Here faithful *Urad*," continued he, "take these Seeds and whenever you are fearful, swallow one of these, and no Dangers shall surround you."

'*Urad* thankfully received the Seeds: "And what" said she, "must I do with the Pepper?"

' "Give them", said the Son of *Houadir*, "to me, and I will endue them with stronger Virtues, and thou shalt by them have Power also over others, as well as to defend thyself."

---

[7] Derived from the Latin, the term 'genius' refers to the tutelary god or attendant spirit allotted to every person at his birth, to govern his fortunes and determine his character, and finally to conduct him out of the world or the tutelary and controlling spirit of a place or institution (*OED*).

'*Urad* pulled the Pepper-corns out of her Bag, and presented them to the Son of *Houadir*, whose Eyes flashed with Joy at the Sight, and he immediately thrust them into the Folds of his Garments.

' "O Son of *Houadir*, what hast thou done?", said *Urad*.

' "I have", answered the false Son of *Houadir*, "gained the full Possession of my lovely *Urad*, and now may address her in my proper Shape"; so saying, he resumed his natural Figure, and became like a Satyr of the Wood.[8]

' "I am," said he, "O beautiful *Urad*, the Enchanter *Repah*, who ranges in the Solitude of the Forest of the *Tigris*, and live and solace myself upon the Beauties, who venture into my Haunts. You I saw surrounded by the Influence of the *Genius Houadir*, and therefore was obliged to use Artifice to gain my dear dear Charmer. But why waste I Time in Words, when the Fulness of thy ripe Beauties tempt my closest Embrace"; so saying, he rushed on *Urad*, and stifled her with his nauseous Salutes.

'The poor deluded Victim, with Tears in her Eyes, implored his Mercy and Forbearance; but he laughed at her Tears, and told her, her Eyes glittered the brighter for them.

' "What," cried the Enchanter, "shall I wish your Sorrows at an End, which so tumultuously heave those Worlds of Bliss, or stop by Kindness those Sighs which send forth more than *Arabian* Perfumes? No, no, I love to enjoy Nature in her fullest Workings, and think it an higher Bliss to ride on the stormy Tempest than through the gentle Breeze."

'As he spake thus, he again clasped the wretched *Urad* in his Arms, and mad with furious Lust, forced her to the Sofa; while she, shrieking and crying, filled the Apartment with vain Lamentations.

'As the Enchanter was dragging the disconsolate Virgin *Urad* to the Sofa, she, in a Fit of Despair, again put her Hands into the Bag, from whence she had fatally resigned the Pepper-corns, and felt about in Agonies for her lost Treasure. And now finding none, and perceiving that the *Genius Houadir* attended not to her Cries, she was drawing out her Hand, when in a corner of the Bag she felt one Pepper-corn, which had before escaped her Search.

---

[8] Satyr of the Wood: a satyr is a demon or god of the wood, part human and part bestial, supposed to be the companion of Bacchus and the type of lustfulness (*OED*).

She instantly drew it out, and throwing it on the Ground, the Enchanter quitted his Hold, and stood motionless before her; the Apartments vanished, and she found herself with him in a dark Hut, with various Kinds of necromantic Instruments about her.

'*Urad*, though fearful, yet was so much overcome with Fatigue and struggling, that she sunk on the Ground, and happily for her the Enchanter was no longer in a Condition to persecute her.

' "Curse on my folly", said he, as he stood fixed to the Ground, "that I neglected to ask for the Bag itself, which held the Gifts of the *Genius Houadir*, her pretty Pupil had then been sacrificed to my Desires, in spite of the many fine Lessons she had been taught by that pitiful and enthusiastic *Genius*; but now by Chance, and not by the Merit of thy Virtues, or thy Education, art thou delivered from my Seraglio, where Vice reigns triumphant, cold Modesty and colder Chastity are excluded, to make Room for the mixed Revels of what pious Cheats call lustful Rioters. But this grieves me not so much, to lose a sickly girl, as that I find a superior Power condemns me to declare to you the Causes of your Error.

' "Know then, *Urad*, (I speak not from myself, but he speaks, who from casual Evil, can work out certain Good) he forces me to declare, that no specious Appearance, no false Colours, should incur the virtuous Heart to listen to the Wiles of Deceit; for Evil then comes most terrible, when it is cloaked under Friendship. Why then had *Urad* so great an Opinion of her own Judgment, as to confide in the false Appearance of the Son of *Houadir*, when she might have consulted her faithful Monitors? The falling of a Pepper-corn would have taught her to trust to no Appearances, nor would she have parted with her Pepper-corns, which were to refresh in her Memory the Sentiments of Virtue, Chastity, and Honor, no, not to *Houadir* herself. No Adviser can be good, who would destroy what he himself has first inculcated, and no Appearance ought to bias us to receive as Truths, those Things which are contrary to Virtue and Religion. How then did *Urad* keep to the Instructions of *Houadir*? But if *Houadir* really had bred her up for the Purposes of Lust, and taught her only the Paths of Virtue to keep her from others, of all Persons they are most to be guarded against, who having the Power of educating the female Mind, too often presume upon the Influence which such intimate

Connexions give them; they, therefore, as the most base and ungrateful, should be most cautiously watched and resolutely repulsed."

'Thus spake the Enchanter, and no more, his Mouth closed up, and he stood fixed and motionless, and *Urad* finding her Spirits somewhat recovered, hastened out of the Hut, and perceived that it was Morning.

'She had now no more Pepper-corns to depend upon, wherefore, she cried to *Houadir* to succour her, but the *Genius* was deaf to her Intreaties.

' "Poor miserable wretch," said *Urad* to herself, "what will become of thee, inclosed in a Forest through which thou knowest no Path? But," continued she, "why should I not examine the Enchanter, who perhaps is yet immoveable in the Cottage: I saw him fold them in the Plaits of his Garments, and they may yet become mine."

'So saying, she returned to the Hut, where entering, the very Sight of the dumb Enchanter affrighted her so much, that it was a long Time before she could venture near him. At length she put forth her Hand, and pulled forth her beloved Pepper-corns, the Enchanter still standing motionless.

'Away fled *Urad* like Lightning from the Hut, and ran till she had again reached the Road from which she had been decoyed.

'She continued her Journeying for seven Days, feeding on the Fruits of the Forest, and sleeping in the most covert Thickets.

'The eighth Day, as she was endeavouring to pass a Ford, where a small Rivulet had been swelled by the rains, she perceived a large body of Horsemen riding through the Woods, and doubted not but it was the Remainder of the Gang of Robbers whom she had before met with.

'*Urad* now was in some measure reconciled to Danger, and therefore, without much fear, dropped a Pepper-corn, and expected Relief.

'The Pepper-corn had been dropped some Time, the Horsemen advanced, and no one appeared to succour her.

' "Alas," said *Urad*, "why has *Houadir* deceived me; neither her Advice, nor her magical Pepper-corns, can relieve me from these lustful and cruel Robbers. Better had I fallen a prey to *Darandu*, better had I sated the Lust of one Enchanter, than undergo the various

Curses of so many Monsters. O *Genius, Genius*, why hast thou forsaken me in my severest Trials!"[9]

'By this Time the Robbers were come up, and were highly rejoiced to find such a beautiful Prize.

' "This only", said the Leader, "was what we wanted, a fair One to regale with, and this dainty Morsel will serve us all. Here is Luxury, my Friends, such as *Almurah* cannot find in his whole Seraglio; let him be dissatisfied with an hundred Females, while we, my Friends, will be satisfied with one! She shall serve us all, and me first."

' "But first," said one, "let us all embrace her, for I never yet had the pleasure to embrace a Virgin, except one that I stabbed first."

'At this he leaped from his Horse, and the trembling *Urad* gave a loud Shriek, which was answered from the Woods by the roarings of an hundred Lions.

' "O *Alla*!" said the Chief, "the lions are upon us."

' "That may be," said he who was dismounted, "but were the whole World set against me, I would secure my Prize"; so saying, he took *Urad* in his Arms to place her on his Horse.

'The roaring of the Lions continued, and many of them came howling out of the Woods; the Robbers fled in Dismay, all but the Ruffian who had seized on the fair *Urad*, who was striving in vain to fix her on his Horse.

'A Lion furiously made at him, and tore him Limb from Limb, while *Urad* expected the same Fate from several others, who came roaring round; "But," said she, "better is Death than Infamy, and the Paw of the hungry Lion than the rude Hands of the lustful Robber."

'The noble beast having devoured his Prey, came fawning at the Feet of *Urad*, who was surprised at his Behaviour and Gentleness, but much more was her Astonishment increased when she heard him speak.

' "O Virgin, for none other can experience the Assistance of our Race, or stand unhurt before us, I am the King and Sovereign of these mighty Forests, and am sent by the *Genius Houadir* to thy Protection; but why did the distrustful *Urad* despair, or why did she accuse

---

[9] Ridley must surely have meant Urad to here echo the cry of Jesus Christ on the cross, 'My God, my God, why hast thou forsaken me?' The story may be a Christian allegory of the temptation of the good Christian female, a kind of oriental *Pilgrim's Progress*.

Providence of deserting her? Should not the Relieved wait with Patience on the Hand that supports him, and not cry out with Impatience and charge its Benefactor with neglect?"

' "True, O royal Lion," answered the fair *Urad*, "but Fear is irresistible, and the Children of Men are but Weakness and Ingratitude; but blessed be *Alla*, who, though justly provoked at my Discontent, yet sent to my Assistance the Guardian of the Fair: Yet how cometh it to pass, O royal Protector, that you who are so bold, and so fierce in your Nature, should yet behave with such tenderness and kindness to an helpless Virgin, whom you might with Pleasure to yourself in a Moment devour?"

' "The truly great and noble Spirit", answered the Lion, "takes a Pride in protecting Innocence, neither can he wish to oppress it. From hence learn, fair Virgin, that of all Mankind, he only is noble, generous, and truly virtuous, who can with-hold his Desires from oppressing or ruining the Virgin that is in his Power. What then must you think of those mean Wretches, who endeavour to undermine your Virtues and pious Dispositions, who cajole you under the Appearance of Affection, and yet tell you, if they succeed not, that it was only to try you. He that is suspicious, is mean; he that is mean, is unworthy of the chaste Affections of the virtuous Maid. Wherefore, O *Urad*, shun him, however honored by Mankind, or covered by the specious Character of Virtue, whoever attempts the Honor of your Chastity, for he cannot be just; to deceive you, he must himself swear falsely, and therefore cannot be good; or if he tell the Truth, he must be weak and ungenerous, and unworthy of you, as he invites you to sin."

'In such Conversation, they passed along the Forest, till after a few Days they were alarmed at the Noise of the Hunters and the Musick of the Chase. "Alas," said the beautiful *Urad*, "what is this that I hear?"

' "It is", answered the royal Beast, "the Noise of the Hunters, and thou shalt escape, but me will they in Sport destroy. The Lion you call cruel, who kills to devour. What then is he, who wantons in the Deaths of those who advantage him not? But Man is Lord of all, let him look to it how he governs!"

' "Nay but", answered *Urad*, "leave me, gentle Protector, and provide for your Safety; nor fear but *Houadir* will prevent the Storms that hover over, from breaking upon me."

' "No," answered the royal Beast, "she has commanded me to follow you till I see her Presence, and where can I better sacrifice my Life, than in the Service of Chastity and Virtue."

'The Hunters were now in Sight, but advanced not towards the Lion; they turned their Coursers aside, and only one, of superior Mien, with several Attendants, rode toward *Urad*.

'The Lion erecting his Mane, his Eyes glowing with vivid Lightnings, drew up the wide Sinews of his broad Back, and with wrathful Front leaped toward him who seemed to have the Command.

'The Horseman perceiving his Intention, poised his Spear in his Right-hand, and spurred his Courser to meet him.

Ere the royal Beast had reached the Horseman, the Rider threw his Spear, which entering between the Fore-paws of the Lion, nailed him to the Ground.

'The enraged Animal tore his Paw from the Ground, but the Spear still remained in his Foot, and the Anguish of the Wound made him shake the Forest with his lordly Roarings.

'The Stranger then rode up to the fair *Urad*, whom viewing, he cried out, "By *Alla*, thou art worthy the Embraces of the viziar *Mussapulta*; take her, my Eunuchs, behind you, and bear her through the forest of *Bagdat*, to the Seraglio of my Ancestors."

'The Eunuchs obeyed, and bore her away, tho' *Urad* dropped her Corn upon the Ground; but still she trusted in the Help of *Houadir*.

'The Viziar *Mussapulta* then ordered that one of his Slaves should stay behind, and destroy and bury the Lion, which he commanded to be done with the utmost Caution, as *Almurah* had made a decree, that if any subject should wound, maim, or destroy any Lion, in his Forests, the same should be put to Death.

'The Eunuchs bore away *Urad* to the Seraglio, taking her through bye ways to the Palace of the Viziar, lest her Shrieks should be heard. *Mussapulta* followed her at a Distance, and the Slave was left with the tortured and faithful Lion.

'In a few Hours they reached the Palace, and *Urad* being conducted to the Seraglio, was ordered to be dressed, as the Viziar intended visiting her that Night.

'*Urad* was thunderstruck at the News, and now began to fear *Houadir* had forgotten her, and resolved, as soon as the Eunuch had left her, to drop a second Pepper-corn. But poor *Urad* had forgotten to take her Bag from her old Garments, which the Eunuch who had dressed her had carried away.

'*Urad* dissolved in fresh Tears at this Piece of Carelessness; "Well," said she, "surely *Houadir* will neglect me, if I so easily neglect myself."

'She waited that Night with Fear and Trembling, but no Viziar appeared. This eased her greatly, and the next Day, when the Eunuchs came, they informed her, that *Mussapulta* had that Evening been sent by his Sultan to quell an Insurrection, and that they did not expect him Home under twenty Days.

'During this Time, no Pains were spared with *Urad* to teach her the Accomplishments of the Country;[10] all which, in Spite of her Unwillingness to learn in such a detestable Place, she nevertheless acquired with the utmost Ease and Facility.

'The Insurrection being quelled, the Viziar returned, and not unmindful of his fair Captive, ordered that she might be prepared for his reception in the Evening.

'Accordingly *Urad* was sumptuously adorned with Jewels and Brocades, and looked more beautifully than the fairest *Circassian*;[11] and the Dignity of her Virtue added such a Grace to her Charms, that even her Keepers, the Eunuchs, dared not look upon her.

'*Mussapulta* in the Evening, came to the Seraglio, where he found his beauteous Captive in Tears.

' "What," said he, "cannot a Fortnight's Pleasure in this Palace efface the Remembrance of your Sorrows! But be gay and chearful, for know, that the Viziar *Mussapulta* esteems you even beyond his Wives."[12]

' "The esteem of a Robber, the Esteem of a lawless Ranger," answered *Urad*, "charms not the Ears of Virtue. Heaven, I trust, will

---

[10] Urad is a Persian Shi'ite, captured by an Ottoman Sunni Vizier. Oriental tales and dramas frequently use the figure of the Persian woman enslaved in Ottoman territories as a figure of embattled virtue.

[11] fairest Circassian: Samuel Croxall's play, *The Fair Circassian* (1721) drew, as Ridley does here, on the myth of the lovely female slave from Circassia, taken from the North Caucasus (Georgian Russia). The term 'Caucasian' has of course come to describe ethnic whiteness.

[12] Commentators of the 18th c. often mention that the Qur'an allows the Muslim man to have four wives but as many concubines as he wishes.

not suffer you to plunder my Body, but no Power can make me look with Pleasure on the Murderer of my Friend, or on the lustful Wretch."

' "What," said *Mussapulta* sternly, "do you refuse my proffered Love? then will I, having first deflowered thee, cast thee forth among my Slaves, and them shalt thou lie down before; thy Body I have, and I will make such full Use of it, as shall sting thy squeamish Virtue to the Soul; I will also have Witness of my Triumph, my whole Seraglio shall be present, and my female Slaves shall be ordered to laugh at thy Cries, as thou liest on the Bed of my Desires; and I too will enjoy thy Screams, and take a Pride in the Sorrows and Throbs of thy departing Chastity; nor shalt thou rise, till many have followed the Example of their Master.

' "Here eunuchs," continued he, "bind that stubborn Piece of Virtue, and stretch her on the Bed; call all my Females here, and bid my Slaves attend. Take off those Trappings from her, and let us see the whole of her Virtuous Composition."

'The Eunuchs advanced to *Urad*, and began their Master's Commands, while she, with the most fearful Outcries, pierced the Air, calling on *Alla*, on *Mahomet*, and on *Houadir* to relieve her.

'The Females arriving, *Mussapulta* gave them their Lesson, who going to the beauteous Victim, began laughing at her Sorrows, and talking to her in the most ungrateful Terms.

'The Slaves also attended, and beheld the lovely *Urad* now almost exposed in all her uncovered Charms to the Eyes of the brutal Company.

' "Why", said the proud Viziar, "do ye delay my Wishes? Haste, Slaves, and lay bare this delicate Piece of Virtue to public View."

'As he said this, an Eunuch came running in haste, crying, "The Sultan, the sultan *Almurah* approaches!"

'All was instant Confusion, *Mussapulta* turned pale and trembling, he ordered the Eunuch to release and cover the fair *Urad*, and ere she was well adorned again, the faithful Lion entered with the sultan *Almurah*.

'The Lion instantly seized on the Viziar *Mussapulta* and tore him Limb from Limb, in the Sight of those very Servants whom he called together to behold his Cruelty and Lust. Yet the generous Animal would not defile himself with the Carcass, but with great Wrath tossed the bloody Remains among the Females of the Seraglio.

'*Almurah* commanded *Urad* to advance, and at the Sight of her, "O royal Beast," said he to the Lion, "I wonder not that thou wert unable to describe the Beauties of this lovely Maid, since they are almost too dazzling to behold.

' "O virtuous Maid," continued *Almurah*, "whose Excellencies I have heard from this faithful Animal, if thou canst deign to accept of the Heart of *Almurah*, thy Sultan will be the Happiest of Mankind; but I swear, by my unalterable Will, that no Power on Earth shall force or distress you."

' "O", sighed *Urad*, "royal Sultan, you honor your poor Slave too much; yet happy should I be were *Houadir* here!"

'As she spoke, the *Genius Houadir* entered the Room; the Face of the sage Instructor still remained, but a glowing Splendor surrounded her, and her Walk was majestic and commanding.

'*Almurah* bowed to the Ground, *Urad* made Obeisance, and the rest fell prostrate before her.

' "My advice", said *Houadir*, "is necessary now, O *Urad*, nor ought young Virgins to enter into such Engagements without Counsel, and the Approbation of those above her, how splendid and lucrative soever the Union may appear. I who know the Heart of *Almurah*, the Servant of *Mahomet*, know him to be virtuous; some Excesses he has been guilty of, but they were chiefly owing to his villainous Viziar *Mussapulta*." Here the Lion gave a dreadful Roar. "Against your Command, *Almurah*, did he wound this Animal, which I endued with Speech for the Service of *Urad*, to teach her, that Strength and Nobleness of Soul would always support the Innocent.

' "*Mussapulta* having wounded him, commanded his Slave to put the royal Beast to Death; but I gave the Slave Bowels of Mercy, and he carried him Home to his Cottage, till the Wound was healed. When the Lion, faithful to his Trust, came toward you as you were hunting, and being endued with Speech, declared the Iniquity of *Mussapulta*; but he is no more.

' "Now *Urad*, if thy Mind incline to *Almurah*, receive his Vows, but give not thine Hand where thy Heart is estranged, for no Splendor can compensate the Want of Affection."

' "If *Almurah*, my gracious Lord," answered *Urad*, "will swear in three Things to do my Desire, his Handmaid will be happy to serve him."

' "I swear," answered the fond *Almurah*, "hadst thou three thousand Desires, *Almurah* would satisfy them or die."

' "What strange Things", said *Houadir*, "has *Urad* to ask of the Sultan *Almurah*?"

' "Whatever they are, gracious *Genius*," said *Almurah*, "*Urad*, the lovely *Urad*, may command me."

' "Then," said *Urad*, "first, I require, that the poor Inhabitants of the Forest be restored to their native Lands from whence thou hast driven them."

' "By the great *Alla* and *Mahomet* the Prophet of the Just," answered *Almurah*, 'the Deed was proposed and executed by the villain *Mussapulta*; yes, my lovely *Urad* shall be obeyed."

' "But now *Urad*," continued the Sultan, "ere you proceed in your Requests, let me make one Sacrifice to Chastity and Justice, by vowing in the Presence of the good *Genius Houadir*, to dismiss my Seraglio, and take thee only to my Arms."

' "So noble a sacrifice", answered *Urad*, "demands my utmost Returns; wherefore, beneficent Sultan, I release thee from any farther Compliance with my Requests."

' "Lovely *Urad*," said *Almurah*, "permit me then to dive into your Thoughts: Yes, by your kind Glances on that noble Beast, I perceive you meditated to ask some Bounty for your Deliverer. He shall, fair virgin, be honored as *Urad*'s Guardian, and the Friend of *Almurah*; he shall live in my royal Palace with Slaves to attend him, and that his Rest may not be inglorious, or his Life useless, once every Year shall those who have ravished or deflowered the Innocent be delivered up to his honest Rage."

'The lovely *Urad* fell at the Feet of her Sultan, and blessed him for his Favors; and the sage *Houadir* approved of *Urad*'s Request and the Promises of *Almurah*. The Lion came and licked the Feet of his Benefactors, and the *Genius Houadir*, at parting, poured her Blessings on the Royal Pair.'

'To guard the soft female Heart from the Delusions of a faithless Sex', said *Iracagem*, 'is worthy of our Race, and the sage *Houadir* has wisely blended Chastity and Prudence in her delightful Instructions; but female Delicacy makes an unequal Opposition to brutal Cunning, unless the Protection of the just One overshadow the Footsteps of the virtuous Maid; wherefore, *Alla* is the first and chief Supporter of the Female Sex, who will assuredly, when requested, confound the vain Artifices of Man, and exalt the prudent Counsels of the modest Fair.

'But most illustrious,' said the sage *Iracagem*, to one of the *Genii* of a superior Mien, 'let me not any longer delay the noble Lessons of thy Tongue, from thee we expect to hear the Adventures of *Misnar*, the beloved of *Alla* and *Mahomet*, his Prophet.'

'Chief of our Race,' answered the *Genius*, 'whose Praises rise earliest and most frequent in the Presence of *Alla*, I am ready to obey thee.'

So saying, the *Genius* thus began her much instructive Tale.

2

THE PSEUDO-ORIENTAL TALE

'The History of the Christian Eunuch'

in *Philidore and Placentia: or, L'Amour trop Delicat* (1727)

Eliza Haywood

Copy-text: vol. ii of the 1st edition (London, 1727)

Eliza Haywood (*c*.1693–1756) was the most prolific British woman writer of the eighteenth century. Her literary career shows a consistent interest in the oriental tale, partly due no doubt to her enthusiasm for French fiction, from which she produced numerous translations. With her long-term lover, William Hatchett, she produced the first English translation of Crébillon fils' *La Sopha* in 1742. The novella *Philidore and Placentia* appeared at the high point of her early career (she was averaging a novel every three months through the 1720s) and, like her other early work, is a racy, sexually driven tale framed by a specious claim to moral intention. It contains an inset story, by a mysterious young man who later turns out to be the heroine's brother; he has been enslaved in Persia where he was castrated as a punishment for his pursuit of an unfortunate passion with a beautiful harem mistress of his master.

The story is one of a number of tales of the early eighteenth century which depict the fortunes of Christian Europeans in eastern (particularly Ottoman and Persian) territories, such as Penelope Aubin's *The Strange Adventures of the Count de Vinevil and his Family* (1721). The vogue for such tales may have been a response to the public concern about Britons taken into slavery by North African corsairs. A redemption procession of December 1721 required former captives (redeemed through ransoms raised through charity in their homeland) to wear their 'Moorish' or 'slavish habits' (see Linda Colley, *Captives: Britain, Empire and the World, 1600–1850* (London: Jonathan Cape, 2002), 79). Accounts of Barbary captivity, as Linda Colley details, appeared in print in numerous forms as newspaper reports, verses, books, and pamphlets, often authored by third parties when the subject was illiterate. Successive treaties in the 1720s with Morocco appear to have reduced the actual threat of such captivity, but the appetite for such accounts did not wane. Haywood is no doubt imitating the captivity narrative by delivering it in the first-person voice of 'the Christian eunuch'. But, in other respects, the tale is pure exotic fantasy and its target is much closer to home than Islamic Persia. The novel offers a critique of Whiggish preoccupations with a balance of powers (between king and Parliament, ministry and monarch, sovereign and subjects) through its satire of the 'too delicate' sensibilities of its hero and heroine, Philidore and Placentia, whose union is constantly deferred when one or the other is not 'equal' in fortune to the other. In the process, it rejects the view that the 'passive' politics of subjection to authority promoted by Tory politics, with which Haywood was in sympathy, was a covert form of absolutism. Haywood represents her own Tory politics as a midway point between the two extremes of delicate distinctions of liberty found in the English setting and despotic ownership of others, figured through the Persian setting.

Philidore, the hero of the frame tale, has left England to make his fortune in Persia, his passion for the wealthy heiress Placentia being too nice to allow him to marry when there is such discrepancy in his fortunes. He intervenes to save a lovely young man who is being assaulted by some bravos, and discovers while his protégé is recovering that the young man has been castrated. The Christian eunuch's story parallels that of Philidore's earlier romance with Placentia, in which Philidore adopted the disguise of an Egyptian servant in order to be close to the woman he had loved from a distance. The English love affair is restrained, chaste, and 'delicate' by contrast with the sexual heat of the Persian illicit relationship. For a reading of *Philidore and Placentia*, along with other exotic tales by the same author, see Jennifer Thorn, ' "A Race of Angels": Castration and Exoticism in Three Exotic Tales by Eliza Haywood', in Kirsten T. Saxton and Rebecca P. Bocchicchio (eds.), *The Passionate Fictions of Eliza Haywood* (Lexington, Ky: Kentucky University Press, 2000), 168–93.

The beautiful Unknown having recover'd his Strength, *Philidore* cou'd no longer contain his impatience for the discovery of Adventures, which promis'd to have something in them very extraordinary: and expressing the desire he had to be inform'd of them, the other hesitated not to gratify it in these or the like terms.

'The History of the Christian Eunuch'

'My Misfortunes', said he, 'being of such a nature, that, tho' innocent of any Crime to draw them on, inflict a lasting disgrace on me, I intreat you will permit me to conceal my Name, and that of my Family. It shall suffice to let you know I was born in *England*, descended from an Ancient and Honourable House, of which I am the last surviving Male Heir. Being left very young in Possession of a large Estate, I fell into the common error of the Age, that 'tis impossible to be an accomplish'd Gentleman, without the improvements of travelling.[1] To which end, with a Train and Equipage

---

[1] From the late 16th c. onward, wealthy young British men in their late teens undertook 'The Grand Tour', often in the company of a tutor, for about a year, centring on travel in Italy and a visit to Paris. There was considerable contemporary criticism of such tourism which saw it as simply the acquisition of a veneer of sophistication. Such travellers often were or became connoisseurs and collectors. See J. M. Black, *The British and the Grand Tour* (London: Croom Helm, 1985).

proportionable to my vanity, I made the Tour of *Europe*, took a pride in collecting the choicest Rarities of every Country I pass'd through, and forgot nothing of their Fashions; but as I was on my way Home from *Constantinople*, the last of my intended Progress, a sudden Storm arising, oblig'd us to shift our Sails, and make towards the *Oguzio*; all the Wind blowing full that way, we were driven much farther out of our way than we at first believ'd: for four and twenty Hours did we Sail on, in spite of our Teeth,[2] and then the Wind ceasing, so great a Calm ensu'd, that all we cou'd do, was to tow the Vessel back: but why should I delay your attention with fruitless Particulars? As great a trouble as the Calm was to us, what follow'd, gave us yet more Pain; a second Tempest overtook us, and with such violence, that our Ship, before very much impair'd, cou'd not sustain the shock; and after combatting, as it were, with the Waves, for almost a whole day, sunk with the weight of Water, which from all sides burst in upon us. Our Captain seeing the danger before it came upon us, threw out the long Boat, and he and I, and as many as cou'd get into it, endeavour'd to save ourselves that way; having the melancholy cry of those we left behind us in our Ears, till eas'd from it, by the sad prospect it gave our Eyes, to see them all swallow'd in the relentless Ocean; we had little reason to think there was any possibility of avoiding the same fate, we were far from shore, and he must have been possess'd of a stronger Faith than any of us, to believe that poor Boat cou'd live long on so rough a Sea—the terror of our expected fate, gave us, without dying, the pangs of death; all our misdeeds came flagrant to remembrance, and the thoughts that we were allow'd no time for penitence, took away the power of making use of that we had—Judge of the horror of our State, encompass'd round with all that can be shocking to the Sense, or staggering to Reason—at last the Tempest ceas'd, but not our danger; for distant from any Shore, and altogether unable to guess where we were, or had we known, without means to steer our Course either one way or the other—with aching Hearts we cast our longing Eyes as far as sight wou'd reach, but nothing appear'd in view but Skies and Waves: in this terrible dilemma, did we continue floating about some six Hours,

---

[2] in spite of our Teeth: notwithstanding one's opposition (*OED*).

and the Night coming on, heightned our Fears and our Confusion; when all at once we spy'd a gallant Ship, making her way directly after us; joy to behold relief so near us, and the terror of being run foul on, by having nothing wherewith we cou'd avoid her, divided every Soul: we cry'd to Heaven for Deliverance, and at the same time to the Men whom we saw on Deck; but sure it can be ascrib'd to nothing less than a miracle, that we were preserv'd; having lost our Oars, we paddled with our Arms as well as we cou'd, to shun the quick approach of that o'er-powering Sail, and rowing in that manner toward the West to escape one danger, run on another; which, however, was not only our own safety, but that also of the Ship; a huge Rock lying out at Sea, our inadvertancy run on it, and the Boat was stav'd in many pieces; having all pretty good skill in swimming, by that means we were sav'd; those in the Vessel being instructed by our damage, steer'd off, and sent the long Boat to take us in. Having escaped so great a Peril, 'tis not to be doubted, but that the first thing we did, was to render thanks to Heaven and its Instruments of our Deliverance. But soon alas! our joys were damp'd, when we found by some *Christians* whom they had taken Prisoners that those People, in whose power we were, were *Persian* Privateers, who made it their business to scower the Seas, and bring all whom they subdu'd, Slaves, not to be redeem'd for any ransome whatsoever—[3] Death now appear'd a less evil, than that to which we were reduc'd; and for my part, I stood in need of all the Religion as well as Philosophy I was master of, to keep my self from throwing my self into the Sea.

'The Weather continuing prosperous, in a small time we cast Anchor at *Liperda*; where being set on Shore, all who were Captives, were chain'd and conducted to a House appointed for the purpose; whence, after taking some refreshment, we were carry'd to the Market-place, there to be dispos'd of to the best bidder. It being nothing material to the History of my adventures to relate the fate of my Companions, I shall only say that mine was to attend the Bassaw of *Liperda*; who, it seems, taking a fancy to my Person, bought me at an

---

[3] Linda Colley (see introduction) records that between 1670 and 1734, 2,200 men and women were returned from North Africa, a considerable proportion of them redeemed by raising ransoms in their native country (*Captives*, 53). However, the practice of redeeming captives was far less common (as was captivity itself) in Persia, where this story is set.

extraordinary Price. When in his Palace, I was treated with a kindness, which left me nothing but the Name of Slave; all the others he
was Master of, were order'd to serve and obey me—all the employment allotted me was, to attend in his Chamber, more for State than
Service, and sometimes entertain him with singing and playing on the
Lute, which I had learn'd in *Italy*, and had been accounted to have
tolerable skill in. The liking he had to me, making him desirous of
talking with me concerning my Country, and those I had travelled in,
with more ease than he cou'd do by an Interpreter: he order'd Masters
to instruct me in the Language of the *Persians*; which when I was
perfect in, never did two intimate Friends, equal in Birth and Fortune,
hold discourse together with less constraint. Such a Slavery had been
a glorious Fortune for some Men, but the remembrance of my Friends
and Country, render'd vain, all the Bassaw's endeavours to make me
happy: and tho' I appear'd before him with as much serenity as
possible in my Countenance, yet did he see through my disguise, and
complain'd of my want of gratitude for the Favours he bestow'd on
me. The kindness with which he treated me, made me sometimes
resolve to ask my Freedom of him; but having reveal'd my Intentions
to a fellow Slave, who had been a long time with him, he deter'd me
from it by these arguments. "You are not acquainted", said he, "with
the disposition of the Persons of this Country; if they show you any
favour, 'tis to please themselves—the Bassaw loves your Company,
because you are capable of diverting him, think you therefore he will
part with you—no, you may as well imagine he wou'd give away a fine
Garden, a Palace, a rich Jewel, or any other thing which affords him
delight—He thinks, on those whom ill fortune has reduc'd to be his
Slaves, but as part of the Furniture of his House—something he has
brought for his Use, and the more necessary to his Contentment, the
more improbable he shou'd quit." The haughty disposition of the
Persians in general, and the little consideration I perceiv'd they had of
any thing but self satisfaction,[4] made me approve the Reasons my

---

[4] Jean de Thévenot comments in a chapter on 'The Nature of the Persians': 'By what I
can find in them, it may be confidently said, that they are extremely vain, and much given
to Luxury, which puts them to vast expences, not onely in Apparel and Furniture, but also
in Servants whom they entertain in great Numbers; and in their Table too, which
(according to their Power,) they fill with Diversity of Dishes' (*The Travels of Monsieur de
Thevenot into the Levant in Three Parts* (London, 1687), pt. 2, ch. 8, p. 90).

Companion had given me, for not urging a request, which 'twas likely, wou'd not only be deny'd me, but also deprive me of all those freedoms, which at present softned my Bondage. But soon alas! had I more prevailing motives to neglect all means of regaining my Liberty: the pleasure the Bassaw took in hearing me Play and Sing, made him keep me so eternally about him, that I cou'd not avoid the opportunity of seeing *Arithea*, the most lov'd and beautiful of all the numerous Train which crowded his Seraglio: taking delight to do every thing which he thought might be obliging to her, he wou'd needs have me frequently entertain her with my Voice and Lute; and tho' whenever I was brought into the Room where she was, she immediately pull'd her Veil over her Face, yet it being made only of a fine thin silk Crepe, I easily discern'd Charms through it, which it was impossible to behold, without becoming devoted to them—Oh *Philidore*! such Eyes, such a Mouth, so many thousand Loves and Graces; but why shou'd I attempt to describe what Language cannot speak.—you have seen the shadow of that adorable Substance;[5] and tho' the Painter's Art but faintly represents the wonders of her Beauty, yet may it give you a better Idea of it, than any thing I am able to say. —Never was a Heart more overwhelm'd with Passion, than was mine; and tho' the utter impossibility that there appear'd of ever possessing her, or indeed of declaring what I felt, might have serv'd to check such desires in their beginning, in any reasonable Man, yet did the new transport afford so much delight, as even Despair had not the power to quell—I attempted not to overcome it—I took pleasure in indulging it—methought it was a Blessing to adore such Excellence—in fine, my infatuation was beyond all bounds, as it was beyond all excuse— wishing still to see her more, and to be more her Slave, I ran hazards, which madness only cou'd have led me into. Every body knows 'tis death inevitable for any Man who enters the Seraglio Walls;[6] and tho' as I have already told you, the Bassaw made me frequently attend him

[5] Earlier in the story, when tending to the wounded eunuch, Philidore found a little picture of a lovely woman worn on the young man's breast.
[6] Thévenot comments of the Persian ruler that 'he is extremely jealous of his Wives though he has a vast number of them, and his Jealousie is so extravagant . . . that if a man had onely looked upon them, he would be put to death without remission' (*Travels* pt. 2, ch. 11, p. 99).

there to entertain *Arithea*, yet had I been detected in an endeavour to have visited either her or any other of his Wives or Concubines without his Licence, the worst of tortures must have been my doom; I knew all this, but I regarded it not, and by some presents making a Friend of one of the Eunuchs, who waited in that forbidden quarter of the Palace, I was admitted in a Mute's disguise,[7] There, Oh *Philidore!* did I behold the Charmer—behold her in a manner, such as I think must have inspir'd the coldest Heart with Love and Adoration; but because it may serve to give you some Idea of the Luxury of those People you are going to live among, as well as in some measure to justify the wildness of my flame for *Arithea*, I will describe to you, as near the truth as I can.

'The heat of the Sun in this Climate not permitting any refreshment from the Air the whole day, the fondness of the Bassaw had contriv'd a place for *Arithea* to enjoy the benefit of the freshest Breezes, at the Noon of Day: a huge mound being cast up at one end of the Garden, an Alcove was built upon it, all compos'd of the most beautiful Shells the Ocean cou'd afford; from a thousand different springs the water was carried up by Aqueducts, which falling down again into a large basin made of Mother of Pearl, edg'd round with Corral, seem'd to form a little kind of Sea, encompassing the throne on which the charmer sat: Vast fans play'd by mutes, who unseen stood behind the Alcove, wafted a pleasing gale like that which *Zephirus*[8] breathes through the Groves. Negligent of her beautys and all unsuspicious of any observing Eyes, she came with Robes ungirt, and loosely flowing; her panting Breast expos'd, unshaded even by the Lawn which hung in careless folds down to her slender fine proportion'd waist—the extreme Heat of the Day added to her Natural Freshness and the Rosy-tincture of her Cheeks set off to vast advantage the matchless whiteness of those parts of her Face and Neck which blushes never Paint—to speak of her Eyes were to describe Lightning; such, and so quick the shining Darts flash'd

---

[7] Mutes were men who were naturally born deaf, and served close to the Persian or Ottoman ruler because silence was meant to be observed in his presence. The sign language they used was reserved for telling stories and repeating the Qur'an. Black eunuchs, taken from Africa and castrated when young, served in the women's quarters of the Ottoman and Persian palaces.   [8] Zephirus is the Greek God of the west wind.

forth their beamy Fires—imagination cannot reach the dazling Beautys which play'd about her; she seem'd the Queen of Love just rising from the Sea to charm the wondering Heavens and diffuse immortal pleasures[9]—It was her custom to sit in this place and posture some hours together every Day—by the assistance of the same friendly Eunuch I miss'd no opportunity of beholding her, and having acquir'd, while I was in *Italy*, some little Skill in Painting, I provided myself with materials; and sitting close under the covert of a large Orange-tree drew her Picture as near the life as Colours cou'd bring it—*Pigmalion* like, I now doated on an Image of my own formation, and cou'd kisses have inspir'd Breath into the inanimate Plate[10] mine must certainly have warm'd it into life—. My time was now wholly taken up between the Shadow and the Substance; when she quitted the Garden, I did so too, and throwing off my disguise either shut myself into my Chamber, or retir'd to some unfrequented shade, and gazing on my dear Picture gave a loose to transports which were little different from frenzy—in fine, I was no longer Master of my reason, all power of reflection and consideration quite forsook me—I neglected every thing—when the Bassaw call'd me, I was not to be found; or if I was, appear'd before him with so wild and so confus'd an Air, made answers to what he said which were so little to the purpose and behav'd in every thing so unlike my self, or as I ought to have done, that he imagin'd my brain was in good earnest disordred; and not suspecting that there cou'd be any other cause for it than the impatience I had to return to my Country, he one Day question'd me concerning it, adding something which made me think it wou'd be no difficult matter for me to obtain my liberty if I desired it; but I had now abandon'd all thoughts of my Religion, Kindred, Friends, Country, and Freedom; and lost in the sweet infatuation of *Arithea*'s charms plac'd all my Heaven in gazing on them, and rather terrify'd than pleas'd at the overture made me by

---

[9] Aphrodite, the Greek goddess of beauty, fertility, and sexual love, was born of the sea-foam.

[10] In Greek mythology, Pygmalion, a king and sculptor, made an ivory statue representing his ideal of womanhood and then fell in love with his own creation, which he named Galatea; the goddess Aphrodite brought the statue to life in answer to his prayer. The term 'plate' refers to any material beaten into a thin sheet so may refer to the paper on which the hero is drawing or suggest he is doing an engraving.

the Bassaw, I threw myself at his Feet, and conjur'd him not to discharge me from his service, assuring him that I thought it greater Honour to be his Slave, than command in any other place. He seem'd to take this testimony of my Fidelity extremely kind; yet had I retain'd any portion of common sense, I might have perceiv'd he was not perfectly satisfied with the earnestness I had express'd. 'Tis certain that from that moment I had a diligent watch put upon my actions. Frequent escapes making me grow secure, easy was it for me to be betray'd the third Day after that in which I had this discourse with the Bassaw. I was seiz'd coming out of the Seraglio-Garden by a Guard of Eunuchs, who, having search'd my pockets and taken thence my Picture, convey'd me to close Prison, where I was kept with no other sustenance than Bread and Water for a whole month; after which I was brought into a large yard and lash'd with Iron whips a hundred strokes upon my naked Back: it was look'd on as a particular grace that my life was preserv'd, tho' sure such a punishment was more terrible than Death, nor cou'd it be accounted less than Miraculous that I surviv'd, so cruelly had the steel tore my Flesh, and such a vast effusion of Blood had follow'd every blow. After this I was carry'd back to the Dungeon with no other support than before, and at the expiration of another month, the same disgracefull painfull Doom inflicted on me: in fine it was three times repeated, which with my manner of living, brought me into such a condition that my Death was hourly expected; intelligence of it being carry'd to the Bassaw he sent orders that I shou'd be carefully attended, saying that he intended not my Death but humiliation. It was however a long time before I recover'd enough to be able to walk, but as soon as I was, the Master of the Eunuchs had command to bring me before him, and having repeated my crime and represented to me the heinousness of such a presumption, extoll'd the goodness of the Bassaw in sparing my Life with such extravagant Hyperboles, that I cou'd scarce acknowledge, as I was requir'd to do, the truth of them, without blushing. After this penance I receiv'd his pardon, and was restor'd to my former office, tho' infinitely short of that respect and favour with which I had before been treated. Nothing cou'd be more deplorable than the state of my thoughts in this juncture, I was now without hope of ever seeing the adorable *Arithea* more; I had lost that dear Picture on which to gaze kept me from the greatest part of the tortures which attend despair; the kind Eunuch who had admitted me into the Seraglio had been put to Death for the favour he had done me—I had nothing to reflect upon but what gave me the most excessive disquiet, and not one dawn of hope to comfort me in the midst of so many Calamitys—strange will you think it that I shou'd still be fond of misery—had I been Master of the least share of Soul, or Spirit, or had been possessed of any part of that fortitude or resolution which every Man ought to have, I shou'd have exerted all the remains of interest I had with the Bassaw to have prevail'd on him to have suffer'd me to depart, or not succeeding in my request, have ventur'd every thing for my escape rather than have tarry'd in a place where I was doubly a Slave. But so strongly had the witchcraft of *Arithea*'s charms wrought on me, that I had no power to form one wish to leave her—tho hopeless of ever seeing her more, to breath in the same Air, to hear her name repeated, to behold those who had the priviledge of beholding her, and tread sometimes in the dear path her Feet had bless'd, all these shadowy Joys were to me felicities preferable to the real ones of Liberty and every laudable desire of Life—my very torments seem'd a Happiness nor wou'd I have parted from them for an Empire—so much I priz'd my pains, that having not the least notion of a possibility of being eas'd of them, I desir'd nothing but to dye a Martyr to them, and had folly enough to think I cou'd not make a more glorious exit from the World; I indulg'd the most unaccountable Chimeras sure that ever were; "when I find I am dying" said I to myself, "I will chuse out the most commiserating and gentle of all who are Witnesses of my Fate, and relating to him the melancholly History of my passion, will entreat to have prefix'd on my Tombstone, that I dyed for love and *Arithea*": it pleas'd me to think how many unhappy Lovers wou'd lament my misfortune and praise my constancy,— "Even *Arithea* herself", thought I, "cannot but pity my unhappy fate, and how glorious wou'd be my Doom", resum'd I, "to draw a sigh or tear from her." I was one Day soothing my lovesick fancy with these Day-Dreams when a Slave whom I very well knew belong'd to *Arithea*, put into my Hand a seal'd paper, which when I had broke open I found contain'd these lines

TO THE CHARMING SLAVE,

That I no sooner sent you a consolation for the ill usage you receiv'd on my account, was owing not to my want of gratitude, but power of doing as I wou'd—the faithfull Slave, who brings you this, will find the means to conduct you to my bed and Arms, if absence, and the severity of my cruel Husband have not effaced that Image in your Breast which cost you so dear to make present to your Eyes—I will not, however so far affront my own Charms as to believe you wou'd not readily undergo greater tortures, if possible, than any you have yet sustain'd, to obtain the recompence I now offer—But I intend, at a proper Season, to chide the coldness of you *Europeans*, who can content yourselves with so little when you so much merit all—it was only the want of a necessary boldness which brought you into any misfortune; since it had been more easy as well as more safe to have had the real substance than the shadow of

ARITHEA

'Ah *Philidore!*' said he, 'it is impossible for you to conceive what 'twas I felt; even tho', as you say, you have known what 'tis to love and to despair—had all the Curtains of the Sky been drawn, and every wonder of futurity reveal'd, my astonishment cou'd not have been more, or more my extacy, had I beheld my name, the foremost in the ranks of the immortal bless'd: the Slave to whom she had imparted her whole mind told me that she was pleas'd with my person the first moment she beheld me, and had often wish'd in secret there were a possibility for her to entertain me without the knowledge of the Bassaw, whose wife she was, not by Choice but constraint—that when she heard of the sufferings I had endur'd on her account she had been like to dye with grief, and that it was only on her request, that my life had been preserv'd—many other particulars he related to me which made me think myself the happiest of mankind; but it being dangerous to be seen to hold any long discourse together, he took his leave after having appointed the time and place where I shou'd meet him in order to be conducted to my expected Heaven.

'The History of the Christian Eunuch'

'The moment, which I then thought bless'd, being arriv'd I posted with a more than common lover's haste to the dear Rendezvous, where the punctual Eunuch immediately appearing we went together into the Seraglio by a back gate of which he had the key: He had taken great care to dispose the greatest part of the guard at distant waiting, and those who kept that quarter being introduc'd by him, took no care to examine me not doubting if I was any other than I seem'd, a mute. Having safely pass'd the avenues I was conducted into the most magnificent Room I had ever seen, where my guide takeing leave of me, the all dazling *Arithea* immediately enter'd. As soon as I saw her, I threw myself at her Feet, and was beginning to express my passion in the most humble terms, but she wou'd not suffer me to proceed, and raising me with a smile, told me I had already suffer'd too much for my humility, it was now time for me to demand that reward my sufferings deserv'd: with these words she led me to an Alcove, and making me sit down by her by a thousand tender words and looks encourag'd my submissive passion to proceed to the greatest libertys with her: I was just on the point of being as happy as the utmost qualification of my desires cou'd make me when suddenly from behind the arras rush'd out the Bassaw attended by five or six arm'd Slaves: not all the respect I had for *Arithea* nor the favours she had bestow'd on me cou'd hinder me in the first emotions of my surprize from believing I had been betray'd by her, and that she had laid this snare for me only to punish the presumption of loving her, but she giving a great shriek as they forc'd me from her Arms, and afterwards falling into a swound, as well as the reproaches made her by the Bassaw, soon convinc'd me of my mistake, and that I had only my own misfortune in this discovery to lament: the Bassaw, who had before resolv'd what to do with me, spoke but little to me; but giving a furious look, orderd I shou'd be taken from his sight; and the doom he had acquainted them with, be immediately executed on me. He had no sooner spoke the word, than the Slaves, seizing all at once upon me, drag'd me from the room and bore me to Prison; where, having bound me, with Instruments proper for the purpose, they deprived me of all power of ever injuring their Lord, or any other person in manner I was about to do, and left me nothing but the name of man:[11] thus wretched, thus become the scorn of both sexes, and incapable of being own'd by either, there was now nothing to wish for but Death, and 'tis certain that I oppos'd all the means made use of, to the cure of my wound as much as the principles of my religion would suffer me do.[12] I recover'd, however, and for my greater mortification was order'd to attend the Beautys I was now depriv'd of all possibility of ever possessing; being qualify'd for the Seraglio, I was compell'd to attend there under the direction of that treacherous Eunuch, who had been entrusted by *Arithea* to bring me to her, and had, as I afterwards learn'd, betray'd us both to the Bassaw. When first I saw *Arithea* after my misfortune, shame and grief overwhelm'd us both; in her expressive looks I read her Pity for my fate, but the fears of falling herself under the displeasure of the Bassaw or bringing on me yet more ill usage prevented her from speaking to me. My post being among the most inferior of the Slaves that waited on her, I had but seldom any opportunity of seeing her; nor did I now much endeavour it. My sentiments had chang'd with my condition, and as I had no longer the power of enjoying had very little of the wish remaining. Slavery also seem'd a less misfortune than it had been; I quitted all thoughts of ever returning to my Country; obscurity was now my only desire, and I chose rather that my friends should believe me to have perish'd by some accident, than enjoy their society with this disgrace upon me—involv'd in a kind of stupid melancholly did I linger on about six Years; at the Expiration of which Time, happening to be walking alone in the Seraglio Garden, near the apartment of *Arithea*, she threw out of the Window a small Bundle, which retiring to a remoter part to open, I found contain'd a Sum of money which in our Country Coin amounted to about a thousand

---

[11] Castration in Persia and Ottoman Turkey was exclusively carried out on boys, usually with stones used to crush the testicles, although European commentators describe operations cutting off the entire genitals. John Fryer says of Persian eunuchs 'they are Gelded so inartificially, or Butcherly rather, that All is cut off, nothing of witness being left, but as clear as the Skin will permit' (*A New Account of East India and Persia, Being Nine Years' Travels, 1672–1681*, ed. William Crooke, Works issued by the Hakluyt Society; 2nd ser., nos. 19–20, 39 (London: Hakluyt Society, 1909), iii. 126).

[12] As a Christian he should not commit suicide if he is to secure grace

Guineas, her Picture set round with Diamonds, and a letter in which was wrote these lines.

TO THE MOST INJURED BUT MOST DEAR OF ALL MANKIND.

Tis not enough to say I pity your misfortune, without I give you some further proof of the sense I have of it—wou'd to God that the best part of my blood, nay all of it, cou'd make you what you were, before my fatal love brought on you this irreparable mischief—gladly wou'd I yield my throat to the remorseless axe or bowstring[13]—but alas it is not in the power of even Heaven itself to restore to you what the cruel Bassaw and his curst Instruments have taken from you—but because it must certainly be an addition to your misfortunes to continue in the place where they befell you, and where every thing but serves to remind you of them and render your disgrace still flagrant, I send you the means of quitting *Persia* for ever—fly this barbarous place, O thou once most charming of thy sex, and still valued, tho' an Eunuch; remember *Arithea*, but lay not the blame of thy ill fate to her—trust no body with your intentions to escape; there's not a Creature depending on the *Seraglio* who has a grain of Honour; we have experience'd the treachery of those who protest most fidelity, else had I not suffer'd in the total disappointment of my wishes, and thou in so severe a manner—if you yet have any remains of tenderness for me, my Picture will deserve your notice; I send it you as a proof of mine, and with it what I hope will be sufficient to bear your expences from this inhumane Court, which I shall never cease to curse while I am

ARITHEA

'How transporting wou'd such an opportunity of returning home have been to me at my first arrival in *Persia*, and how little did I now relish it!—I had no inducements, indeed, to tarry in a place where I had suffer'd so much; yet was I so sensible of my disgrace, which I doubted not but wou'd be soon discover'd, that I cou'd not think of supporting the ridicule, which I thought wou'd be made of it, with any tollerable share of patience; and I can truly aver that no other reason in the World, but the desire I had of being in a place, where

---

[13] The bow-string was the traditional method of execution by strangling for offenders in early modern Ottoman Turkey and Persia.

I cou'd have the free exercise of my religion, won me at last to make use of *Arithea*'s bounty. Having determin'd to quit the service of the Bassaw I stole, one Night, when all the numerous Train but those who were Employ'd as his Body guard, were drown'd in sleep: knowing the watch word, I passed the gates without any difficulty, and before break of Day lost sight of that detested City. I thought myself then secure, and begun to slacken my pace, and travel by easy Journeys; I had, indeed, most certainly escap'd all pursuit had I had foresight enough to have chang'd my habit, but in the Eunuch's garb the badge of servitude[14] had I not been infatuated I cou'd not have hoped to have gone on without being remark'd. Morning was no sooner come, as I afterwards heard, than the Bassaw, being a little indispos'd, call'd for me to play on the flute: I was immediately miss'd and after some hours of fruitless search, several Janizaries were dispatch'd, some one way and some another, with orders to bring me back dead or alive; those whose fortune it was to overtake me, wou'd have perform'd the most favorable part of his injunction; but I refusing to yield myself, they fell upon me altogether and reduc'd me to condition from which your courage and generosity reliev'd me.'

The lovely stranger here ended the Story of his misfortunes, and *Philidore*, truly touch'd with them, omitted no arguments, which he thought might afford him Consolation. And as his friendship was perfectly sincere, what he said, had a force in it, which not all the study'd Compliments of the unaffected can boast—The charming Youth was so much delighted with the Society of *Philidore*, that it seem'd a great addition to his other Woes, that they were oblig'd to part: fain wou'd he have perswaded him to return with him for *England*, assuring him that if he wou'd do so, he shou'd not only be let into the secret of his Name and Birth, but also share with him in all the Goods of Fortune, which, he acknowledg'd to him, were sufficient to glut the Ambition of any two reasonable Men. But this alas! was no temptation to the Love-sick *Philidore*; he cou'd not be prevail'd on to do a thing, which he thought might be a prejudice to the peace of his dear *Placentia*; nor wou'd trust himself a second time with her

---

[14] Eunuchs are commonly depicted in 18th-c. accounts wearing tall turbans and loose robes.

Charms, lest the force of them shou'd compell him to do her an injury, for such he still look'd on becoming her Husband wou'd be without some greater recommendation to her Bed, than mere affection. In fine, he would suffer no Consideration to surmount the niceness of his Passion; and tho' he had the extremest tenderness for this Christian Eunuch, that one Man can possibly have for another, yet he found it no difficulty to part with him, in all probability for ever, when the Interest of *Placentia* was in dispute.

Spectator

no. 512, Friday, 17 October 1712

Joseph Addison

Copy-text: vol. 7 of the 1st edition (London, 1713)

Joseph Addison (1672–1719) was a poet, politician, and essayist. With his collaborator, Richard Steele, the dramatist and journalist, he produced the majority of the periodical papers known as the *Tatler* (published three times a week 1709–11) and the *Spectator* (published daily 1711–12, and 1714). Addison wrote almost half of the 555 papers which make up the 1711–12 run of the *Spectator*. Despite Addison's stronger political connections among the Whig grandees of the early eighteenth century, his contributions were more concerned with culture and taste than those of his collaborator. The periodical presented itself as a coffee-house vehicle for the promotion of manners, morals, and philosophy among the literate middling classes.

Addison was a particular enthusiast for the oriental tale and read avidly in both fiction and travel about the Orient. His papers in both periodicals, but especially the *Spectator*, cite and recirculate stories from writers such as Jean de Thévenot, John Chardin, and Antoine Galland. Martha Pike Conant cites Addison as the founder of the 'moralistic' or 'philosophical' tradition in the English oriental tale, a tradition inherited and promoted by Samuel Johnson in his *The History of Rasselas, Prince of Abyssinia* (1749)

(Martha Pike Conant, *The Oriental Tale in England in the Eighteenth Century*, Columbia University Studies in Comparative Literature (New York: Columbia University Press, 1908)). The tale told here could be compared with the tale of the Ox and Ass delivered by Scheherazade's father in the opening of *The Arabian Nights Entertainments* and the talking animals that populate so many of Pilpay's tales (see Part 1, 'The Framed Sequence'). Addison composed two original tales for his periodical publications: 'The Story of Helim and Abdallah' in *Guardian* no. 167 and 'The Story of Hilpa, Harpath and Shalum' in *Spectator* nos. 584 and 585.

The number given here refers to a tale translated by Jean-François Pétis de la Croix (1653–1713) from an Ottoman source. Pétis de la Croix studied oriental languages from childhood as his father was 'secrétaire-interprête du Rois' for Ottoman Turkish and Arabic. At 16 he went to the Levant to further his study of Arabic and spent three and a half years in Aleppo before leaving in 1674 for Isfahan, the capital of the Safavid Persian kingdom. He spent two years here and a further four in Istanbul, acquiring ancient coins and oriental manuscripts for Colbert before returning to France in 1681. His collection of tales translated into English by William King and others as *Turkish Tales* in 1708 derived from an Ottoman translation of a pre-Islamic Persian cycle known as the *Sindibadnama*, which survives only in a Syriac manuscript translated into Hebrew and thence into European languages as well as Arabic. In this collection seven viziers tell stories to a king to dissuade him from killing, on the persuasions of a wicked wife, his son and heir, Sindibad. The English preface to the 1708 translation insists that they are translated from a text in 'Mr. Petis *Library*' and thus not '*the bare Invention of some French-Man, designing to recommend his Fictions to the World under the Umbrage of a Foreign Title, but the Work of* Chec Zade, *Tutor to* Amurath *the* Second' (n.p.). Murat II reigned 1421–51, acceding to the throne on the sudden death of his father when he was only 17 years old. He spent two years fighting with his four younger brothers for his right to rule and went on to be one of the greatest Ottoman sultans, founding Ottoman power in Europe and Asia. He was a patron of poetry and learning and especially promoted the history of the early Turkish tribes and Turkish antiquities.

In *Spectator* 94 (Monday, 18 June 1712), Addison quoted another of the *Turkish Tales* concerning an Egyptian sultan who lives a full alternative life whenever he plunges his head in water; Addison used the tale to defend his favourite modern philosopher, John Locke, in his contention that our sense of time is derived from reflecting on the succession of ideas in our minds. Addison frequently conflates classical philosophy, oriental narrative, and contemporary empirical thought to produce his distinctive brand of cultured commentary.

Lectorem delectando pariterque monendo.
Hor.[1]

There is nothing which we receive with so much Reluctance as Advice. We look upon the Man who gives it us as offering an Affront to our Understanding, and treating us like Children or Ideots. We consider the Instruction as an implicit Censure, and the Zeal which any one shews for our Good on such an Occasion as a Piece of Presumption or Impertinence. The Truth of it is, the Person who pretends to advise, does, in that Particular, exercise a Superiority over us, and can have no other Reason for it, but that, in comparing us with himself, he thinks us defective either in our Conduct or our Understanding. For these Reasons, there is nothing so difficult as the Art of making Advice agreeable; and indeed all the Writers, both Ancient and Modern, have distinguished themselves among one another, according to the Perfection at which they have arrived in this Art. How many Devices have been made use of, to render this bitter Potion palatable? Some convey their Instructions to us in the best chosen Words, others in the most harmonious Numbers, some in Points of Wit, and others in short Proverbs.

But among all the different Ways of giving Counsel, I think the finest, and that which pleases the most universally, is *Fable*, in

---

[1] Horace, *Ars Poetica*, line 344: 'That in one line instructs and pleases all.'

whatsoever Shape it appears.[2] If we consider this way of instructing or giving Advice, it excells all others, because it is the least shocking, and the least subject to those Exceptions which I have before mentioned.

This will appear to us, if we reflect, in the first place, that upon the reading of a Fable we are made to believe we advise our selves. We peruse the Author for the sake of the Story, and consider the Precepts rather as our own Conclusions, than his Instructions. The Moral insinuates it self imperceptibly, we are taught by Surprise, and become wiser and better unawares. In short, by this Method a Man is so far over-reached as to think he is directing himself, whilst he is following the Dictates of another, and consequently is not sensible of that which is the most unpleasing Circumstance in Advice.

In the next Place, if we look into Human Nature, we shall find that the Mind is never so much pleased, as when she exerts her self in any Action that gives her an Idea of her own Perfections and Abilities. This natural Pride and Ambition of the Soul is very much gratified in the reading of a Fable; for in Writings of this Kind, the Reader comes in for half of the Performance; Every Thing appears to him like a Discovery of his own; he is busied all the While in applying Characters and Circumstances, and is in this respect both a Reader and a Composer. It is no wonder therefore that on such Occasions, when the Mind is thus pleased with it self, and amused with its own Discoveries, that it is highly delighted with the Writing which is the Occasion of it. For this Reason the *Absalon* and *Achitophel* was one of the most popular Poems that ever appeared in *English*. The Poetry is indeed very fine, but had it been much finer it would not have so much pleased, without a Plan which gave the Reader an Opportunity of exerting his own Talents.[3]

This oblique manner of giving Advice is so inoffensive, that if we look into ancient Histories, we find the wise Men of old very often

---

[2] In no. 183 (Saturday, 29 September 1711), Addison had already addressed the importance of fable, but concentrated on Aesop and classical precedents such as Cicero and Plato.

[3] John Dryden's satire in heroic couplets, *Absalom and Achitophel*, was published in 1681. It allegorized the last years of Charles II in terms of the Old Testament story of King David and his rebellious son Absalom (3 Samuel: 13–19), with Charles's illegitimate son, James Scott, duke of Monmouth, featuring as Absalom spurred on by Antony Ashley Cooper, the earl of Shaftesbury, as Achitophel to lead a Whig challenge to the succession of the Catholic James, duke of York, Charles's brother.

chose to give Counsel to their Kings in Fables. To omit many which will occur to every one's Memory, there is a pretty Instance of this Nature in a *Turkish* Tale, which I do not like the worse for that little oriental Extravagance which is mixed with it.

We are told that the Sultan *Mahmoud*,[4] by his perpetual Wars abroad, and his Tyranny at home, had filled his Dominions with Ruin and Desolation, and half-unpeopled the *Persian* Empire. The Visier to this great Sultan (whether an Humourist or an Enthusiast we are not informed) pretended to have learned of a certain Dervise to understand the Language of Birds, so that there was not a Bird that could open his Mouth but the Visier knew what it was he said. As he was one Evening with the Emperor, in their Return from Hunting, they saw a couple of Owls upon a Tree that grew near an old Wall out of an Heap of Rubbish. '*I would fain know*', says the Sultan, '*what these two Owls are saying to one another; listen to their Discourse, and give me an account of it.*' The Visier approached the Tree, pretending to be very attentive to the two Owls. Upon his Return to the Sultan, '*Sir*,' says he, '*I have heard part of their Conversation, but dare not tell you what it is.*' The Sultan would not be satisfied with such an Answer, but forced him to repeat Word for Word every Thing the Owls had said. '*You must know then*', said the Visier, '*that one of the these Owls has a Son, and the other a Daughter, between whom they are now upon a Treaty of Marriage. The Father of the Son said to the Father of the Daughter, in my hearing, "Brother, I consent to this Marriage, provided you will settle upon your Daughter fifty ruined Villages for her Portion." To which the Father of the Daughter replied, "Instead of fifty I will give her five hundred, if you please. God grant a long Life to Sultan* Mahmoud! *whilst he reigns over us we shall never want ruined Villages."*'

---

[4] In Pétis de la Croix, this story is told by the Sultana of Persia to Hasikin, king of Persia, to instruct him how to read allegorically a dream she claims to have had in which his son catches and breaks a ball he holds in his hand (his kingdom), his stepmother gathering up the diamonds from it to return to her husband. The visier of the tale is identified in Pétis de la Croix as Khasayas, visier to Mahmoud Subuktekin, and he tells the tale to make his sovereign realize the dangerous effects of his greedy devastation of the Persian empire. Yamin Al-daula Abu'l-qasim Mahmud Ibn Sebüktigin was sultan of the kingdom of Ghazna (998–1030); he expanded through conquest a kingdom comprising modern Afghanistan and north-eastern modern Iran to include north-western India and most of Iran.

Spectator

The Story says, the Sultan was so touched with the Fable, that he rebuilt the Towns and Villages which had been destroyed, and from that time forward consulted the Good of his People.

To fill up my Paper, I shall add a most ridiculous Piece of natural Magick, which was taught by no less a Philosopher than *Democritus*, namely, that if the Blood of certain Birds, which he mentioned, were mixed together, it would produce a Serpent of such a wonderful Virtue that whoever did eat it should be skill'd in the Language of Birds, and understand every thing they said to one another.[5] Whether the Dervise abovementioned might not have eaten such a Serpent, I shall leave to the Determinations of the Learned.

[5] Addison's source is Peter Bayle, who in his entry on the ancient Thracian philosopher, Democritus, comments that his subject was prone to believing in chimeras: 'Here follow some other idle Fancies of *Democritus*. He said that the Blood of some Birds, which he named, being mixed together, would bring forth a Serpent of such an admirable virtue, that whosoever did eat it might understand what the Birds said to each other' (Peter Bayle, *An Historical and Critical Dictionary* (London, 1710), ii. 'Democritus', Remark H, p. 1081).

'Mi Li. A Chinese Fairy Tale' (1785)

Horace Walpole, 4th earl of Orford

Copy-text: *Hieroglyphic Tales* (Strawberry Hill Press, 1785)

Horace Walpole (1717–97), letter writer, antiquarian, and connoisseur, produced in 1785 just seven copies, including proofs, of his *Hieroglyphic Tales* from his Strawberry Hill Press at Twickenham. The tales were written between 1766 and 1772 for the amusement of his friends after his retirement from politics (he was the son of Britain's first 'prime minister', Robert Walpole, and, like his father, a committed Whig). The collection consists of six tales which demonstrate the enormous hybridity of the eighteenth-century tale as well as Horace Walpole's own eccentric, sometimes vicious, but usually delightful, humour: they satirize the clergy and the literary establishment, play with the reputations of his friends and deploy his antiquarian knowledge, mixing elements from *The Arabian Nights Entertainments*, fairy tales, Shakespeare, the Bible, and travel literature. A postscript asserts that the tales were 'an attempt to vary the stale and beaten class of stories and novels, which, though works of invention, are almost always devoid of imagination'. The preface jokes that the stories were preserved 'by oral tradition' in an uninhabited island 'in the mountains of Crampcraggiri' and were probably the creation in heroic verse of 'Kemanrlgorpikos, son of Quat' otherwise only ever known for a cookery book.

'Mi Li. A Chinese Fairy Tale'

The first tale is an entertaining spoof on the *Arabian Nights Entertainments* in which a Dutch princess enables an insomniac emperor to fall asleep by giving him 'a short account of the troubles that have agitated Europe for the last two hundred years, on the doctrines of grace, free-will, predestination, reprobation, justification, &c'. She and the chief eunuch promptly suffocate the sleeping emperor and she is declared empress, espousing a new husband every night but remitting their execution. The second tale introduces a three-legged dead Egyptian prince, who arrives in England in search of a bride, prompting a craze for Egyptian clothing and cadaverous appearance among the populace. The third tale is a satire on French romances and fairy tales. Here, Pissimissi (Caroline Campbell, 9-year-old daughter of Lord William Campbell, a friend to Walpole who had served as Governor of Carolina (naming his daughter after the region)) sets out in a pistachio shell drawn by an elephant and a ladybird in search of Solomon (the title Walpole habitually conferred on Louis XV) to fulfil a prophecy that she will become his concubine. 'The Peach in Brandy', the fourth tale, was written for the earl of Ossory, whose wife Anne Liddel had miscarried of twin sons: a strange compliment this, since the tale relates how a civil war (caused by a controversy over whether a stillborn child conceived before the succession can be an heir) is averted when an archbishop seized by a fit of cholic swallows the pickled fetus mistaking it for a peach in brandy. The sixth tale is set in Italy and relates the thwarted love of a Milanese hero and a young African slave called Azora (the pair, it transpires, are in fact the pet dogs of a Carmelite nun and a rich Italian widow who are violent rivals).

The tale reproduced here is the fifth in the sequence and it also features Caroline Campbell, as the destined bride of a Chinese prince who is attempting to fulfil a prophecy that he will marry a woman who shares her name with that of her father's kingdom. The story allows Walpole to pursue his enthusiasm for debates about gardening and his fluctuating attitude to the cult for Chinoiserie in mid-eighteenth-century England. An early enthusiast for this craze for porcelain, tea, lacquer-work, and architectural imitation of Chinese forms, Walpole called his goldfish pond at his home in Strawberry Hill Po Yang in reference to a lake in Kiangsi province

127

celebrated for its fish. He counted a number of works about China in his extensive library and received with especial delight a French copy of Jean-Baptiste Du Halde's *General Description of China* from Lord Hervey in 1735. Walpole was also quick to see the potential of the figure of a Chinese informant as a satirical vehicle. A sixpenny pamphlet entitled *A Letter from Xo Ho, A* Chinese *Philosopher at London, to his Friend Lien Chi at Peking* (1757), which went through five editions in the year of its publication, attacks the factionalism of eighteenth-century English politics which, according to Xo Ho's account, led to the court martial and execution of Admiral Byng to assuage public wrath over the loss of Minorca in the Seven Years War. Xo Ho considers the Confucian rationalism of China far superior to the unreasoning pursuit of a scapegoat in England,: 'Reason in *China* is not Reason in *England*' he concludes. Oliver Goldsmith was later to appropriate the name Lien Chi for his *Citizen of the World* series also extracted in this anthology (see Part 4).

However, Walpole appears to have turned against Chinoiserie after the publication of the Tory favourite Sir William Chambers's *A Dissertation on Oriental Gardening* in 1772, which promoted the idea of variety and surprise over classicism or naturalism in garden design. Walpole counters the oriental model with that of the Gothic (arguably an equally whimsical style). For a more extensive discussion than can be provided here, see David Porter, 'From Chinese to Goth: Walpole and the Gothic Repudiation of Chinoiserie', *Eighteenth-Century Life* 23 (1999): 46–58.

Beyond the specific critique of styles in gardening, however, the tale illustrates the complexity and attractiveness of China in the western imagination of the eighteenth century. Walpole captures precisely the paradoxical representation of China. Its image as a territory associated through Jesuit accounts of Confucianism and the longevity of absolutism with hyper-rationalism, conflicts with an equally strong image, prompted by the importation of luxury goods from the region and an ensuing reputation for aesthetic eccentricity, with excesses of fancy bordering on madness. For further discussion of these conflicting images, see David Porter, *Ideographia: the Chinese Cipher in Early Modern*

'Mi Li. A Chinese Fairy Tale'

England (Stanford, Calif.: Stanford University Press, 2001); and Jonathan Spence, *The Chan's Great Continent: China in Western Minds* (London: Allen Lane Penguin Press, 1999).

Walpole's tale is itself a piece of Chinoiserie, a nonsensical fragment which mixes Chinese and European elements like the much-coveted porcelain prepared for the export market which depicted English hunting scenes in the familiar blue-and-white pattern. Like the hero of the tale, whose name 'Mi Li' (my lye) indicates to the reader that he is a mere fabrication, Chineseness is 'lost in translation', becoming an incomprehensible but fascinating sign of otherness. It is not coincidental that this tale about errors in language transmission also exploits the common representation of Chinese language as just such a non-signifying sign system. The Jesuit traveller to China Louis Le Comte complains in his *A Compleat History of the Empire of China* of 'imperfect Hieroglyphicks, that have in a manner no analogy with the things they signifie' (2nd edn., London 1739, 188). Walpole mocks not China but 'Chinoiserie', and with it the superficial learning of travel-writing and the oriental tale in the period. He provides footnotes that assert authenticity rather than demonstrate it and authorial interventions that expose rather than dispel ignorance. The numbering of Walpole's footnotes is given in the text here by letter to distinguish them from my editorial annotations. Where Walpole's notes need further annotation, editorial notes in square brackets are added at the end of Walpole's notes.

TALE V

'MI LI. A Chinese Fairy Tale'

MI LI, prince of China, was brought up by his godmother the fairy Hih,[1] who was famous for telling fortunes with a tea-cup. From that

[1] The name of the Chinese correspondent 'Xo Ho' in Walpole's 1757 pamphlet provides the cue to read this name as an orthographic simulation of laughter. Eliza Haywood

unerring oracle she assured him, that he would be the most unhappy man alive unless he married a princess whose name was the same with her father's dominions. As in all probability there could not be above one person in the world to whom that accident had happened, the prince thought there would be nothing so easy as to learn who his destined bride was. He had been too well educated to put the question to his godmother, for he knew when she uttered an oracle, that it was with intention to perplex, not to inform; which has made people so fond of consulting all those who do not give an explicit answer, such as prophets, lawyers, and any body you meet on the road, who, if you ask the way, reply by desiring to know whence you came. Mi Li was no sooner returned to his palace than he sent for his governor, who was deaf and dumb, qualities for which the fairy had selected him, that he might not instil any bad principles into his pupil; however, in recompence, he could talk upon his fingers like an angel. Mi Li asked him directly who the princess was whose name was the same with her father's kingdom? This was a little exaggeration in the prince, but nobody ever repeats any thing just as they heard it: besides, it was excusable in the heir of a great monarchy, who of all things had not been taught to speak truth, and perhaps had never heard what it was. Still it was not the mistake of *kingdom* for *dominions* that puzzled the governor. It never helped him to understand any thing the better for its being rightly stated. However, as he had great presence of mind, which consisted in never giving a direct answer, and in looking as if he could, he replied, it was a question of too great importance to be resolved on a sudden. 'How came you to know that?' said the prince—This youthful impetuosity told the governor that there was something more in the question than he had apprehended; and though he could be very solemn about nothing, he was ten times more so when there was something he did not comprehend. Yet that unknown something occasioning a conflict between his cunning and his ignorance, and the latter being the greater, always betrayed itself, for nothing looks so silly as a fool acting wisdom. The prince repeated his question; the governor demanded why he asked—the prince had not patience to spell

in a mock-Chinese tale which satirized Walpole's father, *The Adventures of Eovaai* of 1736, named the Chinese mandarin who comments on the narrative 'Hahehihotu'. But the name 'Hih' here may also be a play on 'Her Highness'.

the question over again on his fingers, but bawled it as loud as he could to no purpose. The courtiers ran in, and catching up the prince's words, and repeating them imperfectly, it soon flew all over Pekin, and thence into the provinces, and thence into Tartary, and thence to Muscovy, and so on, that the prince wanted to know who the princess was, whose name was the same as her father's. As the Chinese have not the blessing (for aught I know) of having family surnames as we have, and as what would be their Christian-names, if they were so happy as to be Christians, are quite different for men and women, the Chinese, who think that must be a rule all over the world because it is theirs,[2] decided that there could not exist upon the square face of the earth a woman whose name was the same as her father's. They repeated this so often, and with so much deference and so much obstinacy, that the prince, totally forgetting the original oracle, believed that he wanted to know who the woman was who had the same name as her father. However, remembering there was something in the question that he had taken for royal, he always said *the king her father*. The prime minister consulted the red book or court-calendar,[3] which was *his* oracle, and could find no such princess. All the ministers at foreign courts were instructed to inform themselves if there was such lady; but as it took up a great deal of time to put these instructions into cypher, the prince's impatience could not wait for the couriers setting out, but he determined to go himself in search of the princess. The old king, who, *as is usual*, had left the whole management of affairs to his son the moment he was fourteen,[4] was charmed with the prince's resolution of seeing the world, which he thought could be done in a few days, the

---

[2] Louis Le Comte reports that the Chinese, finding themselves bordered only by barbarous kingdoms, decided '*To have no Commerce with Foreigners and Strangers, but just so much as should be necessary to receive their Homages*' (*Compleat History*, 123), but this attitude resulted in pride whereby they 'lookt upon themselves as a chosen elect People, that Heaven had produced in the Center of the Universe to give them a Law; a People only capable to Instruct, Civilize and Govern Nations' (123).

[3] Jean-Baptiste Du Halde, Jesuit compiler of the *General History of China* from which Walpole derives most of his information refers to a calendar compiled throughout China 'printed in the Form of a Book in red' and sealed by the Tribunal of Astronomy, a copy of which is supplied to every member of the court with great ceremony each year (trans. in 4 vols. Richard Brookes (1736), iii. 94).

[4] Describing the Ch'ing emperor, Shun-chih's minority (ruled 1643–61), Du Halde comments that 'the Emperor being now fourteen Years old . . . was able to govern alone' (i. 484).

facility of which makes so many monarchs never stir out of their own palaces till it is too late; and his majesty declared, that he should approve of his son's choice, be the lady who she would, provided she answered to the divine designation of having the same name as her father.

The prince rode post to Canton, intending to embark there on board an English man of war.[5] With what infinite transport did he hear the evening before he was to embark, that a sailor knew the identic[6] lady in question. The prince scalded his mouth with the tea he was drinking, broke the old china cup it was in, and which the queen his mother had given him at his departure from Pekin, and which had been given to her great great great great grandmother queen Fi by Confucius himself,[7] and ran down to the vessel and asked for the man who knew his bride. It was honest Tom O'Bull, an Irish sailor, who by his interpreter Mr. James Hall, the supercargo,[8] informed his highness that Mr. Bob Oliver of Sligo had a daughter christened of both his names, the fair miss Bob Oliver.[a] The prince by the plenitude of his power declared Tom a mandarin of the first class,[9] and at Tom's desire promised to speak to his brother the king

[5] Jesuit priests like Le Comte were unusual in gaining access to the Chinese mainland because of their astronomical and mathematical skills. European merchants were frustrated by the fact that the Cohong or combined merchant companies established in 1720 at Canton had a monopoly over maritime trade with western countries. From 1760 all foreign trade was restricted to Canton. The British were numerically the largest contingent of the small community living outside the walls of Canton on the south-east coast of China. They were forbidden to live in any other region, could not enter the city of Canton itself, could not bring women from their native countries to live with them, and had to return to Macao or other settlements off the coast of China at the end of every trading season.   [6] Identic: identical.

[7] Confucius (551–479 BC) was viewed by European sources as the most distinguished of oriental philosophers on a par with his classical contemporaries. The Jesuits made much of Confucianism as a secular moralism compatible with their Catholic mission. Du Halde comments that Confucius had the advantage over Pythagoras, Socrates, and Thales 'that his Glory increases with the Succession of Years, and has arrived at the highest pitch that human Wisdom can possibly attain: He at present enjoys the highest degree of Dignity in the midst of the greatest Empire in the World, which thinks itself indebted to this Philosopher for its Duration and Splendor' (*History of China*, iii. 293).

[8] supercargo: an officer on board a merchant ship whose business it is to superintend the cargo and the commercial transactions of the voyage (*OED*).

[a] *There really was such a person.*

[9] Du Halde describes the 'first Order of Mandarins' as 'that of the *Colaos*, or Ministers of State, the Chief Presidents of the Supreme Courts, and other principal Officers in the Army' appointed individually by the Chinese ruler but 'seldom more than five or six' (*History of China*, ii. 32–3).

of Great Ireland, France and Britain, to have him made a peer in his own country, Tom saying he should be ashamed to appear there without being a lord as well as all his acquaintance.

The prince's passion, which was greatly inflamed by Tom's description of her highness Bob's charms, would not let him stay for a proper set of ladies from Pekin to carry to wait on his bride, so he took a dozen of the wives of the first merchants in Canton, and two dozen virgins as maids of honour, who however were disqualified for their employments before his highness got to St. Helena. Tom himself married one of them,[10] but was so great a favourite with the prince, that she still was appointed maid of honour, and with Tom's consent was afterwards married to an English duke.

Nothing can paint the agonies of our royal lover, when on his landing at Dublin he was informed that princess Bob had quitted Ireland, and was married to nobody knew whom. It was well for Tom that he was on Irish ground. He would have been chopped as small as rice, for it is death in China to mislead the heir of the crown through ignorance. To do it knowingly is no crime, any more than in other countries.

As a prince of China cannot marry a woman that has been married before, it was necessary for Mi Li to search the world for another lady equally qualified with miss Bob, whom he forgot the moment he was told he must marry somebody else,[11] and fell equally in love with somebody else, though he knew not with whom. In this suspence he dreamt, *"that he would find his destined spouse, whose father had lost the dominions which never had been his dominions, in a place where*

[10] A manuscript note from Walpole's copy of the first edition annotates the line 'Tom himself married one of them' as follows: 'Alluding to the famous Miss Chudleigh, who married the Duke of Kingston while Maid of Honour to the Princess Dowager of Wales, which post she retained tho married to Mr. Augustus Hervey who was a *Seaman* and who was suspected of having connived at her marrying the Duke that he might himself get rid of her, and marry some other woman which he attempted.' Elizabeth Chudleigh (*c.*1720–85) married privately Augustus John Hervey, 3rd Earl of Bristol in 1744 and then bigamously Evelyn Pierrepont, 2nd Duke of Kingston-upon-Hull in 1769.

[11] 'Whom he forgot the moment he was told he must marry somebody else.' A manuscript note from Walpole's copy of the first edition annotates this phrase as follows: 'Alluding to a certain Prince who had been in love with Lady Sarah Lenox at the same time he consented to marry another person.' George III was thought to be in love with Lady Sarah Lennox (1745–1826) at the time of his marriage to Charlotte-Sophia of Mecklenburg-Strelitz in 1761. Sarah Lennox married Sir Thomas Charles Bunbury in 1762, was divorced in 1776, and married George Napier in 1781.

there was a bridge over no water, a tomb where nobody ever was buried nor ever would be buried, ruins that were more than they had ever been, a subterraneous passage in which there were dogs with eyes of rubies and emeralds, and a more beautiful menagerie of Chinese pheasants[12] *than any in his father's extensive gardens."* This oracle seemed so impossible to be accomplished, that he believed it more than he had done the first, which shewed his great piety. He determined to begin his second search, and being told by the lord lieutenant that there was in England a Mr. Banks,[b] who was going all over the world in search of he did not know what, his highness thought he could not have a better conductor, and sailed for England. There he learnt that the sage Banks was at Oxford, hunting in the Bodleian library for a MS. voyage of a man who had been in the moon, which Mr. Banks thought must have been in the western ocean, where the moon sets, and which planet if he could discover once more, he would take possession of in his majesty's name, under condition that it should never be taxed, and so be lost again to this country like the rest of his majesty's dominions in that part of the world.[13]

Mi Li took a hired post-chaise for Oxford, but as it was a little rotten it broke on the new road down to Henley. A beggar advised him to walk into general Conway's,[14] who was the most courteous person alive, and would certainly lend him his own chaise. The prince

---

[12] Chinese pheasants are probably peacocks or ornamental pheasants, both members of the Phasianidae family of birds. Pheasants were introduced to Europe from China some two thousand years ago.

[b] *The gentleman who discovered Otaheite, in company with Dr. Solander* [Joseph Banks (1744–1820), Secretary of the Society of Dilettanti, natural historian, and traveller. He journeyed to Newfoundland and Labrador (1766), around the world with Captain James Cook (1768–71), and to Iceland (1772). His *Florilegium*, a collection of engravings of plants, was based on drawings by Daniel Solander during Cook's 1768–71 voyage. Otaheite is Tahiti, the largest island of the Windward Group (Îles du Vent) of the Society Islands, French Polynesia, in the central South Pacific, visited in 1767 by Captain Samuel Wallis, of the British navy, who named it King George III Island. James Cook's expedition visited it in 1769.]

[13] Numerous 17th-c. utopian publications presented the moon as a new world discovery: John Wilkins's *The Discovery of a World in the Moone* (1638), Francis Godwin's *The Man in the Moone: or A Discourse of a Voyage thither by Domingo Gonsales* (1638), and Cyrano de Bergerac's *L'Autre Monde* (1657).

[14] Henry Seymour Conway (1719–95) was Horace Walpole's first cousin and closest friend. Leader of the House of Commons, a gardener, and man of letters, he was popular in America because of his part in the repeal of the Stamp Act and Conway, New Hampshire, and Conway, Massachussetts, were named after him.

'Mi Li. A Chinese Fairy Tale'

travelled incog.[15] He took the beggar's advice, but going up to the house was told the family were in the grounds, but he should be conducted to them. He was led through a venerable wood of beeches, to a menagerie[c] commanding a more glorious prospect than any in his father's dominions, and full of Chinese pheasants. The prince cried out in extasy, 'Oh! potent Hih! my dream begins to be accomplished.' The gardiner, who knew no Chinese but the names of a few plants,[16] was struck with the similitude of the sounds, but discreetly said not a word. Not finding his lady there, as he expected, he turned back, and plunging suddenly into the thickest gloom of the wood, he descended into a cavern totally dark, the intrepid prince following him boldly. After advancing a great way into this subterraneous vault, at last they perceived light, when on a sudden they were pursued by several small spaniels, and turning to look at them, the prince perceived their eyes[d] shone like emeralds and rubies. Instead of being amazed, as Fo-Hi, the founder of his race, would have been,[17] the prince renewed his exclamations, and cried, 'I advance! I advance! I shall find my bride! great Hih! thou art infallible!' Emerging into light, the imperturbed[e] gardiner conducted his highness to a heap of artificial[f] ruins, beneath which they found a spacious gallery or arcade, where his highness was asked if he would not repose himself; but instead of answering he capered like one frantic, crying out, 'I advance! I advance! great Hih! I advance'—The gardiner was amazed, and doubted whether he was not conducting a madman to his master and lady, and hesitated

---

[15] incog: incognito.   [c] *Lady Ailesbury's.*

[16] Du Halde gave considerable attention to Chinese flora, especially its medicinal properties, giving chapters to 'Gin Seng' and 'Rhubarb' in vol. iv. Walpole is also suggesting that the gardener may have heard the names of Chinese plants from his employer, Conway, who was a keen gardener and would have been conversant with the book by the royal architect and designer of Somerset House and the gardens at Kew, Sir William Chambers, entitled *A Dissertation on Oriental Gardening* (1772), even though Walpole's description here suggests his garden is largely Gothic rather than Chinese in design.

[d] *At Park-place there is such a passage cut through a chalk-hill: when dogs are in the middle, the light from the mouth makes their eyes appear in the manner here described.*

[17] In his 'Annals of the Chinese Monarchy', Du Halde describes Fo Hi as the first emperor, bringing civilization to his brutish people (i. 269–72). The association of his name here with dogs is a reference to the Chinese stone figures of the snarling lion, usually in a pair, which guard the Buddhist temple, known as the Lion of Buddha, Dog of Fo, or Shishi ('stone lion'). Fo is the name commonly given to the Buddha in 18th-c. European writing.   [e] *Copeland, the gardiner, a very grave person.*

[f] *Consequently they seem to have been larger.*

135

whether he should proceed—but as he understood nothing the prince said, and perceiving he must be a foreigner, he concluded he was a Frenchman by his dancing. As the stranger too was so nimble and not at all tired with his walk, the sage gardiner proceeded down a sloping valley, between two mountains cloathed to their summits with cedars, firs, and pines, which he took care to tell the prince were all of his honour the general's own planting: but though the prince had learnt more English in three days in Ireland, than all the French in the world every learnt in three years, he took no notice of the information, to the great offence of the gardiner, but kept running on, and increased his gambols and exclamations when he perceived the vale was terminated by a stupendous bridge, that seemed composed of the rocks which the giants threw at Jupiter's head,[18] and had not a drop of water beneath[g] it—'Where is my bride, my bride?' cried Mi Li—'I must be near her.' The prince's shouts and cries drew a matron from a cottage that stood on a precipice near the bridge, and hung over the river—'My lady is down at Ford-house,' cried the good[h] woman, who was a little deaf, concluding they had called to her to know. The gardiner knew it was in vain to explain his distress to her, and thought if the poor gentleman was really mad, his master the general would be the properest person to know how to manage him. Accordingly turning to the left, he led the prince along the banks of the river, which glittered through the opening sallows,[19] while on the other hand a wilderness of shrubs climbed up the pendent cliffs of chalk, and contrasted with the verdant meads and fields of corn beyond the stream. The prince, insensible to such enchanting scenes, galloped wildly along, keeping the poor gardiner on a round trot, till they

[18] In Greek legend, the older giant gods, the Titans, engaged in a long war known as the Titanomachia with the god Zeus (Jupiter in Roman mythology) and his younger fellows, resulting in the Titans being banished to the underworld.

[g] *The rustic bridge at Park-place was built by general Conway, to carry the road from Henley, and to leave the communication free between his grounds on each side of the road. Vide last page of 4th. vol. of Anecdotes of Painting.* [Horace Walpole's *Anecdotes of Painting in England* (4 vols. 1765–71) includes in the last volume an essay 'On Modern Gardening'. It concludes with a description of 'general Conway's rustic bridge at Park-place, of which every stone was placed by his own direction in one of the most beautiful scenes in nature' (iv. 151).]

[h] *The old woman who kept the cottage built by general Conway to command a glorious prospect. Ford-house is a farm house at the termination of the grounds.*

[19] sallows: willow trees (*OED*).

'Mi Li. A Chinese Fairy Tale'

were stopped by a lonely[i] tomb, surrounded by cypress, yews, and willows, that seemed the monument of some adventurous youth who had been lost in tempting the current, and might have suited the gallant and daring Leander.[20] Here Mi Li first had presence of mind to recollect the little English he knew, and eagerly asked the gardiner whose tomb he beheld before him. 'It is nobody's'—before he could proceed, the prince interrupted him, 'And will it never be any body's?' 'Oh' thought the gardiner, 'now there is no longer any doubt of his phrenzy'—and perceiving his master and the family approaching towards them, he endeavoured to get the start, but the prince, much younger, and borne too on the wings of love, set out full speed the moment he saw the company, and particularly a young damsel with them. Running almost breathless up to lady Ailesbury, and seizing miss Campbell's hand[21]—he cried, '*Who she? who she?*' Lady Ailesbury screamed, the young maid squalled, the general, cool but offended, rushed between them, and if a prince could be collared, would have collared him—Mi Li kept fast hold with one arm, but pointing to his prize with the other, and with the most eager and supplicating looks intreating for an answer, continued to exclaim, '*Who she? who she?*' The general perceiving by his accent and manner that he was a foreigner, and rather tempted to laugh than be angry, replied with civil scorn, 'Why *she* is miss Caroline Campbell, daughter of lord William Campbell, his majesty's late governor of Carolina'— 'O Hih! I now recollect thy words!' cried Mi Li—And so she became princess of China.

[i] *A fictitious tomb in a beautiful spot by the river, built for a point of view: it has a small pyramid on it.*

[20] In Greek legend Leander of Abydos falls in love with Hero, virgin priestess of Aphrodite at Sestos, and swims the Hellespont at night to visit her, guided by a light from her tower. One stormy night the light is extinguished, and Leander drowned; Hero, seeing his body, drowns herself. Ovid retells the story as does Christopher Marlowe in his poem 'Hero and Leander' (1598).

[21] Caroline Campbell (1721–1803), daughter of the 4th earl of Argyll, unwillingly married the 3rd earl of Aylesbury at the age of 18. A few months after her first husband's death in 1747 she married Henry Seymour Conway keeping her title. The couple had one daughter, Anne Seymour, a favourite and executrix of Horace Walpole. Lady Ailesbury's namesake, Caroline Campbell (1764–89), was the daughter of Lord William Campbell (c.1732–78), MP and Governor of South Carolina. Walpole writes to Horace Mann on 8 January 186 that she 'has always lived with Mr. Conway and Lady Ailesbury, who are as fond of her as their own daughter', *Horace Walpole's Correspondence*, vol. xxv, ed. W. S. Lewis et al. (London: Oxford University Press, 1971), 618.

3

TRAVELS AND HISTORY

'A Voyage to Kachemire, the Paradise of Indostan'

François Bernier

Copy-text: *A Continuation of the Memoires of Monsieur Bernier, Concerning the Empire of the Great Mogol*, translated by Henry Oldenburg (London, 1672) vol. ii of the 1st edition

Seventeenth-century accounts of the Orient often combined a detailed relation of the authors' itinerary in eastern territories with more general descriptions of 'manners', courts, systems of government, and dynastic history, flora and fauna. Travellers also met and travelled together. François Bernier (1620–88)—the author of this account of a journey made with the court of the Mughal emperor Aurangzeb in 1644 from Delhi to Kashmir—travelled with the Protestant jewel-merchant Jean Baptiste Tavernier to Bengal between 1665 and 1666. He also concluded his account of his journey to Kashmir with responses to five questions about Kashmiri Jews, the Indian climate, and the territory of Bengal set by Jean de Thévenot, an independent traveller. *The Six Voyages of John Baptista Tavernier ... Through Turkey into Persia and the East-Indies* was translated into English in 1678 and *The Travels of Monsieur De Thevenot into the Levant* in 1687.

However, Bernier's narrative about the combined luxury and trials of travelling to Kashmir with the Mughal court (he is the first European traveller known to have visited Kashmir) has been selected here because it is by far the most thrilling, revealing, and engaged of such accounts. Tavernier is careful to describe the routes for other traders and the condition of roads, while Thévenot is an illuminating reporter of public events and private manners, but neither enjoyed the access to power nor the enlightened education which make Bernier such a fascinating informant. Moreover, the use of the letter format gives an immediacy and eyewitness freshness to Bernier's descriptions which the retrospective viewpoint of his fellows often lacks.

The translator of Bernier's compendious writings about seventeenth-century India into English, Henry Oldenburg (1626–76), came to England as Consul for Bremen, lost his post, and became tutor to Lord O'Brien. In 1656 he entered as a student at Oxford University and was the first secretary of the Royal Society with responsibility for maintaining correspondences with learned foreigners. He was imprisoned in the Tower under suspicion of treasonable practices as a result of this correspondence but quickly liberated.

Bernier would have been of special interest to Oldenburg because of his philosophical and political connections. He was prepared for his examination in physiology taken in 1652 by the philosopher Pierre Gassendi in Provence and subsequently took a degree as Doctor of Medicine. He visited Palestine and Syria in 1654, returning to tend Gassendi in his last illness. Between 1656 and 1658 he travelled in Egypt and then abandoned his plan to visit Abyssinia, setting sail in an Indian vessel for Surat which arrived early in 1659. India was in the grip of civil war between the rival sons of Shah Jahan (ruled 1628–58) and Bernier was compelled by the eldest, Dara, whom he met near Ahmedabad to accompany him as his physician in his flight towards Sing. At Ahmedabad, he put himself under the protection of a Mughal nobleman, Damishmend Khan, Master of the Cavalry and Secretary of State for Foreign Affairs to the third son, Aurangzeb (ruled 1658–1707), and accompanied him to Delhi. In December 1664 he joined Damishmend Khan in Aurangzeb's journey to Kashmir. Aurangzeb's expedition to Kashmir was part of his overall policy of extending Mughal Islam's reach across India, challenging the Rajputs in the north and the rising Marathas

'A Voyage to Kachemire'

in the south. Thereafter Bernier travelled with Tavernier to Bengal, parted company with him to go on to Masulipatam and Golconda, where he heard of the death of Shah Jahan (1666). He met John Chardin, another Protestant jewel-merchant and travel writer, at Surat where he embarked in 1667 and went on to Shiraz in Persia. He returned to Marseilles in 1669, and his book describing these travels and the Mughal empire in general was published in 1670. After a visit to England in 1685, he died of an apoplexy at Paris in 1688. Bernier learned to speak Persian, the language of the Mughals in India. He translated Gassendi and René Descartes into Persian for Damishmend Khan. In the tradition of his mentor, Gassendi, he is a critic of Aristotle and Descartes, an admirer of Epicurus and Montaigne, a proponent of a compromise between the extremes of scepticism and dogmatism, deriving all knowledge from experience. He presents this philosophy through a series of letters to like-minded Frenchmen in his published memoirs of Mughal India. The letters were not private but public documents, to be read out among his circle, which included the addressee of the letters given here, Monsieur de Merveilles, and Jean Chapelain (literary adviser to Louis XIV's minister Jean-Baptiste Colbert), Samuel Sorbière (the French translator of Thomas Hobbes), and François La Mothe Le Vayer, who had written on the ideas of Confucius and the nature of historical knowledge. The various docu-ments were obviously meant to be read as a whole and Bernier in his letters to Merveilles often mentions other letters or documents also published in the collection which explain or develop a particular term, event, or element in Indian culture. A vigorous opponent of the practice of widow-burning (suttee) among the native Indian population, and indeed of all forms of religious dogmatism in the region including Islam, Bernier reveals a consistent cultural relativ-ism and used his experiences and encounters in India to challenge what he saw as the regressive and unenlightened elements of European culture. See Peter Burke, 'The Philosopher as Traveller: Bernier's Orient', in Jas Elsner and Joan Pau Rubiés (eds.), *Voyages and Visions: Towards a Cultural History of Travel* (London: Reaktion, 1999), 125–37.

The influence of the four-volume translation of Bernier's memoirs which was published in England in 1671 and 1672 can be observed in John Dryden's use of the 'History of the late Rebellion in the States of the Great Mogol' (from vol. i of the memoirs) as a source for his 1675 tragedy, *Aureng-Zebe*. Bernier's depiction of Kashmir as a 'paradise' and admiration of the beauty of its population may also have contributed to the tendency to cast Indian heroines subsequently, as Dryden does in his play, as 'Kashmiri princesses'.

The annotations to this extract have been prepared with the help of *Travels in the Mogul Empire AD 1656-68*, trans. Archibald Constable on the basis of Irving Brock's version, 2nd. edn. revised by Vincent A. Smith (Delhi: Munshiram Manoharlal Publishers, 1992; originally published London: Oxford University Press, 1934).

The first letter to Monsieur de Merveilles Written at *Dehli*, Decemb. 1664. *Aureng-Zebe* being ready to march. CONTAINING *The Occasion and Cause of this Journey of* Aureng zebe; *together with an account of the state and posture of his Army, and the Equipage and ordinary Provisions of the chief of his Cavalry; and some curious particulars observable in the Voyages of the Indies.*

SIR,

Since that *Aureng-zebe*[1] began to find himself in better health, it hath been constantly reported, that he would make a Voyage to *Lahor*, and

[1] In 1658 Aurangzeb (1658–1707) defeated his three brothers in their struggle for power after their father, Shah Jahan, fell ill. Aurangzeb, the third brother, proclaimed himself 'Alamgir' (conqueror of the universe) and imprisoned his father in his fort at Agra until his death in 1666. Bernier compares Aurangzeb to his elder brothers, Dara Shikoh (whom Aurangzeb had murdered in 1659), and Shuja (who took ship to what is now Burma in 1660 and was not heard of again) saying he 'appeared more serious and melancholy, and was indeed much more judicious, understanding the World very well, and knowing whom to chuse for his service and purpose, and where to bestow his favour and bounty most for interest. He was reserved, crafty, and exceedingly versed in dissembling, insomuch that for a long while he made profession to be *Fakire*, that is Poor, *Dervich*, or Devout, renouncing the World, and faining not to pretend at all to the Crown, but to desire to pass his Life in Prayers and other Devotions' (*The History of the Late Revolution of the Empire of the Great Mogol*, trans. Henry Oldenburg (London, 1671), i. 18).

go from thence to *Kachemire*, to change the Air, and to be out of the way of the approaching Summer-heats for fear of a relapse: That the more intelligent sort of men would hardly be perswaded, that as long as he kept his Father *Chah-jean* prisoner in the Fort of *Agra*, he would think it safe to be at such a distance. Yet notwithstanding we have found, that Reason of State hath given place to that of Health, or rather to the Intrigues of *Rauchenara-Begum*, who was wild to breath a more free Air than that of the *Seraglio*, and to have her turn in shewing her self to a gallant and magnificent Army, as her Sister *Begum-saheb* had formerly done during the Reign of *Chah-jean*.[2]

He departed then the 6th of *December*, about three a clock in the after-noon; a day and hour that must needs be fortunate for a great Voyage, if we may give credit to the Gentlemen *Astrologers*, who have so decreed it. And he arrived at *Chach-limar*, his House of Pleasure, distant about two Leagues from hence; where he spent six whole dayes, thereby to give to all sufficient time to make necessary pre-parations for a Voyage, that would take up a year and an half. We have this day news, that he is gone to encamp on the way to *Lahor*; and that, when he hath stay'd there two dayes, he intends to continue his march without any further expectation. He hath with him not only the Thirty five thousand Horse, or thereabout, and 10000 Foot, but also both his Artilleries, the great or heavy, & the small or lighter, which is call'd *The Artillery of the Stirrup*, because it is inseparable from the person of the King, whereas the Heavy sometimes leaveth him to keep the high and well beaten Roads.

The Great Artillery is made up of seventy pieces of Canon, most of them cast; of which some are so ponderous, that they need twenty yoake of Oxen to draw them; and some of them require Elephants to help all those Oxen, by thrusting and drawing the wheels of the Waggons with their Trunks and Heads, when they stick in any deep way, or are to pass some steep mountain. That of the *Stirrup* is

---

[2] Raushan-Ara-Begum, the younger of Aurangzeb's sisters and his greatest supporter within the family. The older sister, Begum-Saheb, supported the oldest brother, Dara, and shared their father's confinement at Agra. Bernier recycles rumours of the two sisters' libertinism, describing Begum-Saheb as 'a great Wit, and passionately beloved of her father', implying a possible incestuous relationship (*History*, i. 20), and Raushan-Ara-Begum as less spirited than her sister, but 'not less cheerful, and comely enough, and hated pleasures no more than her Sister' (*History*, i. 27).

composed of fifty or sixty small Field-pieces, all of Brass, each carried upon a little pritty and painted Charriot (as hath been already said in another place),[3] Beautified with many little red Streamers, and drawn by two very handsom Horses, driven by the Gunner himself, together with a third Horse, which the Gunner's Assistant leads for a relief. All these Charriots go alwaies a great pace, that they may be soon enough in order before the Tent of the King, and discharge all at once at the time of his entry, to give the Army notice.

All these great preparations give us cause to apprehend, that in stead of going to *Kachemire*, we be not led to besiege that important City of *Kandahar*, which is the Frontier to *Persia*, *Indostan* and *Usbeck*, and the Capital of an excellent Country, yielding a very great Revenue, and which for this very reason hath been ever the bone of contention between the *Persians* and *Indians*. Whatever it be, there is now a necessity to dispatch at *Dehli* any business whatsoever notwithstanding; and I should find my self much cast behind the Army, if I should tarry any longer. Besides I know, that my *Navab*, or *Agah Danech-mend-kan* stays for me abroad with impatience: He can no more be without philosophising in the afternoon upon the Books of *Gassendi* and *Des-Cartes*, upon the *Globe* and the *Sphere*, or upon *Anatomy*, than he can be without bestowing the whole morning upon the weighty matters of the Kingdom, in the quality of Secretary of State for forrain Affairs, and of Great Master of the Cavalry. I shall depart this night, after I have given the last order for all my businesses, and provided all necessaries for my Voyage, as all the principal persons of the Cavalry do, that is, two good Tartarian Horses, whereto I am obliged by reason of the one hundred and fifty Crowns of pay, which I have by the month: a Camel of *Persia*, and a Groom; a Cook, and another Servant, which must be had ordinarily to march in these Countries before the Horse, and to carry a Flaggon with water in his hand. I also have provided the ordinary Utensils; such as are a Tent of a middle size, and a proportionate piece of foot-Tapistry;[4] and a little Bed with girdles, made up with four strong and light Canes, and a Pillow for the head; two Coverlets, whereof one folded up fourfold

---

[3] Chapter 25, 'The Artillery of the *Mogol*, great and small, very considerable' of *History*, i.   [4] foot-Tapistry: a carpet of the same size as the tent.

serveth for a Matrasse; a round Table-cloth of Leather to eat upon; some Napkins of dyed Cloth, and three small Sacks for Plate, which are put up in a greater Sack, and this Sack into a very great and strong Sack made of Girdles, in which are put all the provisions, together with the Linnen of the Master and Servants. I have also made provision of excellent Rice for five or six dayes, for fear I should not alwayes find so good; of some sweet Biscuit, with Sugar and Anis; of a linnen sleeve with its little iron-hook, to let, by the means thereof, to run out and to keep curdled milk; and of store of Limons with Sugar to make Limonade; such Milk and Limonade being the two great and soverain refreshments of the *Indies*: All which, as I said, is put into the last named Sack, which is so large and heavy, that three or four men have pains enough to lift it up; though two men do first fold and turn one side upon the other when it is full, and though the Camel be made to stoop very nigh it, and there need no more than to turn one of the sides of that Sack upon the Camel. All this equipage and provision is absolutely necessary in such Voyages as these. We must not look for such good lodging and accommodations as we have in our Country. We must resolve to encamp and live after the *Arabian* and *Tartarian* mode, without expecting any other Inns than Tents.[5] Nor must we think to plunder the Country-man; all the Lands of the Kingdom being in propriety to the King: We are well to consider, that we must be sober and prudent, and that to ruine the Country man, were to ruin the Demesne[6] of the King. That which much comforts me in this march, is, that we go North-ward, and depart in the beginning of Winter before the rains, which is the right season for travelling in the *Indies*, because it raineth not, and we are not so much incommoded by heat and dust. Besides that, I find my self out of danger of eating the bread of *Bazar*, or of the Market, which ordinarily is ill baked, full of sand and dust; nor obliged to drink of those naughty waters, which being all turbid, and full of nastiness of so many people and beasts that fetch thence, and enter into them, do cause such feavers, which are very hard to cure, and which breed also certain very dangerous worms in the legs.[7] They at first cause great inflammation, accompanied with

---

[5] Arabian and Tartarian mode: i.e. nomadic. [6] Demesne: domain.
[7] worms in the legs: the Guinea worm (*Filaria medinensis*), a parisitic worm which lives in the subcutaneous cellular tissue.

a feaver, and ordinarily come forth a little after the Voyage, although there have been some, that have stay'd a whole year and more before they appear'd. They are commonly of the bigness & length of a small Vial-string[8], so that one would sooner take them for some nerve than for a worm; and they must be drawn out little by little, from day to day, gently winding them about a little twig of the bigness of a needle, for fear of breaking them. This, I say, comforteth me not a little, that I find my self exempt from these inconveniencies; my *Navab* having vouchsafed me a very particular favour; which is, that he hath appointed to give me every day a new loaf of his house, and a *Souray* of the water of *Ganges*, with which he hath laden several camels of his train, as the whole Court doth.[9] *Sowray* is that Tin-flagon full of water, which the Servant that marcheth on foot before the Gentleman on horseback, carrieth in his hand, wrap't up in a sleeve of red cloth. Ordinarily it holdeth but one pint; but I had some of them expressly made, that hold two. We shall see, whether this cunning will succeed. The water cooleth very well in this Flagon, provided that care be had always to keep the sleeve moist, and that the Servant that holds it in his hand, do march and stir the air, or else that it be held towards the wind; as is commonly done upon three pretty little sticks, crossing one another, that they may not touch the earth: For the moistness of the linnen, the agitation of the air, or the wind, are absolutely necessary to keep the water fresh; as if this moistness, or rather the water imbibed by the sleeve did keep out the little igneous bodies or spirits that are in the air, at the same time when it giveth entrance to the nitrous or other parts, which hinder the motion in the water, and cause coolness; in the same manner as Glass keeps out Water, and giveth passage to the Light, by reason of the particular texture and disposition of the parts of the Glass, and the diversity there must be between the particles of Light and those of Water. We do not use this Tin-flagon for keeping Water cool but in the field: When we are at home, we have Jars of a certain porous Earth, in which it is much better cooled, provided it be expos'd to the wind, and moisten'd with

---

[8] Vial-string: violin string.

[9] The Mughal emperors were conoisseurs of good water, habitually drinking Ganges water at home and on journeys (the water dispatched in sealed jars from the river) and employing water-tasters.

a Linnen-cloth, as the Flaggon; or else, use is made of Salt-peter, as all persons of quality do, whether in Towns, or in the Army. They put water, or any other liquor, to be cooled, in a round and long-necked Tin-flaggon, such as are the English Bottles, and for the space of half a quarter of an hour this Flaggon is stirr'd in water, into which hath been cast three or four handfuls of Salt-peeter; this maketh the water very cold, neither is it unwholsome, as I did apprehend; but only that sometimes it causeth gripings at first when one is not accustomed to it.[10]

But to what purpose, to play so much the Philosopher, when we should think to depart, and to endure the Sun, which at all seasons is incommodious in the *Indies*, and to swallow the dust, which is never wanting in the Army; to put up, to load, and to unload every day our Baggage, to help the Servants to fasten sticks, to draw Cords, to put up Tents, and to take them down again, to march in the day, and in the night, to devour cold and heat, and in a word, to turn *Arabians* for a year and an half, during which time we are to be in the Field.[11] *Adieu*; I shall not fail to acquit my self of my promise, and from time to time to inform you of our Adventures; and besides, since the Army for this time will make but small Journeys in its march, and pass on with all that pomp and magnificence, which the Kings of *Indostan* do affect, I shall endeavour to observe the most considerable things, that I may impart them to you, as soon as we shall arrive at *Lahor*.

THE SECOND LETTER

Containing the number and magnificence, the order and the disposition of the Tents of the Great Mogol *in the Field: The number of Elephants, Camels, Mules, and Porters, necessary to carry them: The disposition of the* Bazars *or Royall Markets: That of the particular Quarters of the* Omrahs, *or Lords, and of the rest of the Army; The extent of the whole*

[10] Saltpetre is potassium nitrate which occurs as crusts on the surface of the Earth, on walls and rocks, and in caves; and it forms in certain soils in Spain, Italy, Egypt, Iran, and India. An ingredient of gunpowder, and used medicinally in the past as a diuretic and a treatment for asthma, it is white in colour and soluble in water, imparting a cool and salty taste. [11] See Part 1, James Ridley, 'The Adventures of Urad', n. 4.

*Army, when encamped: The confusion there met with; and how it may
be avoided; The order of preventing Robberies; The different Manners
of the March of the King, the Princesses, and the Rest of the* Seraglio:
*The danger there is in being too near the Women: The several wayes of
the Royal Hunting, and how the King hunts with his whole Army: The
abundance of people there is in the Army, and the method of making
them all subsist.*

SIR,

This indeed is called marching with gravity, and as we speak here, *a la
Mogole*: it is no more but fifteen or sixteen dayes Journey from *Dehli* to
Lahor, which make little more than six score Leagues; and yet we have
spent almost two months on this way. 'Tis true, the King with the best
part of the Army went somewhat aside from the high way, the better to
enjoy the divertisements of Hunting, and for the conveniency of the
water of *Gemma*, which we went to look for on the right hand, and
which we leisurely followed long enough in our hunting, crossing
fields of tall grass, full of all sorts of game, where the Horsemen could
scarce be seen. At present, while we are at rest, I am going to make
good what I have promised you in the Title of this Letter; hoping
shortly to make you come to *Kachemire*, and to shew you one of the
best Countries in the world.

When the King is in the field, he hath usually two Camps, I mean
two Bodies of Tents separated, to the end that when he breaketh up
and leaveth one, the other may have passed before by a day, and be
found ready when he arriveth at the place design'd to encamp in: And
'tis therefore, that they are called *Peiche-kanes* as if you should say,
Houses going before: These two *Peiche-kanes* are almost alike, and
there are requisite above threescore Elephants, more than two hundred Camels, above an hundred Mules, and as many more Porters to
carry one of them. The *Elephants* carry the most bulky things, such as
are the great Tents, and their great Pillars,which being too long and
too heavy, are taken down in three pieces. The *Camels* carry the lesser
Tents: The *Mules*, the Baggage and Kitchens. And to the *Porters* are
given all the little moveables, and such as are delicate and fine,
that might easily be broken; as *Porcelain*, which the King usually

imployeth at Table; those printed and guilded Beds, and those rich *Karguais*; which I shall speak of hereafter.

One of these two *Peiche-kanes*, or Bodies of Tents, is no sooner arrived at the place designed for encamping, but the Great Marshal that orders the Lodgings, chuseth some fair place for the Kings Quarters; yet with a regard, as much as is possible, to the Symmetry and order that is to be observed for the whole Army; and he marketh out a Square, of which each side is above three hundred ordinary paces long. An hundred Pikemen presently clear and level this space, making square planes to raise the Tents upon, and surrounding all this great Square with *Kanates* or Skreens seven or eight foot high, which they fasten with cords tyed to sticks, & with perches fix't in the ground, by couples, from ten to ten paces, one without, and the other within, inclining the one upon the other. These *Kanats* are made of a strong cloth lined with stained Linnen. In the middle of one of the sides of this Square is the Entry or Royal Gate, great and magnificent, and the Indian Stuff[12] which 'tis made of, as also those Stuffs, of which the whole side of the Square of the face is lined without, are far better and richer than the others.

The first and the greatest of the Tents, that is reared in this Inclosure, is called *Am-kas*, because it is the place where the King and Lords in the Army do assemble about nine a clock in the morning, when the *Mokam*, that is the usual publick Meeting, is held. For the Kings of *Indostan*, although they are in a march, do not dispense but very rarely with this almost inviolable custom, which is pass'd into a kind of Duty and Law, *viz.* to appear twice a day in the Assembly, there to give order for State-Affairs, and to administer Justice.

The second, which is little less than the first, and a little further advanced into the Inclosure, is called, *Gost-kane*, that is to say, a place to wash in:[13] And here 'tis, where all the Lords every night meet, and where they come to salute and do obeisance to the King, as ordinarily they do when they are in the *Metropolis*. This Assembly in the evening is very inconvenient to the *Omrahs*; but it is a thing that looks great

[12] The 'Indian stuff' is calico printed with large vases of flowers, according to Archibald Constable's translation.

[13] The *ghusl-khána*, or bathroom, was the name given to the private apartment in the Mughal palace.

and stately, to see afar off, in an obscure night, in the midst of a Campagne,[14] cross all the Tents of an army, long files of Torches lighting these *Omrahs* to the Kings Quarters, and attending them back again to their tents. 'Tis true, that these lights are not of wax as ours; but they last very long. They are only an Iron put about a stick, at the end of which are wound raggs of old Linnen from time to time, which is moistened with Oyl, held by the Link men[15] in their hands in a Brass, or Latton-flagon[16] with a long and streight neck.

The third Tent, which is not much less than the two first, and is yet further advanced into the Inclosure, is called *Kalvet kane*, that is to say, a retired or the Privy Council-place, because none but the first Officers of the Kingdom enter into it; and 'tis there where the greatest and the most important Affairs are transacted.

Yet further into the Square are the particular Tents of the King, encompass'd with small *Kanates* or Skreens, of the height of a man, and lined with stained Indian Stuff, of that elegant workmanship of *Maslipatam*, which do represent an hundred sorts of different flowers; and some of them lined with flowred Sattin with large Silk-fringes.

The Tents joyning to the Kings, are those of the *Begum* or Princesses, and the other great Ladies and She-Officers of the *Seraglio*, which are likewise encompass'd, as those of the King, with rich *Kanates*; and amidst all these Tents are placed those of the lower She-Officers, and other serving Women, alwayes, upon the matter, in the same order, according to their Office.

The *Am kas*, and the five or six principal Tents are raised high, that they may be seen at a good distance, and the better fence off the heat. *Without* it is nothing but a course and strong red cloth, yet beautified and striped with certain large stripes, cut variously and advantagiously to the eye: But *within* it is lined with those fine Indian flowred Stuffs, of the same work of *Maslipatam*; and this work is raised and enriched with silk, gold and silver Embroideries having great Fringes, or with some fine flowred Satin. The Pillars supporting these Tents, are

---

[14] Campagne: obsolete form of 'campaign' meaning an open field or plain (*OED*).

[15] Link men: men employed to carry a link (torch made of tow or pitch) to light passengers along a street.

[16] Latton-flagon: latten is a mixed metal of a yellow colour similar to or identical with brass.

painted and guild:[17] One marcheth on nothing but rich Tapistry, having matrasses of Cotton under them four or five inches thick, and round about these Tapestries there are great square rails richly cover'd to lean upon.

In each of the two great Tents where the Assembly is kept, there is raised a Theatre richly adorned where the King giveth Audience under a great Canopy of Velvet, or purfled[18] with gold. In the other Tents are found the like Canopies, and there you may see also set up certain *Karguais*, that is, fine Cabinets, whose little doors are shut with Silver locks. To conceive what they are, you may represent to you two small Squares of our Skreens, set upon one another, and neatly round about fastned to one another with a Silken-string; yet so that the extremities of the sides of the uppermost come to incline upon one another, so as to make a kind of little Tabernacle; with this difference from our Skreens, that all the sides of these are of very thin and slight Firr-boards,[19] painted and guiild without, and enriched round about with gold and Silk-fringes, and lined within with Scarlet, or flowred Satin, or purfled with Gold.

And this is very near what I can tell you of what is contained within the great Square.

What concerns the particulars that are without the Square; there are first two pretty Tents on both the two sides of the great Entry or Royal Gate, where are found two choice Horses saddled, and richly harness'd, and altogether ready to be mounted upon occasion, or rather for State and Magnificence.

On the two sides of the same Gate are placed in order those fifty or threescore small Field-pieces, that make up the *Artillery* of the *Stirrup* above mention'd, and which discharge all together to salute the King entring into his Tent, and to give notice thereof to the whole Army.

Before the Gate there is alwaies left void, as much as may be, a great place, at the end of which there is a great Tent, called *Nagar-kane*, because that is the place of the Timbals[20] and Trumpets.

Near this Tent there is another great one, which called *Tchauky-kane*, because it is the place where the *Omrahs* keep guard, every one

---

[17] guild: gilt, covered in gold.
[18] purfled: having a decorative or enamelled border.
[19] Firr-boards: boards made of fir or pine.   [20] Timbals: drums.

in his turn, once a week twenty four hours together; yet notwithstanding most of the *Omrahs* on the day of their guard, cause, close by, to be rear'd one of their own Tents, to be the more at liberty, and to have more elbow-room.

Round about the three other sides of the great Square are set up all the Tents of the Officers, which are alwaies found in the same order and disposition, unless it be that the place permit it not: They have all their peculiar names; but as they are hard to pronounce, and I pretend not to teach you the language of the Country, it will be sufficient to tell you, that there is a particular one for the Arms of the King; another for the rich Harnesses of Horses; another for Vests purfled with Gold, which are the ordinary Presents bestow'd by the King. Besides, there are four more, near one another; the first of which is designed for keeping Fruit; the second for Comfits;[21] the third for *Ganges* water, and the Salt-peter to cool it; and the fourth for the *Betele*, which is that Leaf, whereof I have spoken elsewhere, which is offered to friends, as *Coffee* is in *Turky*, and chew'd to make ruddy lips, and a sweet breath.[22] Next to these, there are fifteen or sixteen others that serve for kitchins and what belongs in them. Almost all these Tents are those of a great number of Officers and Eunuchs. Lastly, there are four or five long ones for led Horses, and some others for the best Elephants; and all those that are for hunting. For there must needs be a retreat for all that great number of Birds of prey, that are alwaies carried for Game and Magnificence; and so there must be for those many *Dogs*, and those *Leopards* serving to take wild Goats; for those *Nilgaus*, or gray Oxen, which I take for *Elks*; for those *Lions* and *Rhinoceroses*, that are led for greatness; for those great *Buffaloes* of *Bengale* fighting with Lions; and lastly for those tamed wild Goats, they call *Gazelles*, that are made to sport before the King.

This vast number of Tents, now spoken of, together with those that are within the great Square, make up the King's Quarter, which is alwaies in the middle, and as 'twere in the center of the Army, except

---

[21] Comfits: sweetmeats made with a root or fruit, preserved with sugar (*OED*).

[22] In ch. 1 of his *History* vol. i, Bernier describes Shah Jahan conferring poisoned betel on a suitor for his eldest daughter's hand. Betel is a leaf chewed with the dried areca-nut. The term 'betel' comes from the Portuguese 'betle' itself derived from the Malayalim 'vettila' for simple leaf.

the place do not allow it. It will easily be thence concluded, that this Quarter of the King must needs be something great and royal, and afford a very fine prospect, if one behold from some high place this great body of red tents in the midst of the Army, encamped in a fair and even Campagne, where may be fully seen all that order and disposition that is to be observed in the whole.

After that the Great Marshal of the Camp hath chosen a place fit for the King's Quarter, and hath made the *Am-kas* to be set up highest of all the Tents, and by which he is to take his measure for the ordering and disposing the rest of the Army accordingly; He then marketh out the Royal *Bazars* or Markets, whence the whole Army is furnisht with necessaries; drawing the first and the chief of all, like a great street running straight, and a great free way traversing the whole Army, now on the right hand, and by and by on the left of the *Am-kas* and the king's Quarter, and alwaies in the straightest line that may be towards the encamping of the next day. All the Royal *Bazars*, that are neither so long nor so broad, commonly cross this first, some on this, others on the other side of the king's Quarter; and all these *Bazars* are discern'd by very high Canes like great perches, which are fixt in the ground from three hundred to three hundred paces or there about, with red Standards, and Cows-tails of the great *Tibet* fastned on the top of these Canes like Perriwigs.[23]

The same Marshal designs, next, the place of the *Omrahs*, so as they may alwayes keep the same order, and be ever as near as may be the king's quarter; some on the right, others on the left hand, some on this side of him, others beyond him; so that none of them may change the place that hath been once appointed for him, or that himself hath desired in the beginning of the Voyage.

The quarters of the *Omrahs* and *Rajas*, as to their particular order and disposition, are to be imagined in a manner like that of the King: For commonly they have two *Peiche-kanes* with a Square of *Kanates*, which incloseth their principal Tent and those of their Women; and round about these are put up the Tents of their Officers and Cavaliers, with a peculiar *Bazar*, which is a street of small Tents for the lower

---

[23] The valuable tails of the Tibetan ox or yak were used by the court as fly-flappers or mounted on silver as marks of dignity.

sort of people that follows the Army, and furnisheth the Camp with Forrage, Grains, Rice, Butter and the other things that are most necessary; whereby they are so accommodated, that they need not alwayes go to the royal *Bazars*, where generally all things are to be found as in the Capital City. Each *Bazar* is marked at the two ends by two Canes planted in the ground, which are as tall as those of the Royal *Bazars*, that so at a good distance the particular Standards fastned to them may be discover'd, and the several quarters distinguish't from one another.

The Great *Omrahs* and *Rajas* affect to have their Tents very high. But they must beware, lest they be too high, because it may happen, that the King, passing by, might perceive it, and command them to be thrown down; of which we have seen an example in this last march. Neither must they be altogether red without, since those of the King alone are to be so. Lastly, out of respect they must all look towards the *Am-kas* or the Quarter of the King.

The residue of the space between the Kings Quarter, and those of the *Omrahs* and the *Bazars*, is taken up by the Tents of the *Mansebdars* or little *Omrahs*, and of that infinite number of great and small Merchants that follow the Army; of all those that belong to the Law; and lastly, of all such as serve both the Artilleries: Which maketh indeed a prodigious number of Tents, and requireth a very great extent of ground. Yet it is not all true what is said of either of them. And I believe, that even the whole Army is in a fair and even Campagne, where it may encamp with ease, and that, following the ordinary plot, it comes at length to be lodged, as near as may be, in a round (as we have often seen it does upon this road) the compass of it will not be above two Leagues, or two Leagues and an half; and with all this there will be left here and there several void places. But then the great Artillery, which taketh up a great tract of ground, doth very often a day or two go before.

Nor is all true, what is said of the strange confusion, which commonly strikes an astonishment into all new comers. For a little acquaintance with the method of the Army, and some heeding of the order observed in the Camp, will soon enable one to avoid all embarassment, and to go to and fro about his business, and to find his quarter again; forasmuch as every one regulateth himself by the King's

Quarter, and the particular Tents and Standards of the *Omrahs*, that may be seen afar off, and by the Standards and Perriwigs of the Royal *Bazars*, which may also be seen at a great distance.

Yet for all these marks it will sometimes fall out, that one shall be extreamly perplexed, and even in the day time, but especially in the morning, when a world of people do arrive, and every one of those is busie and seeks to lodge himself: And that not only, because there is often raised so great a dust, that the King's Quarter, the Standards of the *Bazars* and the *Omrahs* (which might serve for Guides) cannot be discover'd: But because a man finds himself between Tents that are putting up, and between cords, which the lesser *Omrahs*, that have no *Peiche-kane*, and the *Manseb-dars* stretch out to mark their lodgings, and to hinder, that no way may be made nigh them, or that no unknown person may come to lodge near their Tents, where often they have their Women: If in this case you mean to get by on one side, you will find the wayes obstructed by those stretched-out cords, which a troupe of mean Serving-men, standing there with big cudgels, will not suffer to be lower'd, to suffer your Baggage to pass: If you will turn back, you'l find the ways shut since you passed. And here it is, where you must cry out, storm, intreat, make as if you would strike, and yet well beware of doing so, leaving the men, as well as you can do, to quarrel against one another, and afterwards to accord them for fear of some mischief, and in short, to put your self into all imaginable postures to get away thence, and to make your Camel pass: But the great trouble is, when a man is obliged to go in an evening to a place somewhat remote, because that those offensive smoaks of the fire of green Wood, or Cow-shares,[24] of Camel-dung, which the common people then make in their kitchins, do raise a mist (especially when there is no wind) so thick, that you can see nothing at all. I have been three or four times surprized with it, so as not to know what to do. Well might I ask the way; I knew not whither I went, and I did nothing but turn. Once, among other times, I was constrained to stay till this mist passed, and the Moon risen. And another time I was forced to get to the *Aguacy-die*, to lie down at the foot thereof, and there to pass all the night as well as I could, having my Servant and

---

[24] Cow-shares: cow-shard or cow-sharn is cow dung (*OED*).

Horse by me. This *Aguacy-die* is like a tall Mast, but very slender, which can be taken down in three pieces, and 'tis planted toward the King's Quarter, near that Tent which is called *Nagar-kane*: In the evening is drawn up to the top of it a Lanthorn with a light burning in it all night long; which is very commodious, as being seen a great way off, and thither it is that people gone astray do retire, from thence to get again to the *Bazars*, and to ask the way, or there to pass the rest of the night; for no body hinders one from doing so, and a man may be there in safety from Robbers. It is called *Aguacy-die*, as if you should say, *light of Heaven*, in regard that from afar it appears like a Star.

For the prevention of Robberies, each *Omrah* causeth a guard to be kept all the night long, in his particular Camp, of such men that perpetually go the round and cry '*Kaber-dar*', 'have a care'. Besides, there are round about the Army set guards, at five hundred common paces from one another, that keep a fire, and cry also, '*Kaber-dar*'. And over and above all these, the *Cotoual*, who is, as 'twere, the great Provost, sends out troupes of guards every way, that pass through all the *Bazars*, crying out and trumpetting all night long. Yet for all this, some robberies there are now and then committed; and 'tis necessary alwayes to be upon ones guard, to go to sleep by times, that so you may be awake the rest of the night, and not to trust your servants too much to keep guard for you.

But let us now see, how many different wayes the Great *Mogol* is carried in the Field.

Ordinarily he causeth himelf to be carried on men's shoulders, in a kind of Sedan or Litter, upon which is a *Tact-raven*, that is a Field-throne, on which he is seated: And this is like a magnificent Taber-nacle with pillars, painted and guilded, which may be shut with glass, when 'tis ill weather; the four branches of the Litter are cover'd with Scarlet or purpled[25] Gold, with great Gold and Silk-fringes; and at each branch there are two robust and well-cloathed Porters, that change by turns with as many more that follow.

Sometimes also he goeth on Horseback, especially when 'tis a fair day for hunting. At other times he rideth on an Elephant, in a *Mik-dember*, or *Hanze*; and this is the most splendid appearance: For, the

---

[25] purpled: probably a typesetter's error for 'purfled' (see n. 18).

Elephant is decked with a very rich and very magnificent Harnass; the *Mik-dember*, being a little square House or Turret of Wood, is alwaies painted and guilded; and the *Hanze*, which is an Oval seat, having a Canopy with Pillars over it, is so likewise.

In these different Marches he is alwaies accompanied with a great number of *Omrahs* and *Rajas* following him close and thick on horse-back without any great order: And all those that are in the Army are obliged to be at the *Amkas* at break of day, unless he do exempt them from it upon the account either of their peculiar Office, or their great Age. This march is very inconvenient to them, especially on hunting dayes; for they must endure the Sun and Dust as the simple Souldiers, and that sometimes until three of the clock in the afternoon; whereas, when they do not attend the King, they go at ease in their *Palekeys*, close cover'd, if they please, free from the Sun and Dust; sleeping in them couched all along as in a bed, and so coming in good time to their Tent, which expects them with a ready dinner, their kitchen being gone the night before, after supper. About the *Omrahs*, and amongst them, there is alwaies a good number of Horse-men well mounted, call'd *Gourze-berdars*, because they carry a kind of Silver-Mace of Armes. There are also many of them about the person of the King, together with store of Foot-men. These *Gourze-berdars* are Choice-men, of a good meen and a fair stature, appointed to carry orders, and having all of them great sticks in their hands, whereby they put people aside at a good distance, and hinder that no body march before the King to incommode him.

After the *Rajas* march a train mixed of a great number of Timbals and Trumpets. I have already said in another place, that this train consists of nothing but of figures of Silver representing strange Animals, Scales, Fishes, and other mysterious things, that are carried at the end of great Silver-sticks.[26]

At last a great troup of *Manseb-dars*, or little *Omrahs*, well mounted, and furnisht with Swords, Arrows and Quivers, follow after all the former: And this Body is much more numerous than that of the *Omrahs*, because, besides that all those that are of the guard dare not

---

[26] In his 'Description of Dehli and Agra' earlier in the *Continuation*, Bernier described in more detail the 'Kours', silver figures mounted on large silver sticks that precede the evening march past the Mughal emperor of his guard.

fail to be at break of day, as the *Omrahs*, at the gate of the King's Tent to accompany him, there are also many, that come amongst them, to make their Court, and to become known there.

The Princesses and the great Ladies of the *Seraglio* are also carried in sundry fashions; some are carried, like the King, on men's shoulders, in a *Tchadoule*, which is a kind of *Tactravan*, painted, guilded, and cover'd with great and costly Net-work of Silk of divers colours, enriched with Embroidery, Fringe, and thick pendant tufts. Others are carried in very handsome *Palakeys* closed, that are likewise painted and guilded, and cover'd with that rich silken net-work. Some are carried in large Litters by two strong Camels, or by two small Elephants, instead of Mules: And in this manner I have sometimes seen carried *Rauchenara-Begum*; when I also observed, that in the fore-part of her Litter, being open, there was a little She-slave, that with a Peacock's-taile kept off from her the Flyes and Dust. Lastly, others are carried upon Elephants richly harnessed, and cover'd with embroider'd deckings, and great Silver-bells; where these Ladies sit, raised, as 'twere, into the middle region of the Air, four and four in *Mik-dembers* latticed, which alwaies are cover'd with silken Net-work, and are no less splendid and stately than the *Tchadoules and Tact-ravans*.

I cannot forbear relating here, that in this Voyage I took a particular pleasure in beholding and considering this pompous march of the *Seraglio*. And certainly nothing more stately can be imagined, than to see *Rauchenara-Begum* march first, mounted upon a lusty Elephant of *Pegu* in a *Mik-dember*, all shining of Gold and Azur, attended by five or six other Elephants with their *Mik-dembers*, almost as splendid as hers, filled with the principal She-Officer of her House; some of the most considerable Eunuchs, richly adorned, and advantagiously mounted, riding on her side, each with a Cane in his hand, a Troupe of *Tartarian* and *Kachemirian* Maids of Honour about her,[27] oddly and fantastically dressed, and riding on very pretty Hackney-horses; and lastly, many other Eunuchs on Horseback accompanied with store of Pages and Lackeys, with great sticks in their hands, to make

[27] Tartar and Kashmiri maidens are not Muslim and therefore do not have to travel in purdah.

way a far off. After this *Rauchenara-Begum*, I saw pass one of the
principal Ladies of the Court, mounted and attended in proportion:
And after this, a third in the same fashion; and then another, and so on
to fifteen or sixteen, all (more or less) bravely mounted and accompanied according to their quality, pay, and office. Indeed this long file
of Elephants to the number of fifty, or sixty, or more, thus gravely
marching with paces, as 'twere, counted, and withal this gallant train
and equipage, does represent something that is Great and Royal; and
if I had not beheld this Pomp with a kind of philosophical indifference, I know not, whether I should not have suffered myself to be
carried away to those extravagant sentiments of most of the *Indian*
Poets who will have it, that all these Elephants carry as many hidden
Goddesses. 'Tis true, one can hardly see them, and they are almost
inaccessible by men; it would be a great misfortune to any poor
Cavalier whatever, to be found in the Field too near them in the
march; all those Eunuchs, and all the crew of Servants are to the
highest degree insolent, and desire nothing more than such a pretext
and occasion to fall upon and man and give him some Bastinadoes.
I remember, I was once thus unfortunately surprized, and certainly
I had been very ill used, as well as many other Cavaliers, if at length I
had not resolved to make my way out by my sword, rather than suffer
my self to be thus maimed as they began to order the matter; and if by
good luck I had not been provided with a good Horse, that carried me
vigorously out of the press, when I put him on thorow a torrent
of people, that was to be repassed. And it is grown in a manner
a common Proverb of these Armies, That, above all, one must beware
of three things: *First*, not to let one self to be engaged amongst the
troops of the chosen led Horse, they never failing to strike: *Secondly*,
not to come into the places of Hunting: *Thirdly*, not to approach too
near the Women of the *Seraglio*. Yet notwithstanding by what I hear,
it is much less dangerous here than in *Persia*; for there 'tis death to be
found in the field in sight of the Eunuchs that attend them, although
you were half a league distant from them.[28] It is required, that as many

---

[28] In ch. 11 of the second part of his *Travels into the Levant* (1687), Jean de Thévenot
describes the inconvenience caused by the strictness of the eunuchs of the Persian court
who clear the streets when the women of the royal court are being moved to join the ruler
in the country (99).

men as there are in the Villages and Burroughs, where they pass, do all abandon them, and retire a far off.

As to the *Hunting* of the King, I knew not first how to imagine what is commonly said, which is, that the Great *Mogol* goes to hunt with an hundred thousand men: But now I see, it may very well be said, that he goes to hunt with above two hundred thousand; nor is it a thing hard to comprehend. In the neighbouring places to *Agra* and *Dehli*, along the river *Gemma* as afar as to the mountains, and even on both sides of the high way to *Lahor*, there is abundance of untilled Lands, some of Copse-wood, and some of Grass above a man's height: In all these places there are great number of Guards, uncessantly roving up and down, and hindering all other people from hunting, except Partridges, Quailes and Hares, which the Indians know to take with nets: So that every where in those places there is very great store of all kind of Game. This being so, the hunting guards, when they know the King is in the field, and near their quarters, give notice, to the Great Hunting-master, of the quality of the Game, and of the place where most of it is; then the Guards do line all the avenues of that quarter, and that sometimes for above four or five Leagues of ground, that so the *whole Army* may pass by, either this or that way, and the King being in his march may at the same time enter into it with as many *Omrahs*, Hunters and other persons as he should please, and there hunt at his ease, now in one manner and then in another, according to the difference of the Game. And now behold first, how he hunteth the *Gazelles* or wild Fawns with tamed *Leopards*.[29]

I think, I have elsewhere told you, that in the *Indies*, there is store of *Gazelles*, that are in a manner shaped as our Hinds or Fawns; that these Gazelles commonly go in several troupes, and that every troupe, which never consists of above five or six, is alwaies follow'd by one only male, discernable by the colour. One of such troupes being discover'd, they endeavour to make the Leopard see them, who is held chain'd upon a little chariot. This crafty animal doth not presently and directly run after them, but goes winding and turning, stopping and hiding himself, so to approach them with more

---

[29] The tamed leopards were in fact cheetahs. The Mughal emperors also used the lynx for this purpose.

advantage, and to surprize them: And as he is capable to make five or six leaps with an incredible swiftnes, when he finds he is within reach, he lanceth[30] himself upon them, worrieth them, and gluts himself with their blood, heart and liver: If he faileth (which often happens) he stands still, and it would be in vain for him to attempt to take them by running after them, because they run much faster, and hold out longer than he. Then the Master comes gently about him, flattering him, and throwing him some pieces of flesh, and thus amusing him, puts something over his eyes to cover them, and so chains him, and puts him upon the charriot again. One of these Leopards gave us once in our march this divertisement, which frighted store of people. A troupe of Gazelles appear'd in the midst of the Army, as they will do every day; it chanced that they passed close to the two Leopards that were carried, as they use to be, upon their little charriot. One of them not blinded, made such an effort that he burst his chain, and darted himself after them, but without catching any of them: Yet the Gazelles not knowing which way to escape, being pursued, cried after, and hunted on every side, there was one of them that was forced to repass again near the Leopard, who, notwithstanding the Camels and Horses, that pestred all the way, and contrary to what is commonly said of the Beast, that it never returns to its prey when it hath once failed of it, flew upon it and caught it.

The hunting of the *Nilgaux* or gray Oxen, which I said were a kind of Elks, hath no great matter in it. They are inclosed in great Nets, that are by little and little drawn closer together, and when they are reduced to a small compass of enclosure, the King, the *Omrahs*, and the Hunters do enter and kill them at pleasure, with Arrows, Half-Pikes, Sables[31] or Musquets; and sometimes in so great numbers that the King sends quarters of them for presents to all the *Omrahs*.

The Game of the *Cranes* hath something of divertisement. 'Tis a pleasure to see them defend themselves in the Air against the Birds of prey; they sometimes kill some of them; but at length, not being nimble in turning, many strong Birds master them.

Of all the Games that of the *Lion*[32] is the most Royal, because there is none but the King and the Princes that can exercise it (unless it be

---

[30] lanceth: throws, flings.   [31] Sables: sabres (*OED*).
[32] Lions are only found in India in Kathiawar, a peninsula in Gujerat, west-central India.

by a particular leave;) but it is also the most dangerous. The manner of it is this. When the King is in the field, and the Hunting-guards have discover'd the place of the Lion's retirement; they tye fast an Ass thereabout, which the Lion soon comes to devour, and without caring to look out for other prey, as Oxen, Cows, Mutton or Shepherds, he goes to seek for drink, and returns to his ordinary lodging place, where he lyes down and sleeps until next morning, when he finds another Ass in the self same place, which the Hunters have fastned there as the day before; and when they have thus baited and fed him several dayes in the same place, and now know that the King is nigh, they at length tye fast another Ass, but whom they have made to swallow a quantity of *Opium*, to the end that his flesh may the better lull to sleep the Lion, and then all the Country-men of the circum-jacent Villages spread large and strong nets, made for that purpose, which they also by degrees reduce to a small compass, as is practised in the hunting of the *Nil-gaux*. All things thus prepar'd, the King mounted on an Elephant trap'd[33] with iron, being attended by the great Hunting-master, some *Omrahs* riding also on Elephants, by abundance of *Gourze-berdars* on Horseback, and by a numerous Hunting-guard on foot, arm'd with Half-pikes, approacheth to the Nets from without, and with a great Musquet shoots at the Lion; who when he finds himself wounded, comes directly to the Elephant, as his custom is; but he meets with those big Nets stopping him, and the King shoots so often at him, that at last he kills him. Yet in this last hunting there was a Lion that leapt over those Nets, fell upon an Horseman whose Horse he kill'd, and then ran away. But the Hunters met with him, and inclosed him again in the Net, which caused a great disturbance to the Army; we were three or four dayes padling in small torrents running down the mountains, betwixt under-wood and such long grass as that Camels hardly can be seen therein; and happy were these that had some provision of victuals; for all was in disorder: The *Bazars* could not range themselves, and the Villages were remote. The reason why we were to stop there so long, was, that as it is a good *Omen* with the Indians when the King kills a Lion, so it is a very ill one, when he faileth, and they think that the State would run great

---

[33] trap'd: adorned with trappings (*OED*).

hazard if they should not master him. Hence 'tis also that they make many Cerimonies upon the account of this Hunting; for they bring the dead Lion before the King in the general Assembly of the *Omrahs*, and after he hath been well viewed & exactly measur'd, 'tis recorded in the Archives, that such a King, at such a time, slew a Lion of such a bigness, of such hair, of so long and large teeth and claws, not omitting the least circumstances.[34]

I shall here add only a word in reference to what is commonly said of the *Opium*, that the Ass is made to swallow, *viz.* That one of the chief Hunters assur'd me, that it was but a tale of the vulgar, and that the Lion slept sufficiently without it, when he had his belly full.

Now to return to our march; when the great Rivers, which in these quarters commonly have no Bridges, are to be passed, there are made two Boat-bridges, about two or three hundred paces distant from one another; which they know well enough how to chain and fasten together. Upon them they cast earth and straw mingl'd together, which preventeth the sliding of the animals. The first passing upon, and the coming from it are only dangerous, because, that besides the great crowd, which then commonly throngeth, and the great confusion and embarrassment, it often happens that pits or holes are made when 'tis moving earth; and then you shall have Horses and burthen'd Oxen tumble upon one another, over whom people do pass with an incredible disorder; which would be yet greater, if all were to pass in *one* day: But ordinarily the King encampeth but half a League from the Bridge, where he stays a day or two, and he never almost encampeth farther than half a League from the River on the other side of the Bridge, that so the Army may have at least three dayes and three nights to pass more conveniently.

Lastly, as to the number of people that is found in the Army, it is not so easie a thing to determine it. It is so differently spoken of, that one knows not what to judge of it. What I can tell you of it in the general, that is most probable, is this: That in this march there were at least, as to Souldiers and others, an hundred thousand Horsemen, and above

[34] Constable details that Akbar (reigned 1556–1605) ordered an account to be kept of the game he shot and his successor, Jahangir (reigned 1605–27), caused the officials of the Hunting Department to draw up a 'game book' covering his kills from the age of 12 to 50. He shot 17,167 head of game of all kinds over this period.

an hundred and fifty thousand Animals, as Horses, Mules or Elephants; that there were near fifty thousand Camels, and almost as many Oxen or Asses, that serve to carry the grain, and other provisions of these poor people of the *Bazars*, their wives and children: For they lugg all with them, as our *Bohemians* do.[35] Upon this measure you may reckon pretty near the number of serving people, supposing that nothing is there done but by the force of servants, and that I, who am but in the rank of a Cavalier of two Horses, can hardly do my business with less than three men: Some say, that in the whole Army, there is scarce less than between three or four hundred thousand persons. Others reckon more; others less. No body ever told them to determine the precise number. I can say nothing of certainty, but only that 'tis a prodigious and almost incredible number; but then you are to imagine, that 'tis all *Dehli*, the Capital City, that marcheth, because that all the Inhabitants of that Town, living upon the Court and the Army, are obliged to follow them, especially when the voyage is to be long, as this is; or else they must starve.

The difficulty is to know, whence and how so great an Army can subsist in the Field, so vast a number of people and beasts. For that, we must only suppose (which is very true) that the *Indians* live very soberly, and observe a very simple diet, and that of all this great number of Cavaliers there is not the tenth, no not the twentieth man, that in his march eats flesh: provided they have their *Kichery*, that is, their mixture of Rice and of other legums,[36] upon which they pour butter when they are boiled, they are content. We are also to know, that Camels endure labour, hunger and thirst extreamly well, live upon little, and eat almost any thing: and that assoon as the Army encampth any where, the Camel-drivers let them go into the field to brouze,[37] where they eat whatever they light upon. Besides, that the Merchants that entertain *Bazars* in *Dehli*, are obliged to entertain them in the field; and that all the small Merchants, that keep shop in the *Bazars* of *Dehli*, keep them also in the Army, either by force, or out of necessity; and lastly, that as to Forrage, all these poor people goe roving up and down every where in the Village, to buy what they

---

[35] The French word 'bohème' refers to a gypsy.
[36] legums: from French 'legumes' for vegetables.
[37] brouze: browse, i.e. graze.

can get, and to gain something by it; and their great and common refuge is, with a kind of Trowel to raspe[38] or knock down whole fields, to beat and wash what they have there gotten, and so to carry it to sell to the Army, which they do sometimes very dear, and sometimes very Cheap. I forgot to mention one thing that's remarkable: *viz.* that the King enters into the Camp, now on one side, then on another; and that to day he passeth near the Tents of certain *Omrahs*, and to morrow near those of others, Which he doth not without design; for the *Omrahs*, which he passeth so near, are obliged to meet him, and to make him some small present or other; so that some will present him with twenty Roupies of Gold, which maketh thirty Pistols:[39] others with fifty, and so others in proportion, according to their generosity, and the greatness of their pay.

For the rest, you will excuse me, that I do not observe to you the Towns and Burroughs that are between *Dehli* and *Lahor*. I have seen in a manner none of them, for I went almost alwaies cross the fields, and in the night, because my *Agah* was not placed in the middle of the Army, where often is the high way, but very forward in the right Wing. We went as well as we could by Star-light cross the fields to gain the right wing of the Camp, without seeking for the high way; though sometimes we found our selves much perplexed, and in lieu of three or four Leagues, which is the ordinary distance of one encampment from another, we sometimes made five or six; but when the day comes on, we soon found our selves where we should be.

THE THIRD LETTER

A Description of Lahor, *the Capital of* Penjeab, *or,* The Kingdom of the Five Waters.

SIR,

It is not without reason, that this Kingdom, of which *Lahor* is the Capital City is called *Penje-ab*, or the *Country* of the *Five Waters*, because there are actually Five considerable Rivers coming down from

---

[38] raspe: scrape or scratch (*OED*).   [39] Rupees are Indian coins and pistoles French.

those Mountains, within which the Kingdom of *Kachemire* is lock'd up, and that run cross this tract of Land to fall into the River *Indus*, discharging themselves together into the Ocean at *Scymdi*, towards the entry of the Persian Gulph. Whether *Lahor* be that ancient *Bucephalos*, I decide not. Mean time, *Alexander* is sufficiently known here under the name of *Sekander Filifous*, that is, *Alexander*, Son of *Philip*; but as to his Horse, they know it not.[40] The City of *Lahor* is built upon one of these Five Rivers,[41] which is not less than our River *Loire*, and for which there is great need of a like bank, because it maketh great devastation, and often changeth its bed, and hath but lately retired it self from *Lahor* for a quarter of a League; which very much incommodeth the Inhabitants. The Houses of *Lahor* have this peculiar above those of *Dehli* and *Agra*, that they are very high, but most of them are ruinous, because 'tis now more than twenty years that the Court is always at *Dehli* or at *Agra*,[42] and that in these later years the rains have been so excessive, that they have overthrown many of them, whereby also much people hath been killed. 'Tis true, there remain still five or six considerable Streets, of which there are two or three that are above a League long; but in them also are many buildings found that fall down. The Kings Pallace is no longer upon the River side, as it was formerly, because that the River hath left it.[43] It is very high, and magnificent; yet those of *Agra* and *Dehli* do much surpass it. It is now above two months that we are here, expecting the melting of the Snow of the mountains of *Kachemire*, for a more convenient passage into that Kingdom. But at length we are to depart to morrow. The King hath been gone these two dayes. I have got a little *Kachemirian* Tent, which I bought yesterday. I was advised to do like

[40] Bucephala is the city founded in Alexander's conquest of Asia. In spring 326, crossing the Indus near Attock, Alexander entered Taxila, whose ruler, Taxiles, furnished elephants and troops in return for aid against his rival Porus, who ruled the lands between the Hydaspes (modern Jhelum) and the Acesines (modern Chenab). In June Alexander fought his last great battle on the left bank of the Hydaspes. He founded two cities there, Alexandria Nicaea (to celebrate his victory) and Bucephala (named after his horse Bucephalus, which died there); and Porus became his ally.

[41] Lahore sits on the banks of the river Ravi, a tributary of the Indus. The Mughals captured the city in 1524.

[42] After the death of Jahangir, who often resided at Lahore, in 1627, and the accession of Shah Jahan who preferred Agra and Delhi, the population of the city began to decline.

[43] Aurangzeb built an embankment to prevent flooding, which deflected the course of the river Ravi.

others, and to leave here my ordinary tent, which is big and heavy enough, because, they say, that between the mountains of *Kachemire*, whither we are now marching, it will be difficult to find room enough, and that the Camels not having place enough to pass, we shall be obliged to get our Baggage carried by Porters, and that so my large Tent would cost me much to carry. *Adieu.*

THE FOURTH LETTER

SIR,

I Believed [*sic*], that after we had overcome the heats of *Moka*, near *Babel-mandel* I could defie those of the rest of the Earth, but since these four dayes that the Army left *Lahor*, I find I come very short of my reckoning, and I have experimented to the hazard of my life, that it is not without reason, that the Indians themselves did apprehend the eleven or twelve dayes march of the Army, from *Lahor* to *Bember*, the entry of the mountains of *Kachemire*. I protest unto you, without any exaggaration, that the heats have been so excessive, that sometimes they have reduced me to extremity, insomuch that I knew not in the morning whether I should live till night. The cause of this extraordinary heat is, that the high mountains of *Kachemire* being on the *North* of our road, keep from us all the cool wind that might come and refresh us from that quarter, and do reflect the sun-beams upon us, and leave the field burnt up and choaking. But to what purpose, to play the Philosopher, and to seek reasons for that, which perhaps will kill me to morrow.

THE FIFTH LETTER

SIR,

I Passed yesterday one of the greatest Rivers of the *Indies*, called the *Tchenau*. The excellency of its water, of which the great *Omrahs* make provision in lieu of that of the *Ganges* (whereof they have drunk hitherto) keeps me from believing this to be some River to pass to

Hell,[44] rather than to *Kachemire*, where they would make us believe
we shall find Snow and Ice: For I find it grow worse and worse each
day, and that the more we advance, the more heat we feel. 'Tis true
that I pass'd the Bridge at Noon-day; but I almost knew not, which was
best, to march in the field, or to keep ones self stuff'd up under a Tent:
At least, I have succeeded in my design, which was to pass the Bridge
with ease, whilst all men did repose themselves, expecting to leave the
Camp towards evening when the Heat is not so violent; whereas if I had
staid as the rest did, some mischief perhaps might have befallen me.
For it hath been, I hear, the most terrible confusion, and the greatest
disorder that ever was in any the like former passage from *Dehli*, the
entring upon the first Boat, and the going off from the last, having been
made very difficult, because it was meer moving sand, which as the
people marched upon it, and stirr'd it, did slide away into the water,
and left a pit; insomuch that a great number of Camels, Oxen and
Horses were in the crowd overthrown and trampled under foot, and
store of blows distributed besides: There are ordinarily, upon such
occasions, some Officers and Cavaliers of the *Omrahs*, who to make
way for their Masters and their Baggage, are not sparing of them. My
Navab hath lost one of his Camels with the Iron Oven[45] it carried;
which maketh me apprehend, I shall be reduced to the bread of the
Bazar. Farewel.

THE SIXTH LETTER

SIR,

It is too much curiosity, 'tis folly, or at least temerity in an European to
expose himself to such heats and dangerous marches. It is putting
one's self into manifest peril of life. Yet notwithstanding, misfortune
is good for something. Whilst we stayed at *Lahor*, I was seized on by
a Flux, and by gripings, which did much incommode me; caused by
my constant lying upon a *Terrasse*, and taking the cool of the night, as

[44] Religious mythologies from ancient Egypt, Greece, and Rome all depict the journey
to the underworld as a water-crossing.
[45] The oven known as a 'tandur' made of sheet iron for the baking of flat bread.

we use to do at *Dehli* without danger, But since we have been marching these eight or nine days, the sweat hath dissipated all these humors. My body is become a right Sieve, very dry, and I have no sooner taken into my stomach a pint of water (for less will not serve our turn) but I see it at the same time issue out of my limbs like a dew to the very ends of my fingers. I believe I have this day drunk above ten pints. And this is some comfort, that one may drink of it as much as one lists without danger, provided it be good water.

THE SEVENTH LETTER, TO THE SAME

Written from the Camp of the Army, marching from Lahor *to* Kachemire, *the tenth day of the* March *in the morning.*

SIR,

The Sun is but just now rising, yet he is intolerable; there is not a Cloud in the Sky, not a breath of Wind; my horses are spent, they have not seen a green Herb[46] since we came out of *Lahor*; my *Indians* for all their black, dry and hard Skin, sink under it. My face, hands and feet are peeled off, and my body is covered all over with pimples, that prick me as so many needles. Yesterday one of our poor Cavaliers, that had no Tent, was found dead at the foot of a small Tree he had seized on. I doubt, whether I shall outlive this days journey; all my hope is in a little dry curdled Milk, which I am going to dilute with Water and Sugar, and some Limons, I have left, to make Limonade, Farewel; the Ink dryeth at the end of my Pen, and the Pen falls out of my hand. Farewell.

THE EIGHTH LETTER, TO THE SAME

Written from Bember, *the Entry of the Mountains of* Kachemire, *after having two days encamped there. What* Bember *is; the change of carriages for the Mountains; the incredible number of Porters, and the order observed in the Army.*

---

[46] Translated from French 'herbe', in other words, not a blade of grass.

SIR,

We are at length arriv'd at *Bember*, the foot of a steep, black and burn'd Mountain, and we are encamped in the channel of a large Torrent dried up, full of sand and stones burning hot. It is like an hot oven: And if it were not for the shower of Rain we had this morning, and for the curdled Milk, the Limons and the Fowl brought to us from the mountains, I know not what would have become of me, and you would perhaps never have seen this Letter. But, God be thanked, I feel the Air a little cooler; my Stomach, Strength and Tongue are returned. So then take this account of our new kind of march and trouble.

Yester-night the King first of all, together with *Rauchenara-Begum*, and the other Women of the *Seraglio*, The *Raja Ragnat*[47] that performs the Office of the Vizir, and *Fasel-kan*[48] the High Steward, went away from this burning place, and last night the great Hunting-master departed with some of the greatest and most necessary Officers of the Royal Family, and many considerable Women. This night 'tis our turn; my *Navab Danech-mend-kan* will go away, and *Mahmet Emir-kan*, the Son of that famous *Emir-jemla*, of whom I have spoken so much in another place, will be of our Company;[49] *Dianet-kan*,[50] our good friend, with his two Sons, and many other *Omrahs*, *Rajahs*, and *Manseb-dars:* And after us, all the other Lords, that are bound for *Kachemire*, will be gone all in their turns, to avoid in these difficult and narrow ways of the mountains, the trouble and confusion, during

[47] Named by Constable as Raja Raghunath, but I have no further information and Bernier does not refer to him elsewhere in his four volumes.

[48] In his account of events after Aurangzeb's rebellion (*History*, ii), Bernier refers to Fazelkan's promotion to the office of 'Khànsàmàn' or Grand Chamberlain of the royal household in recognition of his service to the new emperor.

[49] Emir-jemla: Mohammed Sayyid Mir Jumla, a Persian adventurer and former diamond merchant, entrusted by Shah Jahan with advancing Mughal interests in the Deccan, planned with Aurangzeb (whose father had given him government of the territory) to seize power from the sultan of Golconda in 1655. The pair were forced by Shah Jahan at the urging of Dara Shukoh to reinstate the sultan of Golconda but Mir Jumla became Shah Jahan's chief minister and his son, Mahmet, was released from imprisonment. Mir Jumla seized Bijapur in 1657 in a campaign directed by Aurangzeb and then aided Aurangzeb in his rise to power. Bernier describes him as immensely wealthy because of his control of the diamond mines and names him as the principal agent of Aurangzeb's rise in the 12th chapter of the *History*, vol. i.

[50] In the second volume of his *History*, Bernier makes reference to Dianet-Khan's being awarded the governorship of Kashmir by Aurangzeb after the latter's victory over his brothers in 1658.

these five days of marching between this place and *Kachemire*. All the rest of the Court, as *Fedaykan*, the great Master of the Artillery,[51] three or four great *Rajas*, and many *Omrahs*, are to stay here about, for a guard, during three or four months, until the King do return after the great heats are over. Some shall go to dress their Tents on the one side of the River *Tchenau*, others in the neighbouring Towns and Burroughs, and others will be obliged to camp here in this Fire of *Bember*.

The King for fear of starving this small Kingdom of *Kachemire*, first carries with him the least number of Women he can, the greatest Ladies, the best friends of *Rauchenara-Begum*, and those that are most necessary for service. Nor doth he carry more of the *Omrahs* and *Militia* than needs he must: And the *Omrahs* that have leave to come with him, cannot take with them all the Cavaliers, but only 25 of 100, yet without comprehending therein the particular Officers of their Family. And that is to be religiously observ'd, because there is an *Omrah* upon the Guard at the entry of the Mountains, that reckons all that pass, one by one, and hinders the passing of that great number of *Manseb-dars* and other Cavaliers, that would fain go and enjoy the cool Air of *Kachemire*; as also all those small Merchant and little people of *Bazar* that seek to gain a livelyhood. The King, for the carriage of necessaries and the Women of the *Seraglio*, taketh with him some of the strongest and best Elephants: These Beasts, though gross and unwieldy, are very sure-footed, and in ill way they march very warily, assuring themselves first of one foot before they remove the other. He taketh also some Mules with him; but Camels, the most necessary, he cannot make use of in this passage; these Mountains being too steep and craggy for their long-shanked and stiff legs: Porters must supply their places; and what number, you think must there be, if the King alone, as they say, hath above six thousand for his occasions, and I, a private man, though I have left at *Lahor* my ordinary Tent and much of my baggage, as every one hath done, even the King himself and the *Omrahs*, find my self obliged to have three of them? 'Tis believed, there are already no less here than fifteen

---

[51] Fidai Khan, foster-brother to Aurangzeb. He was given the title of Azim Khan in 1676 and made governor of Bengal where he died in 1678.

thousand, partly of those which the Governour of *Kachemire* and the *Rajas* here about have compelled to be here, partly of those that came hither of their own accord out of the neighbouring Villages to earn something; for a man is obliged, following the Kings order, to give them ten Crowns for an hundred pound weight. 'Tis said, that, in all, there are above thirty thousand of them, without reckoning that a month ago the King and *Omrahs* sent away some bagage [*sic*] before, and the Merchants, all sorts of Commodities.

From *The General History of the Mogol Empire* (1709)

compiled by François Catrou from the memoirs
of Niccolo Manucci

Copy-text: 1st edition (London, 1709)

The Venetian Niccolo Manucci (1639–1714) was, like the
Frenchman Bernier, a physician who spent many years in
India, but here the resemblance ends. Manucci left Venice in
1653 at the age of 14, and took ship on a vessel bound for
Smyrna where he came under the protection of Viscount
Bellamont, an English nobleman, and travelled with him from
Persia to India. When Bellamont died in 1656, Manucci
found employment as an artilleryman in the service of Prince
Dara Shukoh, eldest son of the Mughal Emperor Shah Jahan.
When Dara was executed by his newly sovereign younger
brother Aurangzeb in 1659, Manucci refused service with
Aurangzeb and retrained as a physician. The profession
proved unlucrative, however, and he became captain of
artillery for Rajah Jai Singh. This post he resigned after a
few years and thereafter he travelled around India, narrowly
escaping the Inquisition, until he took service with Kirat
Singh, son of Jai Singh. Manucci moved to Lahore at the end
of 1670 when his employer was ordered to Kabul.

His next unlucky venture in Bandora on Salsette Island
resulted in financial losses and he returned to the Mughal
court, where he was appointed as a physician attached to Shah

Alam, following him to the Deccan when Shah Alam was made governor there in 1678. Shah Alam was recalled in 1680 to join a military campaign, but Manucci took leave and went to Goa where the Portuguese used him in negotiations with a Mahrattah chief. In 1684 he received a knighthood from the Portuguese but was thereafter detained by Mughal forces as a deserter and obliged to join Alam in a campaign against the king of Golconda. He escaped Shah Alam's service once more and took refuge at the English Fort St George at Madras. Here he married a Catholic widow in 1686 named Clarke and they had one son who died in infancy. At Madras he negotiated with Indian rulers, Mughal and Hindu, on the part of the English governors Gyfford and Pitt. He became absorbed in disputes between the Capuchins and Jesuits in the early years of the eighteenth century. His wife died in 1706 and some time before 1712 he moved to Pondicherry. By 1712 he was back in Madras having received a leasehold on his wife's first husband's house and gardens there. He died in India in 1717.

All this time, Manucci was keeping copious manuscript memoirs, written in French and Portuguese rather than his native tongue because of a lack of amanuenses in that language, which he sent back to Europe in two forms. In 1701, André Boureau-Deslandes (*c*.1640–1706), a Pondicherry official with the French Company in India, took a three-volume manuscript to Venice, which he lent to Father François Catrou (1659–1737), a Jesuit priest. The latter published an edited version of the manuscript as a book in 1705 entitled *Histoire Générale de l'Empire du Mogul*, which was rendered into English by an anonymous translator in 1709. Catrou sent Manucci an advance copy which enraged the latter who saw it as an attempt by the Jesuits to take the glory of his own labour (the memoirs reveal a marked hostility to the Jesuits, the Portuguese, and Aurangzeb). In 1706 he sent original drafts of the first three parts to which Catrou had had access, along with a fourth part written since 1701, to the Venetian Senate at Paris, Lorenzo Tiepolo, followed by a fifth part in 1712. Tiepolo became librarian of San Marco Library in 1736 and the manuscripts were housed there by him. Manucci also sent a volume of portraits with the 1701 manuscript which the San Marco Library had acquired by 1741; this became in 1797 the

property of the French nation and was kept at the Bibliothèque
Nationale. The original Manucci manuscripts were located in
the early twentieth century by William Irvine, who translated
and edited them as *Storio do Mogor, or Mogul India, 1653–1708*
in 4 vols. (London, 1907–8).

In the first two parts of his manuscript, Manucci mixes
accounts of the lives of the Mughal emperors from Timur to
Aurangzeb, in the third he provides a treatise on the Mughal
court, and he devotes much of the fourth and fifth to disputes
between the Capuchins and Jesuits in India. Catrou
produced a continuation (which he calls the third part) from
the three volumes he received in 1701 in 1715. However, his
1705 compilation (the text of the English translation of 1709)
only uses Manucci as a foundation; it departs considerably
from its source, omitting most of the travel narrative to
concentrate on dynastic history and using many other
informants (including François Bernier and Jean-Baptiste
Tavernier) to supplement and develop Manucci's version of
events, manners, and customs in Mughal India.

Catrou obviously had an interest in the history of empire,
since he also produced a *History of the Romans* in French
between 1721 and 1737 (translated into English in 6 vols.
1728–37). He also edited a literary organ called the *Journal de
Théroux* for twelve years. In his author's preface to the 1709
General History, he presents the work as part of what
Raymond Schwab has termed the 'Oriental Renaissance'
(*The Oriental Renaissance: Europe's Rediscovery of India and
the East, 1680–1880*, trans. Gene Patterson-Black and Victor
Reinking (New York: Columbia University Press, 1984));
a Europe tired of ancient Greece and Rome can turn to the
Orient for new accounts of glory:

> *we are tired of seeing Heroes on the Stage always in an*
> European *Dress; and that those of* Asia *are not without
> their Beauty's, where they but tolerably drawn to the Life;
> that the History of the remotest Country is no less capable of
> Ornaments than that of our own; that perhaps it has some
> of an uncommon kind, and which are peculiar to it that
> the human Passions, which are the Soul of great Events, are
> the same in* Asia *as in* Europe; *that we may be instructed in*
> France *by Examples of* Indian *Vertue, as others had been*

heretofore in Greece *by the illustrious Patterns of Probity and Generosity among the* Scythians; *in fine, that the Example of* Padmani *might be as useful a Lesson of conjugal Fidelity, as the Constancy of the Heroes of* Toxaris *was among the* Athenians *of the highest Friendship.* (n.p.)

The example of Padmani is illustrated in the text below. This is a romanticized account of the Mughal Emperor Akbar's (reigned 1556–1605) siege of the Rajasthani hill fort Chitor between 1567 and 1568. The story of the intrepid actions of the Hindu wife of the Rana is one that clearly resonated with European readers. A version of the same story, possibly derived from Catrou, is the 'History of Commladeve' told by Alexander Dow and given in this anthology (more likely Dow's source was the version of it in the sixteenth-century Mughal chronicle of Firishtah, which Dow translated in 1768). The Padmani story in Dow's translation is that of the heroic daughter of the Raja of Chitor in 1304 who used the same method described here to liberate her father from the clutches of the Delhi sultan, Nasir-ud-Din (Firishtah, *History of Hindostan*, i. 280–1), a story with which Manucci was clearly acquainted.

Padmani's combination of subtlety and self-sacrifice (resulting in the act of suttee) was to prove enduringly attractive to European writers about India. This representation of the 'Indian' (Hindu) woman allowed European powers with nascent colonial ambitions in the territory both to figure themselves as saviours of the Hindu population from Mughal/Muslim despotism and as civilizers of a culture still observing cruel practices such as widow-burning. In fact, the story was a rather different one.

The Rana of Mewar, Udai Singh, presented in Manucci/Catrou's story as a hero, fled when Akbar's forces besieged the city and founded a new capital named Udaipur, where he died in 1572. Akbar massacred some twenty thousand non-combatants having fired the city of Chitor, which was never reoccupied. Udai Singh's son, Rana Pratap, is, however, a hero of Rajasthan and may be here elided with his father. Rana Pratap was Maharaja (1572–97) of the Rajput confederacy of Mewar and sought to avenge the pillage of Chitor, in contrast to his fellow Hindu princes, who had submitted to the Mughals. He reorganized the government, improved the forts, and directed his subjects to take refuge in the mountain country when attacked by Mughals. Defeated in June 1576 by Mughal forces at Haldighat, he fled to the hills but continued to harass the Mughals and promote non-cooperation with Mughal taxation among his people. On his death in 1597, he was succeeded by his son, Amar Singh, who submitted in 1614 to Jahangir, son of Akbar. Although Akbar plays the role of villain in this narrative, this Indian-born ruler, married to a Hindu and tolerant of religious difference, was probably the most powerful and liberal of the Mughal emperors. He was determined, however, to consolidate Mughal power from its uncertain base in the Punjab, resulting in a combination of an aggressive military campaign and wide-ranging administrative reform.

Agra, at this Day, the ordinary Residence of the *Mogol* Emperors, is Situate in a vast Plain upon the same River which runs by *Dely*; it extends it self along the Banks of the *Gemma* in the form of a *Crescent*. At one end of it Stands the Imperial Palace, and the House of the principal Lords of the Court. The City takes up in Length about Nine Italian Miles, so that it's much longer than Broad. It's true, it was not surrounded with a Wall in the Days of *Akebar*: But a large Ditch always fed with Water by a Communication with the River Encompass'd it on every Side.

The Number of Inhabitants soon amounted to Six Hundred and Sixty Thousand, without including Strangers, whom the Conveniency of *Caravanseras,* and the Freedom of Trade, had drawn thither from all the Countries of *Asia*.

The Emperor's Palace which serves as a Citadel to the Town of *Agra*, may pass for one of the finest in the World, whether we consider its Situation, Building or Riches. It Stands upon an Eminence, and its Walls which are Twenty Five Foot in Heighth, are built of a Stone of a reddish Colour, not very unlike Marble; the Masonry is incomparable, 'tis not Possible to discover the joining of the Stones. In Fine, this vast Edifice seems to be one Entire Rock. On the Side towards the River, the Palace makes the noblest Front in the World. The Windows and Balcony disposed with Symmetry enough have a particular Grace. From these the Emperor sees the Combats of his Elephants on a Strand which reaches from the Palace to the River; on the other Side of the River is to be seen a Second Town, as long, though not as broad as the first. Here the *Banianes* and Tradesmen have their Dwelling. 'Tis almost incredible what they turn in Trade.

Akebar lookt upon the City of *Agra*, of which he was Founder as the noblest Monument of his Glory. He did not disdain to give it his own Name. 'Twas call'd, during his life, *Akebarabad*, that is to say, the Town of *Akebar*, but after his Death, when Flattery did no longer constrain *Akebarabad*, resum'd its ancient Name of *Agra*, and retains it to this Day.[1]

Those Employments of Peace did not abate the Emperor's natural Inclination for War. He cou'd not indure that an *Indian* Prince, of the Race of the famous *Rana*, who formerly submitted to the Power of *Tamerlane*,[2] shou'd hold a kind of Soveraignty in his Neighbourhood; that Prince was called *Rana*, after the Name of his Ancestors, and boasted of being lineally descended from the antient *Porus*.[3] The Territories of the *Raja* were not above Twelve Days Journey from *Dely,* and the Capital of his Country was called *Chitor*. 'Twas rather a Fortress, than a Town of Trade. It's Situated on a high Mountain

[1] In fact, the city of Agra was founded in the early 18th c. by Sikander Lodi, but Akbar did construct a magnificent fort there. He made Fatehpur Sikri near Agra his capital in 1569, the place where his Rajput wife gave birth to their first child (the future Emperor Jahangir). Here, he began in 1571 to build a magnificent palatial complex to which Catrou may be referring since it is indeed largely built of a ruddy sandstone.

[2] Catrou recounts how the Mongol nomad Timur (he names him Tamerlane) returned to the Indies in AD 1399 at the age of 64 and crushed the resistance of the Hindu princes led by Prince Rana, forcing him to become tributary to Tamerlane's rule (14–19). Akbar was the eighth Mughal ruler in descent from Timur. In fact, no such conflict took place and Timur did not penetrate far into the Indian interior. Manucci also refers to this mythical event in his manuscript memoir and his modern editor, William Irvine, suggests he is superimposing a version of the previous Mughal emperor Babur's contest with Rana Sanga in 1527 (*Storio do Mogor*, i. 101).

[3] Porus was an Indian prince who ruled the region between the Hydaspes (Jhelum) and Acesines (Chenab) rivers at the time of Alexander III the Great's invasion (327–326 BC) of the Punjab. Porus resisted Alexander so bravely at the battle of the Hydaspes, that Alexander allowed him to retain his kingdom.

surrounded with Water on every Side in the midst of a vast Plain. The top of the Mountain on which the Town was Built is a Flat. It's about a League and a half in Circumference, and half a League over in some Places. At the Foot of the Mountain, the *Nug*, a pretty large River, but very deep, glides gently a long. A Rivulet of the best Water in the World takes its source in the Town. It makes a great many windings within it; and at last having form'd several natural *Cascades* on the break of the mountain, throws it self into the River. Within the Compass of the Fortress, are several beautiful Fields sow'd with *Rice*, and water'd by the overflowing of the *Rivulet*; it affords Provisions enough to supply an indifferent large Garrison. A place inaccessible, which wants neither Victuals nor Water, passes in the *Indies* for impregnable. However; this was the place of which *Akebar* undertook the Conquest. It's thought, that the young Emperor's Love for the Princess *Padmani*,[4] the Wife of *Rana*, Sovereign of *Chitor*, represented that Enterprise easy, which otherwise might seem impracticable. Before he wou'd attempt so dangerous a Siege, *Akebar*, by his Ambassadors, let *Rana* understand, that Ambition alone was not the Motive of this Undertaking; that the *Indian* might preserve his Country from the Ruine which threatn'd it, by giving up the most beautiful Princess of the *East*, to the most potent Monarch of the World. A Proposal of this kind is not so shocking in the *Indies*, as it would be in *Europe*. Their Laws allow Divorce. However, *Rana* had too great a Passion for *Padmani*, to part with her to a Rival, and wou'd hear nothing more upon that Subject, but the Dictates of his own Valour, and the Tears of his Wife. 'Can you find in your Heart to abandon me' (says the virtuous Princess) 'to a Tyrant whom I detest? Have we not Strength enough in *Chitor* to consume your Enemy's Forces, and extinguish his Flame, by the length of a fruitless Siege? At worst, if I must loose my Life, I'll loose it without Regret, provided I am not so unhappy as to survive you.' Words so moving, determin'd *Rana* to prefer an honourable War to an ignominious Peace. He

---

[4] The term 'Padmini' refers to the highest of the four female castes accorded to women in Hinduism. Irvine suggests that the name is also meant to invoke Padamawati, a heroine of romance and poetry, who lived about 1303 and was taken by Ala-ud-din Khalji, the Delhi sultan (1296–1316), when he conquered Chitor. Irvine suggests Manucci conflated the story of Ala-ud-din with the attack on Chitor by Bahadur Shah of Gujarat in 1533 and Akbar's 1568 siege (*Storio do Mogor*, i. 124).

answer'd the Ambassador of *Akebar*, that he wou'd not advise his Master to sit down before *Chitor*: But if his Passion had the Ascendant of his Reason, *Akebar* shou'd find in the Person of *Rana* a true *Ragepute*, capable of maintaining his Rights, and incapable of an Infidelity to *Padmani*. The Emperor was surpris'd at so haughty a Reply. He was not accustom'd to meet with any Opposition to his Will, or be cross'd in his Desires. 'Can it be possible', cry'd he, 'that there is a Man upon Earth, audacious enough to disobey me?' He quickly assembl'd his victorious Troops, which had newly conquer'd Two Kingdoms.[5] *Rana* for his part was not asleep, and made Preparation for maintaining a long Siege in *Chitor*. He rous'd up by his Ambassadors the sloathful *Rajas* in his Neighbourhood. He gave 'em to understand, that their negligence must soon expose 'em to the Tyranny of a *Mahometan*. That the *Mongols* were a Race of People but lately arriv'd in the *Indies*,[6] and who grew formidable only by the division of the *Indians*; that if the Princes Votaries of *Brama*,[7] wou'd Unite against the Sectaries of *Mahomet*, they might easily destroy 'em. *Jamal* and *Tata*, both *Rajas* and Princes of two Provinces bordering on *Chitor*,[8] join'd their Troops to those of *Rana*, and came in Person to make War against *Akebar*. They appear'd in the Field at the head of their Armies; but the *Mogol*, who advanced by long Marches towards *Chitor*, quickly dispers'd 'em. The Two Brothers had no other Remedy, but that of retiring into the strong Places of their Provinces, and there expect the Enemy whose Force they were not able to withstand in the Field. Never was seen in *Indoustan* a finer, nor a

[5] Manucci refers in his manuscript to conquests in Gujerat, the Deccan, and Kashmir prior to the siege of Chitor (*Storio do Mogor*, i. 120–3). The reference may be to Akbar's defeat of Malwa which commanded the route through the Vindhya hills to the Deccan in 1561 and marriage in 1562 to the daughter of Raja Bihari Mal of Amber (Jaipur), the first of the Rajput chiefs to acknowledge Akbar's suzerainty.

[6] The Mughal (Mongol) or Timurid state was founded by Babur between 1526 and 1530. Babur was a Chagathay Turk who claimed descent from Timur and, on his mother's side, from the Mongol leader Genghis Khan.

[7] i.e. Hindu princes, followers of the one God, Brahma.

[8] Manucci's manuscript says that the Raja of Chitor and husband of Padmani is called Jamel or Jai Mall and he and his brother called Fata fought bravely against Akbar (*Storio do Mogor*, i. 124). Bernier refers in his 'Description of Delhi and Agra' (*Continuation*) to two statues outside the fortress of Delhi of Jemel and Polta, princes of Chitor, who he says resisted with their mother (presumably the Padmani of the tale) Akbar's siege and died in the resulting battles. Catrou converts the brothers into neighbouring princes in his version.

more numerous Army than that of the *Mogol. Akebar* spar'd no Cost to shew himself before *Chitor* in the utmost Splendor.

The Richness of his Tents is hardly to be conceiv'd by us in *Europe*. All was Gold about 'em. He thought by his magnificent Equipage to dazzle the Princess *Padmani*, and by the Numbers of his Army to frighten the *Rana* into a Submission. *Akebar* found by Experience, that Virtue and Valour are sometimes Proof against the greatest Hopes, and the greatest Fears. The gallant *Indians* beheld without Emotion from the Top of their Mountain the Magnificence and prodigious Extent of the Enemies Camp. The *Mogol*, in the Beginning of his Siege, acted the Soldier and the Lover. It's said, he shot Arrows into the Town, which carry'd his Letters for *Padmani*. The Princess took no Notice of 'em. He push'd the Siege like one in Despair. He fired terribly upon the Place from several Batteries. But his Cannon shooting upwards had little or no Effect. The *Indians* from their Ramparts insulted the *Mahometans*, and reproach'd 'em with their want of Bravery, though animated to the Fight by more Passions than one. A *Portuguese* Historian tells us, that the Siege of *Troy* was acted over again in that of *Chitor*.[9] He adds, that it lasted Twelve long Years, and that *Padmani* had time to grow old, while the *Mogol* endeavour'd to conquer her by his Arms. This is an Exaggeration which the *Mogol* Chronicle does not confirm.[10] The Siege lasted at most but Two Years, and then concluded by a very extraordinary Adventure. The Truth of it is what I can't warrant.

It's said, that *Akebar* weary'd out by so obstinate a Resistance, made Shew of raising the Siege of *Chitor*, and that he writ to *Rana* a

---

[9] The earliest accounts of India from the 16th c. derived from Portuguese traders and were governed by the conventions of classical epic. The exact reference here has not been located but likely sources are Joao de Barros, Luis de Camoes, and Fernao Lopez de Castanheda.

[10] In his 'Author's Preface', Catrou makes much of Manucci's privileged access to Mughal sources. In reading the manuscript, he says, '*I found by it that* M. Manouchi *had had the Perusal of the Chronicles of the* Mogol *Empire; that he had got 'em translated into the* Portuguese; *and that they were inserted in the Work which I had in my Hands*' (*General History* (1709), n.p.). The Chronicles to which he refers may well have been the *Golshan-e Ebrahimi* by Firishtah, a Persian army officer of the late 16th c. who produced an account of the Muslim rulers of India from the 10th c. to the late 16th. Alexander Dow translated the account up to the death of Akbar as *The History of Hindostan* (2 vols., 1768). Manucci may have been acquainted with Firishtah's work since Firishtah also produced a medical treatise on phramacology and therapy.

very obliging artful Letter. He commended the *Raja* for his Courage, but desir'd he'd grant him Two Favours, before he quitted an Enterprise which he did not abandon but to his Confusion. First, that the *Raja* wou'd give him a Sight of the Princess, whom he had not known but by her publick Fame: Next, that he wou'd permit him to go into *Chitor* and see the only Place of the World capable of resisting his Power. The *Raja* granted him the second Demand very freely, but refus'd the first. He consented, that the *Mogol* shou'd enter *Chitor*, attended by only Fifty of his Officers, but wou'd not promise that he shou'd see *Padmani. Akebar* accepted the *Raja's* Offer, and having receiv'd Hostages for the Security of his Person, he enter'd *Chitor* with a smaller number of Attendants than was allow'd him. The Emperor receiv'd from *Rana* all the Respect and all the Distinction due to his Rank. He was regaled in the Palace after the Indian Manner.[11] The Entertainment was civil on both Sides; but *Akebar* whose Eloquence was perswasive, had the Art to make *Rana* grant him more than he had promis'd. When he saw the *Indian* warm'd with good Cheer, he entreated him to send for *Padmani*, if but for one moment. The *Raja* was willing, but they had a deal of Difficulty to get the Princess's Consent. At last, in Complaisance to her Husband, she shew'd her self, but disappear'd in an Instant. The Indiscretion of *Rana* cost him dear. *Akebar's* Passion was much more inflam'd upon Sight of the Princess; however, he had command enough over himself to dissemble it. He made *Rana* believe that he was resolv'd to raise the Siege from a Place which had cost him too dear already. He had besides Prudence enough not to intermix his Discourse with any Praises of *Padmani*, but such as were cold and indifferent. *Rana* thus deceiv'd by Appearances, treated his most cruel Enemy without the least Mistrust. He received his Presents, and made him others in Return. *Akebar* gave the Prince a Scimitar set with Diamonds, and *Rana* made the Emperor accept of some Jewels in Return. And now the Hour of their Parting drew near. *Akebar* renew'd his kind

[11] Manucci says that Akbar entered with five hundred rather than fifty, 'was well received, and great honours were paid him. The rajah gave him a great feast, and laid before him many presents of valuable jewels' which Akbar responded to with gifts of 'several elephants and caparisoned horses, a sword and decorated shield and other rarities' (*Storio do Mogor*, i. 125).

Protestations. At last they came to the Gate of the Fortress, where the *Mogol*, as a further Testimony of his Friendship, wou'd put about the Neck of *Rana* one of those large Pearl Necklaces, which the Men wear in the *Indies* as well as the Women. He took care to string it with some of the strongest Twist.[12] He dragged him by this Collar out of the Gate, while his forty Bravos opposed the Guard, who made a Motion to rescue their Prince. The *Mogols* forc'd the *Indian* to mount a Horseback, and after having receiv'd some Discharges from the Musquets on the Ramparts, they conducted *Rana* alive to the *Mogol*'s Camp.

In the mean time, the Uproar made at the Gate put the whole Town into a Consternation. The People thought the Enemy had surpris'd it, and certainly had the *Mogol* been but a little better provided with an arm'd Force to second his Design, he might easily have carry'd the Place. Fame which ever magnifies brought to *Padmani*'s Ears the News of a sudden Irruption of the Enemy. She was even told that her Husband was missing in the Fray. The Gallant Princess did not suffer herself to be overwhelm'd with this unexpected Disaster. She immediately got a Horseback, and with her Lance in her Hand, appear'd at the Head of her Troops, resolv'd to conquer or die. She did not learn the Truth of *Akebar*'s Treachery, and the forcing away of *Rana*, till she came upon the very Spot. *Padmani* perceiv'd plainly enough, that she had been the true Cause of his Misfortune, but she thought fit to conceal that Part. Full of Constancy, 'he is dead', she cry'd, 'that dearest Husband is dead whom my Tenderness has undone. Let's think no more of recovering him by a dishonourable Composition, but revenge his Death by seeing the Authors of it fall in heaps about us.' She spake, and without shedding a Tear, tho' pierc'd with the sharpest Sorrow, she walk'd round the Ramparts, gave all the necessary Orders, encourag'd the Soldiers, and animated the Principal Leaders. In fine, she shew'd herself as much Superior to the Men in Prudence and Courage, as she surpass'd in Beauty all those of her own Sex.

Akebar had now flatter'd himself with becoming quickly Master of the Fortress. And gave the besieged to understand, that if they did not

---

[12] Twist: cord, string (*OED*).

deliver up the Place and the Princess, he wou'd first cause *Rana*'s Head to be struck off, and conclude his Revenge in the sacking of the Town and putting the Inhabitants to the Sword. The brave *Amazon*[13] answer'd, that her Husband falling into the Hands of a perjur'd man, she was no longer in doubt of his Death; but still there remain'd *Rageputes* enough of his Nation to revenge their Soveraign.

That for her part she wou'd employ all the Authority Heaven had given her over her People to raise up to the *Mogol* Enemies yet more formidable than *Rana*: and besides that the Principal Leaders of her Army, had sworn to loose their Lives rather than surrender the Place.

Akebar was not ignorant of the Firmness of the *Rageputs* in all their Resolutions. He chose therefore to raise the Siege, and endeavor to obtain the Princess by way of negotiation. An Ambassador was sent to *Padmani* loaded with rich Presents, and the most passionate Letters. *Akebar* represented to the Princess that she had given Proofs enough of the Fidelity due to a Husband; that it was now time to make some condescension in Favor of a great Emperor, and her own Interest; that her tenderness for *Rana* cou'd not better appear than by procuring the Liberty of her Captive Husband: That by redeeming *Rana* from his Captivity, she might make her self the greatest Queen in the World.

They shew'd her at the same time Letters extorted from the Captive Prince, by which he exhorted her to make her self Happy by setting him at Liberty. The *Heroine* rightly apprehended that *Rana*'s was only a forc'd Consent; and that her own Glory depended on an inviolable Fidelity to him. Yet she thought it not unlawful to play the Hypocrite, and deceive a Deceiver, who had robb'd her of her Husband by a Wile. She let the *Mogol* understand that she began to waver in her Resolution, and that Ambition had shaken her Constancy: That if her Vows did not bind her indispensably to *Rana*, she cou'd think herself happy in being *Sultaness* to so great a Prince. But

---

[13] In Greek mythology the Amazons were a nation of female warriors ruled by a queen. No man was permitted to dwell in their country, which was located on the south coast of the Black Sea. Male infants were sent to their fathers, the Gargareans, in a neighbouring land. The girls were trained in agriculture, hunting, and the art of war. According to the myths, Amazons invaded Greece, Syria, the Arabian Peninsula, Egypt, Libya, and the islands of the Aegean. Catrou continues his tendency to make analogies between classical myth or epic and Indian history by describing Padmani as an Amazon.

that she had sworn to her first Husband by all their Gods that she wou'd never be the Wife of another without an express Consent from his own Mouth: That the Emperor might chuse either to permit *Rana* to come to *Chitor*, or permit *Padmani* to goe and demand her Husband's Consent, in the Place of his Captivity. *Akebar* embrac'd the last Proposal, and consented that the Queen might come with a good Guard to pay her Husband a Visit.

A Castle in the Neighbourhood of *Agra* was *Rana*'s Prison. It's impossible to express the Impatience of *Akebar* for the Arrival of a Princess at his Capital, for whom he had been at so much Expence, and expos'd to so many Dangers. Couriers upon Couriers were dispatch'd to desire her not to defer her Departure. The *Mogol* sent her Presents every Hour, of Jewels, of Fruits, and of a mysterious kind of Nosegays, which are made use of in the East to express by matching of Flowers the Sentiments of the Heart. The Queen got ready her Equipage with all possible Speed. The most sumptuous *Pallanquin's* were prepar'd for her Journey. These are a kind of *Indian* Chaises, in which People of Quality are carry'd on the Shoulders of ten or a dozen Slaves. They are long enough to sleep in, as in a Litter. Those for the Men are open at top, but the Women's are close, and of a much larger Size. Four may conveniently fit in one of 'em, so that there's need of twenty Slaves to bear those in which the Princesses are carry'd.

Padmani shut up eight of the bravest of her Subjects in the two *Pallanquin's*, and enjoyn'd 'em into a profound Silence during their Journey.[14] For her own Part she remain'd at *Chitor*, and sent away the *Pallanquin's* with a good Guard. The Project was executed with so much Secrecy that the whole Town was deceiv'd. The People were all in Tears at the supposed Departure of their Princess, and follow'd the *Palanquins* in crowds out of the Town. Mean time *Padmani* keeping very private in her Palace, had the Pleasure to see the Sorrow of her People for their imaginary Loss.

---

[14] Manucci says that there was no one in the handsome palanquin that Padmani had prepared but three thousand Rajput horse accompanied it to Fatehpur Sikri, followed by numerous other closed palanquins as if each held a lady of state. When they approach the palace two men are put into the palanquin to liberate the Rana and lead him to waiting horses (*Storio do Mogor*, i. 127–8).

As soon as the Emperor was inform'd that the Princess was set out for *Agra*, he appointed several Persons to meet and compliment her. The Princesses first Eunuch who manag'd the Intrigue, and was shut up in the *Pallanquin*, in which the Princess was suppos'd to be, made Answers for her. Among other things, he let the Emperor know, in the Name of *Padmani*, that if she met with the least Interruption in her Journey; or was hindred from proceeding directly to her Husband, without going thro' the Capital; or even, if she was disturb'd in her Entertainment with *Rana*, that she was determin'd to stab her self with a Dagger which she had brought for that purpose, and held ready in her Hand for Fear of any Surprise. *Akebar* had not a Thought of making the least Opposition to the Princesses Will. He sent her Word, that she shou'd be at full Liberty to see *Rana*, to discourse him and bid him adieu.

The nearer the *Pallanquins* approach'd towards *Agra*, the more Courtiers were dispatched to wait on them. They were met by 'em at every Village, and still the Eunuch gave Answers to the Letters of *Akebar*. About half a days Journey from *Agra*, and three or four Leagues from the Castle where *Rana* was Prisoner, they met a magnificent Equipage which the Emperor had sent to receive the Princess. 'Twas compos'd of Elephants train'd to War,[15] of Camels, and several Squadrons which were to conduct *Padmani* to the Royal Palace, and supply the place of the *Rageputes* of her Guard, while her Husband took the way of *Chitor* with these. In fine, they arriv'd about Night-fall at the Place where *Rana* was Prisoner. The two *Pallanquins* only and some Officers of *Padmani's* Guard were permitted to enter the Castle. These Officers together with the *Bravos*, shut up in the *Pallanquins*, dispatch'd the Governor of the Castle, who first advanc'd to receive the Princess; Afterwards becoming Masters of the Guard, they quickly delivered *Rana* from his Imprisonment. They mounted him on a very fleet Horse; and as they had posted change enough on the Road, the *Raja* soon arriv'd at *Chitor* where he made *Padmani* all the Acknowledgments due to his Deliverer. Mean time *Akebar* was

---

[15] The description of the Mughal court at the end of the *General History* (1709) comments that five hundred of the Mughal emperor's elephants 'are another Article of his Forces, and an Ornament of his Palace' (344) and that they are 'equall train'd for Hunting or for Battle' (345).

waiting impatiently in a Garden for the Arrival of the Princess, When word was brought him that *Rana* had made his Escape; and that some arm'd Men had been conceal'd in the *Pallanquins* instead of *Padmani*, he immediately commanded the Messenger's Head to be struck off who first brought this News; but coming to himself a Moment after, he was contented to forbid him his Presence for ever. 'Pursue, pursue *Rana*', crys he; but *Rana* was got too far on his Road to be overtaken. As to the *Rageputes*, who had serv'd as Convoy to the *Pallanquins*, after having march'd all Night with great Expedition, They found themselves about Morning in the Territories of a *Raja*, and Friend to the Prince of *Chitor*, and at last got safe into their own Country. As soon as *Rana* was return'd to his Fortress, he wrote an insulting Letter to *Akebar*. He reproach'd him with Perfidiousness, and rally'd him on the ill Success of his Amours. He made him a Defyance likewise of coming a second Time to try his Fortune against the Cittadel of *Chitor*; he added that after having been baffled and outwitted by a Woman, he might very well expect to be overcome by an Army of *Rageputes*, who waited his Coming with Impatience. *Rana* did more than insult his Enemy by Letters. He erected in the Market Place of *Chitor* a Pillar, on which were ingraven these Words in the Language of the Country, *Never trust the Mogols who have once betray'd you.*

The behavior of *Rana*, and the Slights of the Princess *Padmani*, provok'd *Akebar* to such a Degree, that he was no longer Master of himself. Once more he assembl'd his Troops; he augmented his Artillery; he prepar'd Machines; in fine, he made such Provision for the Siege of *Chitor*, that he believ'd the taking of it Infallible. In this Assurance he surrounded the Place on every Side, he raised Platforms on which he planted his Engines. The Assaults were furious and were equally sustain'd. The *Mogol* was now no more that amorous Prince, who seem'd tender of the Lives of his Princesses People, but an Emperor outrag'd to the last degree, who came to revenge a personal Affront. The Two Principals were continually attentive, one to push the Siege, and the other to defeat it. *Rana* was continually upon the *Ramparts* where he encourag'd his Men and repair'd the Breaches. *Akebar* of his Side often mounted on the *Platforms*, and gave his Orders for forming the Attaques. One Day as *Akebar* was taking a View of the Place, from one of those *Platforms* almost equal in Heighth to the Walls of *Chitor,* he perceiv'd an Officer walking carelessly on the *Ramparts*; he took Aim with his *Fusee,*[16] and Shot the *Raja* Dead upon the Spot. *Akebar* had an Account about Two Days after, that he had Kill'd his Rival, that his Body was burnt in great Pomp, and that the generous *Padmani* according to the Custom of the *Ragepute* Princesses, had thrown herself into the Flames and mingled her Ashes with those of her Husbands.[17] *Chitor* still made some Resistance, but at last was forc'd to yield to the Valour and Fortune of *Akebar.*

This Relation which we find as well in *European* as in *Indian* Histories (says M. *Manouchi*) seems to have an Air of Fable invented to Amuse; and yet it has nothing of the Stile of those Romances which are commonly Written in the *Indies,* and are for the most part stuff'd with Discourses between Monkies, tales of other Animals, and Miracles of the Gods of the Country,[18] without the least Appearance of Reality. However, as this Adventure of *Akebar* and *Padmani* is not found in the Chronicle of the Empire, the Reader may give it what Credit he Pleases. As to the taking of *Chitor* and the Death of *Rana* they are incontestable Facts.

---

[16] Fusee: a light musket or firelock (*OED*). In Alexander Dow's account of Akbar's siege of Chitor, translated from Firishtah's chronicle, it is the town's governor, Jeimal (another version of Jai Mall, the Rana in Manucci or Jemal, the son of the Rana, in Bernier) who is killed by Akbar's deadly shot, while the Rana and his family have escaped to a safe place away from Chitor (*History of Hindostan* (1768), ii. 254).

[17] Padmani commits 'suttee', the custom of a widow burning herself on her husband's pyre or after his death. The name is thought to derive from the Sanskrit term *sati,* which means 'chaste wife' and which is also the name of a Hindu goddess. Akbar and his father, Humayan, took steps to restrain the practice and the first law passed by the British administration in India in 1829 was designed to abolish it. European accounts were fascinated by suttee, and, while they condemned it, also often celebrated the chastity and loyalty of Indian wives supposedly demonstrated by their willingness to become sati by contrast with European widows.

[18] The discourses between monkeys is presumably a reference to the *Ramayana,* in which the monkey general Hanuman, later revered as a god, is instrumental in restoring Sita to Rama; the tales of other animals invokes the *Pañcatantra* (of the same family of tales as the fable from Pilpay extracted in Part 1 of this anthology) in which a series of animal fables are used to debate the nature of good government and especially the role of the courtier; and the miracles of the Gods of the country are contained in the *Mahabharata, Harivamsa,* and *Puranas* as well as the Pali *Jatakas* (episodes in the Buddha's earlier lives).

From *Letters of the Right Honourable Lady M——y W——y M——e* (1763)

Lady Mary Wortley Montagu

Copy-text: vol. iii of the 1st edition (London, 1763)

Lady Mary Wortley Montagu (1689–1762) travelled to Istanbul in 1716 with her husband, Edward Wortley, and their infant son. Wortley had a tricky commission as ambassador to the Ottoman court, to try and broker a peace between the long-standing rival empires of Austria and Turkey. The family travelled via the courts of Hanover and Vienna, to Belgrade, Sophia, and Adrianople. In 1717 they arrived in the Ottoman capital.

During the second decade of the eighteenth century Lady Mary was at the height of her creative powers, which were clearly fostered by her encounters with the melting pot of eastern and western cultures in the Ottoman capital. She had experienced considerable success as a society hostess in London prior to her departure, a magnet for young political and literary minds (her circle included Alexander Pope, John Gay, and Baron John Hervey). Lady Mary's letters and the journal she later destroyed, written during her travels abroad, provided the basis for the collection of 'Embassy Letters' she prepared on her return to Britain in 1718. They are thus a document prepared for circulation, if not publication. She was to give the two-volume manuscript, accompanied by a preface from the celebrated feminist Mary Astell and an anonymous prefatory poem, to a Presbyterian minister, Benjamin Sowden, in 1761 as she passed through Rotterdam en route to England, aware that her death from cancer was not far off. He returned them to her daughter Lady Mary Bute after her mother's death on 21 August 1762. This manuscript was published by Becket and De Hont on 7 May 1763 and the letters were an immediate hit, resulting in a rapid second edition and a piracy in the same year with a second volume containing five alleged extra letters (in fact imitations).

Apparently Montagu wrote up her travel experiences between 1719 and 1724 from her journal records. She chose fourteen addressees, disguising them with initials (though most are identified today), only ten of whom did she actually write to from Turkey. She excluded many she had written to, including her father, William Congreve, and Frances Hewet. These letters no longer survive with the exception of one to Frances Hewet where the content is quite different from the letters she prepared for publication, being more homely and domestic. She shared out her material, avoiding duplication and tailoring letters to each addressee: her sister Lady Mar gets descriptions of costume, Alexander Pope literary discussions, the savant Enlightenment priest, Abbé de Conti, accounts of the Ottoman administration and classical learning. The 'letters' prove to be a cover for a travel treatise which challenges and rewrites those that have gone before, especially Paul Rycaut's *The Present State of the Ottoman Empire* (1668), Jean Dumont's *A New Voyage to the Levant* (1696), and Aaron Hill's *A Full and Just Account of the Present State of the Ottoman Empire* (1709).

The text given here is that of the first edition of the published text rather than the letters transcribed and edited by her into the two volumes she passed on to Sowden and which are available in the second of Robert Halsband's three-volume edition of *The Complete Letters of Lady Mary Wortley Montagu*, 3 vols. (Oxford: Clarendon Press, 1965-7). Halsband dates this letter as May 1718, written from Lady Mary's residence outside Istanbul in Pera to the countess of Bristol,

From Letters of Lady Mary Wortley Montagu

i.e. Elizabeth Felton, second wife of John Hervey, and close friend of Lady Mary.

Lady Mary had fallen victim to the smallpox in the British winter of 1715 at considerable cost to her celebrated beauty, and in March 1718, while her husband was away, Lady Mary had her young son inoculated against smallpox with a live vaccine following the Turkish practice. The smallpox matter was taken from a sufferer with a mild strain and administered by an old nurse in Istanbul. She chose at that point not to have her recently born daughter inoculated since the child's Armenian nurse did not have immunity. After her return, however, when a smallpox epidemic swept England in April 1721, she enlisted the help of the surgeon Charles Maitland and had the virus 'ingrafted' into her daughter. She and Princess Caroline became the leading advocates of the practice of inoculation in their circle to great effect. Lady Mary was widely acknowledged as the importer of the practice of inoculation into English society and accordingly fêted or vilified (some claimed that inoculation caused rather than prevented deaths). Her one identified contribution to the print war, 'A Plain Account of the Innoculating of the Small Pox by a Turkey Merchant' (*Flying Post*, 13 September 1722), was an attack on doctors who either refused to administer the smallpox or applying it in such large quantities on gashes cut in the skin (rather than the needle pinprick observed in Turkey) as to risk the lives of their patients. Mary Wortley Montagu advocated its administration by lay operatives, even women, and sensible domestic nursing care rather than excessive bleedings and treatments. In the matter of inoculation, Lady Mary champions folk knowledge and all-female circuits of information and action. The same principles guide many of her 'Turkish Embassy Letters' written by a woman to other women, providing inset narratives which illustrate her sense of the agency and authority women could secretly command in a culture habitually represented as only oppressive to women.

Lady Mary was fascinated throughout her life with stories. She was an avid novel reader, and a particular enthusiast for the oriental tale, producing her own manuscript variants such as the charming 'Sultan's Tale' (available in *Lady Mary*

Wortley Montagu: Romance Writings, ed. Isobel Grundy (Oxford: Clarendon Press, 1996). As with inoculation, she saw the absorption of elements of matter from the 'other' as a means of protecting and indeed strengthening the European body politic, and especially the place of women within it. In this letter, the inset story of a Catholic European lady who chooses marriage to her abductor-rapist over incarceration in a convent after her defloration, is a means of articulating her passionate commitment to a Whiggish concept of 'liberty' (freedom to self-determination within the political contingencies of the moment) and of attacking Catholic absolutism in Europe. Equally, she uses customs among the different populations living in and around Istanbul to challenge some of the securities and pieties of Eurocentrism. For example, she presents the practice of adoption among Turks, Greeks, and Armenians, as a more sure way of passing on one's estate than the systems of entailment in England that see distant and unknown relatives succeed to unearned wealth. This comment challenges the seventeenth- and eighteenth-century commonplace that oriental absolutism was a disincentive to a profitable economy. In 1603, Richard Knolles is one of the earliest of the many commentators who complained that 'the Great Sultan is so absolute a Lord of all things within the compass of his Empire, that all his Subjects and People, be they never so great, so call themselves his Slaves and not his Subjects; neither hath any man power over himself, much less is he Lord of the House wherein he dwelleth, or of the Land which he tilleth . . . .' (*The Turkish History* (1687; first pub. 1603), 982). However, Lady Mary is not free from all prejudice. Her republicanism was strictly autocratic and she reveals in this letter, as elsewhere, contempt for the labouring and urban working classes in Turkey, confirming prejudices about their propensity to lie and cheat.

For biographical information about Lady Mary's long and colourful life, see Isobel Grundy, *Lady Mary Wortley Montagu: Comet of the Enlightenment* (Oxford: Oxford University Press, 1999). There has been vigorous and prolific discussion of the relationship of Lady Mary's writings to what Edward Said terms 'Orientalism', the systematic privileging of West over East. For this debate and some of the most insightful contributions to it, see Srinivas Aravumudan, ch. 4 'Lady Mary in the Hammam', in his *Tropicopolitans: Colonialism and Agency, 1688–1804* (Durham, NC: Duke University Press, 1999); Meyda Yegenoglu, 'Supplementing the Orientalist Lack: European Ladies in the Harem', in her *Colonial Fantasies: Towards a Feminist Reading of Orientalism* (Cambridge: Cambridge University Press, 1998); and Lisa Lowe, 'Travel Narratives and Orientalism: Montagu and Montesquieu', in her *Critical Terrains: French and British Orientalisms* (Ithaca, NY, and London: Cornell University Press, 1991). On religious argument in the 'Turkish Embassy Letters', see Jane Shaw, 'Gender and the "Nature" of Religion: Lady Mary Wortley Montagu's Embassy Letters and their Place in Enlightenment Philosophy of Religion', *Bulletin of the John Rylands University Library of Manchester* 80/3 (1998): 129–45.

LETTER 42

To the Countess of—

I am now prepareing to leave Constantinople, and perhaps you will accuse me of hypocrisy, when I tell you, 'tis with regret; but as I am used to the air, and have learnt the language, I am easy here; and as much as I love travelling, I tremble at the inconveniencies attending so great a journey, with a numerous family, and a little infant hanging at the breast.[1] However, I endeavour, upon this occasion, to do as

---

[1] Lady Mary gave birth to a daughter, also called Mary, in January 1718. She was to become her mother's major correspondent during Lady Mary's long absence living and travelling in Europe between 1739 and 1762. The younger Mary married against her father's wishes, but enjoyed a much happier union than the obviously strained and difficult relationship between her parents. She married John Stuart, 3rd earl of Bute (1713–92), an impoverished Scottish aristocrat, in August 1736; his close friendship with the prince of Wales led to his elevation to the post of Prime Minister under George III in 1762. Lady Mary's son, Edward (1713–76), proved a constant trial to his parents despite sharing

I have hitherto done in all the odd turns of my life; turn them, if I can, to my diversion. In order to do this, I ramble every day, wrapped up in my *Ferige* and *Asmak*, about Constantinople, and amuse myself with seeing all that is curious in it. I know you will expect that this declaration should be followed with some account of what I have seen. But I am in no humour to copy what has been writ so often over. To what purpose should I tell you, that Constantinople is the antient Bizantium?[2] that 'tis at present the conquest of a race of people, supposed Scythians?[3] that there are five or six thousand mosques in it? that *Sancta Sophia* was founded by Justinian?[4] &c. I'll assure you 'tis not for want of learning, that I forbear writing all these bright things. I could also, with very little trouble, turn over *Knolles* and Sir *Paul Rycaut*, to give you a list of Turkish Emperors;[5] but I will not tell you

his mother's enthusiasm for things oriental (his collection of oriental tales were acquired by William Beckford); he constantly petitioned his parents for money, was forced to live abroad for long periods as a result of financial indiscretions, married unsuitably, was cut out of his father's will, and, after a chequered career in the army, converted to Islam.

[2] The name Byzantium appears to derive from the name of the Greek leader Byzas who, according to legend, captured the peninsula from pastoral Thracian tribes and built the city about 657 BC. In AD 196, having razed the town for opposing him in a civil war, the Roman Emperor Septimius Severus rebuilt it, naming it Augusta Antonina in honour of his son. In 330, when Constantine the Great dedicated the city as his capital, he called it New Rome.

[3] The Scythians were a nomadic people originally of Iranian stock who migrated from Central Asia to southern Russia in the 8th and 7th c. BC. The Scythians founded a powerful empire centred on the region now known as the Crimea and which at its height stretched from west Persia through Syria and Judaea to the borders of Egypt. They were eventually destroyed by the Sarmatians in the 2nd c. BC. In fact the term Ottoman, for the race which conquered Constantinople in 1453, is a dynastic appellation derived from Osman, the nomadic Turkman chief who founded both the dynasty and the empire. Both the Scythians and the Ottomans were originally nomadic tribes, admired for their horsemanship and military aggression. The confusion for a literary mind such as Lady Mary's may stem from the reference to Timur, another nomadic empire-builder but in fact a member of a Turkicized Barlas tribe, a Mongol sub-group that had settled in Transoxania (now roughly corresponding to Uzbekistan), as a Scythian in Christopher Marlowe's *Tamburlaine the Great* (1590). Timur fought with and subdued the Ottoman Emperor Bayazid I in the mid-14th c.

[4] Sancta Sophia: Hagia Sophia, the cathedral built at Constantinople under the direction of the Byzantine Emperor Justinian I. The structure, a domed basilica, was completed in AD 537. The architects were Anthemius of Tralles and Isidore of Miletus.

[5] Richard Knolles's *Generall Historie of the Turks* appeared in 1603, consisting of detailed accounts of the lives of the Ottoman emperors. Paul Rycaut produced a continuation, *The History of the Turkish Empire from the Year 1623 to the Year 1677* in 1680, and a final volume written by Rycaut entitled *The History of the Turks beginning with the Year 1679* appeared in 1700. Rycaut was a career diplomat attached to the Levant company who served as ambassador to Smyrna.

From Letters of Lady Mary Wortley Montagu

what you may find in every author that has writ of this country. I am more inclined, out of a true female spirit of contradiction, to tell you the falsehood of a great part of what you find in authors; as for example, in the admirable Mr. *Hill*, who so gravely asserts, that he saw in *Sancta Sophia*, a sweating pilar, very balsamic for disordered heads. There is not the least tradition of any such matter; and I suppose it was revealed to him in vision, during his wonderful stay in the Egyptian Catacombs; for I am sure he never heard of any such miracle here.[6] 'Tis also very pleasant to observe how tenderly he and all his brethren voyage-writers, lament the miserable confinement of the Turkish ladies,[7] who are perhaps more free than any ladies in the universe, and are the only women in the world, that lead a life of uninterrupted pleasure, exempt from cares, their whole time being spent in visiting, bathing, or the agreeable amusement of spending money and inventing new fashions. A husband would be thought mad that exacted any degree of oeconomy from his wife, whose expences are no way limited but by her fancy. 'Tis his business to get money, and hers to spend it; and this noble prerogative extends itself to the very meanest of the sex. Here is a fellow that carries embroidered handkerchiefs upon his back to sell. And as miserable a figure as you may suppose such a mean dealer; yet I'll assure you, his wife scorns to wear any thing less than cloth of gold; has her ermine furs, and a very handsome set of jewels for her head. 'Tis true, they have no places but the bagnios, and these can only be seen by their own sex; however, that is a diversion they take great pleasure in.

[6] Aaron Hill, *A Full and Just Account of the Present State of the Ottoman Empire* (1709). Hill had travelled as a teenager with the embassy of Heneage Finch to Istanbul and his is an apprentice work. Lady Mary may have disliked him also as the leader of a circle of largely Tory wits named the Hillarians. He writes of the sweating column (138) and the Egyptian catacombs (263–71). Hill tends to collect his insights from rumour and his reading rather than empirical evidence.
[7] In ch. 14, 'Of the Turkish Women in General', in his *Full and Just Account*, Aaron Hill concludes his account of the confinement of Turkish women as follows: ' 'TIS an awful *Fear and Duty*, that obliges them contentedly to live *at Home*, without the smallest Power in Domestick matters, shut up *together* in a long Appartment, divided *like our Hospitals* for several Beds, where free from *Envy, Pride* or *Jealousy*, they *Eat, Drink*, and *Work together*, Guarded by the Watchful Observation of *Industrious Eunuchs*, and excluded from the Society of *Men*, above Ten Years Old, never Stirring from their Houses, nor making Visits to their Neighbours, but all entirely bent to please by *turns* the Wandring will of their Respected Husband' (109–10). Hill's description is typical of accounts of Turkey by European men.

I was, three days ago, at one of the finest in the town, and had the opportunity of seeing a Turkish bride received there, and all the ceremony used on that occasion, which made me recollect the *Epithalamium* of *Helen*, by *Theocritus*;[8] and it seems to me, that the same customs have continued ever since. All the she friends, relations and acquaintance of the two families, newly allied, meet at the bagnio; several others go, out of curiosity, and I believe there were that day two hundred women. Those that were, or had been married, placed themselves about the rooms, on the marble sofas; but the virgins very hastily threw off their cloaths, and appeared without other ornament or covering, than their own long hair braided with pearl or ribbon. Two of them met the bride at the door, conducted by her mother and another grave relation. She was a beautiful maid of about seventeen, very richly dressed, and shining with jewels, but was presently reduced to the state of nature. Two others filled silver gilt pots with perfume, and began the procession, the rest following in pairs, to the number of thirty. The leaders sung an *Epithalamium*, answered by the others in chorus, and the two last led the fair bride, her eyes fixed on the ground, with a charming affectation of modesty. In this order they marched round the three large rooms of the Bagnio. 'Tis not easy to represent to you the beauty of this sight, most of them being well proportioned and white skin'd; all of them perfectly smooth, and polished by the frequent use of bathing. After having made their *tour*, the bride was again led to every matron round the rooms, who saluted her with a compliment and a present, some of jewels, others of pieces of stuff, handkerchiefs, or little gallantries of that nature, which she thanked them for, by kissing their hands. I was very well pleased with having seen this ceremony; and you may believe me, that the Turkish ladies have, at least, as much wit and civility, nay liberty, as among us. 'Tis true, the same customs that give them so many opportunities of gratifying their evil inclinations (if they have any) also put it very fully in the power of their husbands to revenge themselves, if they are discovered; and I do not doubt but they suffer sometimes for their indiscretions in a very severe manner. About two months ago, there

[8] An epithalamium is a poem written to celebrate a wedding. Here the reference is to Theocritus' (fl. *c*.270 BC) *Idylls*.

was found at day-break, not very far from my house, the bleeding body of a young woman, naked, only wrapp'd in a coarse sheet, with two wounds of a knife, one in her side, and another in her breast. She was not quite cold, and was so surprisingly beautiful, that there were very few men in Pera, that did not go to look upon her; but it was not possible for any body to know her, no woman's face being known. She was supposed to have been brought, in the dead of night, from the Constantinople side, and laid there.[9] Very little inquiry was made about the murderer, and the corpse was privately buried without noise. Murder is never pursued by the King's officers, as with us. 'Tis the business of the next relations to revenge the dead person; and if they like better to compound the matter for money (as they generally do) there is no more said of it. One would imagine this defect in their government, should make such tragedies very frequent, yet they are extremely rare; which is enough to prove the people not naturally cruel. Neither do I think, in many other particulars, they deserve the barbarous character we give them. I am well acquainted with a Christian woman of quality, who made it her choice to live with a Turkish husband, and is a very agreeable sensible lady. Her story is so extraordinary, I cannot forbear relating it; but I promise you it shall be in as few words as I can possibly express it.

She is a Spaniard, and was at Naples with her family, when that kingdom was part of the Spanish dominion.[10] Coming from thence in a *Feloucca*, accompanied by her brother, they were attacked by the Turkish Admiral,[11] boarded and taken. —And now how shall I modestly tell you the rest of her adventure? The same accident happened to her, that happen'd to the fair Lucretia so many years

[9] Istanbul is a walled sea-bordered city. Across the Golden Horn lies the region of Galata. From the 10th c. onward, Galata was an enclave for foreign traders. After the Ottomans took the city in 1453, all foreigners who were not citizens of the empire were restricted to this quarter, which housed embassies, schools, churches, and hospitals for the various nationalities. Eventually Galata became too crowded, and extended into the area of Pera. This is where Lady Mary's family resided during their stay at the Ottoman capital.

[10] The Spanish Habsburgs governed Naples from 1503 to 1704. It was conquered by Austria in 1707 and in 1734 became, under the Spanish Bourbons, the capital of an independent kingdom of Sicily.

[11] Halsband speculates that this is Ibrahim Pasha, Lord Admiral from 1706 to 1709 and again from February 1717 to February 1718. He was succeeded by Suleyman Kodja, who held office until 1721.

before her.[12] But she was too good a Christian to kill herself, as that Heathenish Roman did. The Admiral was so much charmed with the beauty, and *long-suffering* of the fair captive, that, as his first compliment, he gave immediate liberty to her brother and attendants, who made haste to Spain, and in a few months sent the sum of four thousand pound sterling, as a ransom for his sister. The Turk took the money, which he presented to her, and told her she was at liberty. But the lady very discreetly weighed the different treatment she was likely to find in her native country. Her relations (as the kindest thing they could do for her in her present circumstances) would certainly confine her to a nunnery for the rest of her days. —Her Infidel lover was very handsome, very tender, very fond of her, and lavished at her feet all the Turkish magnificence. She answered him very resolutely, that her liberty was not so precious to her as her honour, that he could no way restore that but by marrying her, and she therefore desired him to accept the ransom as her portion, and give her the satisfaction of knowing that no man could boast of her favours without being her husband. The admiral was transported at this kind offer, and sent back the money to her relations, saying he was too happy in her possession. He married her, and never took any other wife,[13] and (as she says herself) she never had reason to repent the choice she made. He left her some years after, one of the richest widows in Constantinople. But there is no remaining honourably a single woman, and that consideration has obliged her to marry the present Capitan Bassa (i.e. Admiral) his successor. —— I am afraid that you will think my friend fell in love with her ravisher; but I am willing to take her word for it, that she acted wholly on principles of honour, tho' I think

[12] In the Roman tradition, Lucretia, wife of the nobleman Lucius Tarquinius Collatinus, was raped in 509 BC by Sextus Tarquinius, son of Lucius Tarquinius Superbus, the tyrannical Etruscan king of Rome. After exacting an oath of vengeance against the Tarquins from her father and her husband, she stabbed herself to death. Lucius Junius Brutus then led a rebellion that drove the Tarquins from Rome and founded the Republic.

[13] Paul Rycaut comments that 'the *Turks* of themselves, though they have the liberty of *Polygame*, and freer use of divers Women allowed them by the Law, than the severity of the Christian Religion doth permit, are yet observed to be less fruitful in Children, than those who confine themselves to the chaste embraces of one Wife' (*The Present State of the Ottoman Empire* (1668), 81). Muslim men are entitled to take up to four wives and any number of concubines.

she might be reasonably touched at his generosity, which is often found amongst the Turks of rank.

'Tis a degree of generosity to tell the truth, and 'tis very rare that any Turk will assert a solemn falsehood. I don't speak of the lowest sort; for as there is a great deal of ignorance, there is very little virtue amongst them; and false witnesses are cheaper than in Christendom, those wretches not being punished (even when they are publickly detected) with the rigour they ought to be.

Now I am speaking of their law, I don't know, whether I have ever mentioned to you one custom peculiar to their country, I mean, *adoption*, very common among the Turks, and yet more amongst the Greeks and Armenians. Not having it in their power to give their estates to a friend or distant relation, to avoid its falling into the Grand Signior's treasury, when they are not likely to have any children of their own, they chuse some pretty child of either sex, amongst the meanest people, and carry the child and its parents before the *Cadi*, and there declare they receive it for the heir. The parents, at the same time, renounce all future claim to it; a writing is drawn and witnessed, and a child thus adopted, cannot be disinherited. Yet I have seen some common beggars, that have refused to part with their children in this manner, to some of the richest among the Greeks; (so powerful is the instinctive affection that is natural to parents!) though the adopting fathers are generally very tender to these *children of their souls*, as they call them. I own this custom pleases me much better than our absurd one of following our name. Methinks 'tis much more reasonable to make happy and rich, an infant whom I educate after my own manner, *brought up* (in the Turkish phrase) *upon my knees*, and who has learnt to look upon me with a filial respect, than to give an estate to a creature without other merit or relation to me than that of a few letters. Yet this is an absurdity we see frequently practised. —Now I have mentioned the Armenians, perhaps it will be agreeable to tell you something of that nation, with which I am sure you are utterly unacquainted. I will not trouble you with the geographical account of the situation of their country, which you may see in the maps; or a relation of their antient greatness, which you may read in the Roman History. They were, as they say, converted to the Christian religion by St. *Gregory*, and are perhaps the devoutest Christians in the whole world.[14] The chief precepts of their priests enjoin the strict keeping of their Lents, which are, at least, seven months in every year, and are not to be dispensed with on the most emergent necessity; no occasion whatever can excuse them if they touch any thing more than mere herbs or roots (without oil) and plain dry bread. That is their constant diet. —Mr. W[ortle]y has one of his interpreters of this nation, and the poor fellow was brought so low by the severity of his fasts, that his life was despaired of. Yet neither his master's commands, nor the doctors entreaties (who declared nothing else could save his life) were powerful enough to prevail with him to take two or three spoonfuls of broth. Excepting this, which may rather be called a custom, than an article of faith, I see very little in their religion different from ours. 'Tis true, they seem to incline very much to Mr. *Whiston*'s doctrine;[15] neither do I think the Greek church very distant from it, since 'tis certain, the Holy Spirit's proceeding *only* from the Father, is making a plain subordination in the Son. —But the Armenians have no notion of *Transubstantiation*, whatever account Sir *Paul Rycaut* gives of them (which account I am apt to believe was designed to compliment our court in 1679)[16] and they have a great horror for those amongst them that change to the Roman religion. What is most extraordinary in their customs, is their matrimony; a ceremony, I believe, unparallel'd all over the world. They are always promised very young; but the espoused never see one another, till three days after their marriage. The bride is carried to church with a cap on her head, in the fashion of a large trencher, and over it a red silken veil, which covers her all over to her feet. The priest asks the bridegroom whether he is contented to marry that woman, *be she deaf, be she blind?* These are the

[14] Gregory (240–332) converted the Armenian King Tiridates around AD 300. Armenia lost its autonomy in the 14th c. and its territories fell under Ottoman or Persian rule. Armenians were a significant Indo-European minority in Istanbul with a thriving independent community.

[15] William Whiston supported the Arian doctrine that denied that Christ's body was not of the same essence or substance as that of God.

[16] Paul Rycaut paralleled Armenians and Catholics in their belief in transubstantiation in an account of the Armenian and Greek Churches written at the command of Charles II (*The Present State of the Greek and Armenian Churches* (1670), 433). Lady Mary interprets Rycaut as 'complimenting' the diplomatic shunning of public Catholicism on the part of Charles II in the midst of anxiety about Catholic conspiracy in England in the late 1670s which led to the Exclusion Crisis of 1681, an attempt to exclude Charles's Catholic brother, James duke of York, from the succession.

literal words; to which having answered *yes*, she is led home to his house, accompanied with all the friends and relations on both sides, singing and dancing, and is placed on a cushion in the corner of the sofa; but her veil is never lifted up, not even by her husband. There is something so odd and monstrous in these ways, that I could not believe them till I had inquired of several Armenians myself, who all assured me of the truth of them, particularly one young fellow who wept when he spoke of it, being promised by his mother to a girl that he must marry in this manner, tho' he protested to me, he had rather die than submit to this slavery, having already figured his bride to himself, with all the deformities in nature. —I fancy, I see you bless yourself at this terrible relation. I cannot conclude my letter with a more surprising story, yet 'tis as rigorously true, as that I am,

Dear sister,[17]
Yours, &c. &c.

---

[17] Two lines scored out in the manuscript version of this letter (and hence not appearing in print) make it clear that Lady Mary's sister, Lady Frances Mar (1690–1761), was not the addressee of this letter when drafted. However, Lady Mary seems to have decided to make her the addressee in scoring out the sentences addressed to 'Your Ladyship'. This may be an oblique reference to her sister's own unhappy marital situation. In apparent reaction to Mary's elopement with Edward Wortley in the summer of 1713, her father married off her sister in July 1714 to an ageing Jacobite peer (John Erskine, earl of Mar); Frances lived much of her life abroad with him in exile in great unhappiness over their union. This letter is full of discussion of customs of marriage among the different populations in the Ottoman capital and Lady Mary no doubt saw parallels betweeen Armenian marriages and her sister's unhappy fate. In any case, the drift is to suggest that Turkish Muslim marriage arrangements afford women more liberty and autonomy than those offered in Catholic Christian cultures.

4

LETTER FICTIONS

The Eight Volumes of Letters Writ by a Turkish Spy (1687–1694)

Giovanni Paolo Marana

Copy-text: 1st edition of the eight volumes complete (London, 1694)

The six hundred letters in eight volumes supposedly written by an Arabian living in Paris from 1637 to 1682 to a number of correspondents, the majority functionaries at the Ottoman Porte, have a complex and enigmatic publication history which leaves their authorship in some doubt. There is no confusion that a Genoese journalist named Giovanni Paolo Marana (1642–93) produced the letters which make up the first volume published in English translation in 1687. This volume was composed of letters found in four slim volumes (1684, 1685, and 1686 in Paris, and a fourth at Amsterdam in 1688). They were translated by the hack writer William Bradshaw (fl. 1700) into English under the supervision of an 'editor', Robert Midgley (1655–1723), who owned the copyright of the work. The remaining seven volumes appeared first in English between 1691 and 1694 with a preface to the second volume reprinting a letter from a Daniel Saltmarsh (of whom we have no other record) which claims to have discovered an Italian edition from which the text is purportedly translated (no such edition has since been uncovered). The earliest French edition of the last seven volumes (with the first) appeared in Cologne in 1696–7 in four volumes and asserts that it is a translation from the English. Bradshaw and/or Midgley are likely contenders; William McBurney suggests a bookseller named Hindmarsh, from whom the name Saltmarsh is cryptically derived ('The Authorship of *The Turkish Spy*', *PMLA* 72 (1857): 915–35). The Tory hack Delariver Manley claimed that her father, a Royalist cavalier named Roger Manley, was the 'genuine author of the first volume of that admired and successful work' (*The Adventures of Rivella*, ed. Katherine Zelinsky (Peterborough, Ont.: Broadview Press, 1999), 51). However, the consistency of voice, preoccupations, and narrative across all eight volumes leads most readers to view it as the work of a single pen and the most likely candidate remains Marana, who may have had difficulty in getting the later volumes published in France and turned to England to secure their continuing appearance (at least until his death in 1693).

Whoever wrote the letters, they had an abiding popularity through the eighteenth century and had gone into fifteen complete editions by 1801, after which point (and the decline in the vogue for epistolary spy narrative which *The Turkish Spy* inaugurated) they disappear from literary history. Daniel Defoe was an admirer, commenting in a letter to his employer, the Tory minister Robert Harley in 1704 that the letters might serve as a model for the spy network Defoe was charged to establish across the British Isles (*The Letters of Daniel Defoe*, ed. George Harris Healey (Oxford: Clarendon Press, 1955), 38), and producing his own *A Continuation of Letters Written by a Turkish Spy at Paris* in 1718.

Part of the popularity of the Turkish spy in Europe may have lain in the compendious, encyclopedic nature of the volumes, which provide a form of popular European history for its readers. For English readers they provide a window into the long reign of Louis XIV, always a figure of both threat and fascination for a minor Protestant power across the channel. Mahmut's letters cover the period in France from the last years of the Regency of Anne of Austria and Cardinal Richelieu through the long reign of Louis XIV under the influence of Cardinal Mazarin and after 1661 without a first minister. This account, along with others concerning the Hapsburg empire,

From *Letters Writ by a Turkish Spy*

Italian states, England, Sweden, as well as the Ottoman empire, are held together by a conceit of a life led in disguise, which is largely uneventful and can be swiftly summarized. In the course of the eight volumes which take Mahmut from the age of 28 when he first arrives in Paris to his early seventies his cover is nearly blown when he encounters his old Christian slave master at Notre Dame; he renews his acquaintance and passion for the lovely Greek Lady Daria; he is imprisoned in the Bastille; he loses a box of letters; he is reunited with his mother and cousin Isouf in Paris; he is suspected of being of the prince of Condé's party and has his apartments searched; he is attacked on the street and kills his attacker to discover later that the assailant was Daria's husband driven by jealousy; he falls prey to the treachery of his cousin Solyman, who joins with his enemies at the seraglio in Istanbul to try and discredit him; he grieves the death of his mother just a day after her wedding to his Jewish ally in Paris; and he closes the sequence in fear of his life with the discovery of the probable murder of Nathan ben Saddi, his fellow spy in Vienna. At several intervals, his hopes are raised of a likely recall from a posting which has brought him nothing but misery, but they all come to nothing. His spying activities are in the main general rather than particular, although he does for several years employ the services of a dwarf named Osmin who can hide under tables and sneak into chambers to read private papers.

One attraction of the letters probably lies in the well-developed persona of the spy himself. A Cartesian rationalist yet still attracted by theories of transmigration, always questioning and speculating at the same time as he displays a paranoid fear of discovery of his own secret mission, Mahmut holds his reader's attention throughout. The letters extracted here are designed to show the range of Mahmut's correspondence. I include the opening and closing letters that set up Mahmut's persona and leave his ultimate fate an enigma, and two letters from the third volume, the first an example of his political activity in Paris which illustrates the kind of private/insurrectionary history that is the trademark of the 'spy' informant, and the second an example of his interest in the genre of travel literature which points to the generic hybridity of the new mode of 'reverse ethnography' he introduces. I also provide here Marana's preface which illustrates the carefully developed context of the letters' discovery and circulation. Mahmut's letter to his brother from the third volume also provides an interesting example of a fictional letter which establishes a productive contrast between two oriental cultures, the Ottoman world to which Mahmut reports and the Mughal state about which his brother, Pestelihali, has written.

Although Mahmut's correspondence is the opening salvo in a succession of writings which deploy the voice of a foreign informant to produce an Enlightenment perspective of curiosity and alienation about the familiar world of European politics and manners, he is also unusual in that his voice is *not* that of a disinterested party. The representation of Mahmut feeds into anxiety in Europe about the proximity and power of Muslim governments (for the English in North Africa, the Austrians on their very border, and the French in mainland Europe). As the century progressed, that threat waned and by the late seventeenth century with the publication of all eight volumes, Turkish expansionism appeared to have been halted with the defeat of Ottoman forces at Vienna in 1683 (Mahmut's letters stop just one year before this event). Accordingly, through the course of his letters (their publication beginning one year after the defeat at Vienna), Mahmut's incendiary political purpose becomes less apparent and he is figured less as a devoted agent of the Ottoman Porte—contemptuous, critical, and mocking of his adopted culture in Paris—and more as a mediating figure who makes connections between the speculative philosophical traditions of West and East and who finds himself in a strategically advantageous position to make illuminating contrasts between a variety of cultures.

The *Letters Writ by a Turkish Spy* have received little critical attention to date. See, for further information, the introduction to the only modern anthology of the letters, *Letters Writ by a Turkish Spy*, ed. Arthur Weitzman (London: Routledge & Kegan Paul, 1970) and my own reading of the work in *Fabulous Orients*.

From *Letters Writ by a Turkish Spy*

I here offer you a Book written by a *Turk*, whose Manner is as instructive and delightful, as the Manner of finding it was strange and surprizing.

I do not doubt but you would know where 'twas written; and perhaps, whether the Author be living; and whether you must expect a *Romance* or a *real History*. Here then in short, what will fully satisfie you.

The Curiosity of seeing *Paris*, made a Man of *Letters* leave *Italy* in the Year 1682; where being arrived, he found such Diversions, as caused his stay longer than he intended.

Scarce had he been Two Months in *Paris*, when, by changing his Lodging, he discovered, by meer chance, in a Corner of his Chamber, a great heap of Papers; which seem'd more spoil'd by Dust than time.

He was at first surprized to see nothing but barbarous Characters, and was upon the Point of leaving them without any further search, if a *Latin* Sentence, which he perceived on the top of a Leaf, had not retained him:

Ubi amator, non laboratur; & si
Laboratur, labor amatur[1]

The Surprize of the *Italian* was yet greater, when after having considered these Characters with more Attention, he found them to be *Arabick*; which Language was not altogether unknown to him, which made him look narrowlier into them, where he found, That they treated of Affairs of State: That they contained Relations of War and Peace; and discoursed, not only of the Affairs of *France*, but those of all *Christendom*, till the Year 1682.

The curious *Italian* was in no small Impatience, to know how, and where these *Memorials* had been writ, and by what adventure they came to lie so neglected in a Corner of his Chamber. But, before he further informed himself, he thought it expedient, to transport these Manuscripts into another House, as a place of greater Security.

He afterwards questioned his Landlord with great Precaution, concerning the Papers, and he inform'd him even to the least Circumstances.

---

[1] From St Augustine, *De Bono Viduitatis* 21.26 'In quod amatur, aut non laboratur aut et labor amatur' (Marana gives the translation later in this preface). With thanks to Professor Oliver O'Donovan, Christ Church College, Oxford University.

He told him, That a Stranger, who said he was a Native of *Moldavia*,[2] habited like an *Ecclesiastick*, greatly Studious, of small Stature, of a very course Countenance, but of surprizing Goodness of Life, had lived long at his House. That he came to lodge there in the Year 1664, and had staid Eighteen Years with him; that being gone abroad one day, he returned no more, and they had no certain News of him since. He was about Seventy Years old, had left Manuscripts, that no Body understood, and some Moneys, which was an Argument, that his Departure was not premeditated.

He added, That he had always a Lamp Day and Night burning in his Chamber; had but few Moveables, only some Books, a small Tome of St. *Austin, Tacitus,* and the *Alcoran* with the Picture of *Massaniello,* whom he praised very much, calling him the *Moses* of *Naples*.[3] He said further, That this Stranger's greatest Friend, and whom he saw often, was a Man which most People took for a Saint, some for a *Jew,* and others suspected to be a *Turk*. According to the Landlord's Report, he came to Paris in the Year 1637, being then but Twenty eight Years of Age. At first he had lodg'd with a *Flemming*;[4] he went oft to Court; Moneys never fail'd him; he had Friends, and passed for very Learned. As for his End, this Man thinks he died miserably; it being suspected that he had been thrown into the River.

[2] Moldavia, although nominally an independent territory, was under the sway of the Ottomans in the 17th and 18th c. and Christian Moldavians of high rank lived in a manner very similar to Ottoman Turks which makes Mahmut's disguise particularly effective. Marana may have also chosen this disguise because his native culture, Genoa, had founded commercial outposts in the 14th c. which made possible the first connections with old Moldavia, known as Bassarabia.

[3] St Austin is St Augustine of Hippo (354–430), and the work most likely his *Confessions* which are the foundation of medieval and modern Christian thought. Apart from providing an acquaintance for the Arabian with the dominant strain of western Christian thought, Augustine's writings may also be seen as attractive to him because of their articulation of divine predestination (which was seen as a common link between Islam and Christianity). Tacitus is Publius (or Gaius) Cornelius Tacitus (56–120), Roman orator and public official, recognized as the greatest historian (as well as outstanding prose stylist) in Latin. His best-known works are the *Germania*, describing the Germanic tribes, the *Historiae*, concerning the Roman empire from 69 to 96, and the *Annals*, dealing with the empire in the period 14–68. Massaniello is Tommaso Aniello (1620–47), a Neapolitan fisherman who led an insurrection in Naples against the nobility when they sought to raise tribute money to the Spanish through a tax on fruit; when Massaniello urged the slaughter of the noblemen in a drunken outburst he was murdered by an assassin hired by his antagonists. [4] Flemming, i.e. someone from Flanders, Belgium.

From *Letters Writ by a Turkish Spy*

This *Italian* being sufficiently instructed by what he had heard, applied himself to the Study of the *Arabian* Language; and as he had already some Knowledge in it, he quickly learned enough to translate these Manuscripts, which he undertook a while after; and he examined with care the Truth of what the *Moldavian* had writ; confronting the Events he met, with the Histories of those Times; and to succeed the better, searched the most approved *Memorials*, having had Access into the Cabinets of Princes and their Ministers.

These Letters contain the most considerable Intrigues of the Court of *France*, and the most remarkable Transactions of *Christendom*, which have been sent to several Officers of the *Ottoman* Court.

By these may be known the Perspicacity of this Agent of the *Turks*; and by him the Prudence of those that command in that Nation, who chose (the better to penetrate into the Affairs of *Christians*) a Man, who could not be suspected by his Exterior; who was deform'd, but prudent and advised; and for the better concealing him, destined his ordinary Abode in one of the greatest and most peopled Cities of *Europe*.

During his being at *Paris*, which was Forty Five Years, he has been Eye-witness of many great Changes; has seen the Death of Two great Ministers of State;[5] has seen that Kingdom involved in War, without and within.[6] He was scarce landed in *Paris*, but he was Witness to the birth of a King, who surpasses those that preceded him; in a time, when the Queen's Barrenness, caused the King, her Husband, to despair of ever having a Son that should succeed him.[7]

[5] Two great Ministers of State: Cardinal Richelieu, Armand du Plessis (1585–1642) and Cardinal Jules Mazarin (1602–61). Richelieu served with the Queen Mother before becoming first minister of Louis XIII in 1628 and leading a campaign against the Protestants in France. He concentrated power in the royal government and extended the frontiers of France by opposing Spanish interests, a policy which led him into alliances with German Protestant states. He was also a patron of the arts and instrumental in founding the French Academy in 1634–5. Mazarin served under Richelieu and then succeeded him as first minister in 1642, remaining in the post until his death in 1661, after which point Louis XIV chose to rule without a first minister. He was responsible for selecting and training administrators who established Louis XIV's absolutist reign and was a patron of the opera and letters.

[6] War, without and within: Louis XIV was at war with the Spanish Netherlands and the Dutch Republic in the early part of his reign to 1679. The years 1648–53 saw a period of civil insurrection during the minority of Louis XIV known as the 'Fronde', led by Condé, the king's uncle.

[7] Louis XIV was born in 1638, the son of Louis XIII and Anne of Austria, who married in 1615.

During the Course of so many Years, he hath seen Cities Revolt, and return again to the Obedience of their Sovereign; Princes of the Blood, make War against their King; and Queen *Mary de Medicis*, Wife, Mother, and Mother in Law to some of the greatest Kings in *Europe*, die in Exile in *Cologne*.[8]

He speaks frankly of the Princes of *Christendom*, and explains his Sentiments with Liberty. He saith, The *Emperor*[9] commands Princes, the King of *Spain* Men, and the King of *France* sees Men, and even Kings, obey his Orders. He adds, That the First commands and prays, the Second sees oft times more effected than he commanded, and that the Third commands many brave Soldiers, and is well nigh obey'd by Crown'd Heads. There appears no Hate or Animosity in him, in what he writes against the *Pope*. In discoursing of the *Emperor* and King of *Spain*, he says, That both of them having Provinces of such vast Extent, they are not much concerned at the Losses they sustain.

He believed that *England* was more powerful than the Empire, and *Spain* at Sea. He apprehended more the Counsels of the *Republick* of *Venice*, than their Arms. He magnifies what passed in the Wars of *Candy*, which the *Venetians* supported with so much Bravery against the Forces of the *Ottoman* Empire.[10] The *Genoeses* with him are perfect *Chymists*. He speaks of the last Plague, and last War that this

[8] Maria de Médicis (1573–1642) was queen consort of Henri IV, first Bourbon king (reigned 1589–1610), and their first son born in 1601 became Louis XIII. Her daughter, Henrietta Maria, married Charles I of England. She served as Regent during the latter's minority from 1610 to 1614 but her previous alliance with Richelieu turned sour when the latter sought alliances in Protestant Europe against the Spanish. When she demanded Richelieu's removal from office in 1630, Louis XIII banished her and she took up residence in the Spanish Netherlands where she died destitute in 1642.

[9] The Emperor refers to the Holy Roman Emperor, then a Habsburg. The Holy Roman Emperor was crowned by the Pope and his territories at this stage were largely Germanic with some claims in Italy. Between 1618 and 1648 the Holy Roman Empire was embroiled in the Thirty Years War, begun in Bohemia when the Protestants refused to accept the Catholic Ferdinand II as emperor. England, Holland, Denmark, and eventually France defended the Protestant cause and the war virtually ruined the Holy Roman Empire. In 1648 Ferdinand III brought the war to a conclusion with the Peace of Westphalia, leaving France dominant in Europe thanks to Cardinal Richelieu's statesmanship over the conflict.

[10] Always a rival with Marana's native land, Genoa, Venice was in decline by the early 16th c. when new trade routes to the East meant they lost their monopoly over European access to oriental trade. The Ottoman Sultan Ibrahim (1640–8) appointed Semin Mehmet Pasa as grand vizier in 1646 who embarked on an effort to capture Crete from Venice, resulting in a long and debilitating siege of the island's capital, Candia. The conflict was not resolved until a peace was agreed in 1669 and Venice evacuated the island in return for restoration of trade privileges with the Ottoman empire.

From *Letters Writ by a Turkish Spy*

Commonwealth hath been afflicted with; he touches something of the late Conspiracy against this State by *Raggi* and *Torne*; and to shew, that he understood their History, he says something of *Vacchero* and *Baldi*.[11]

Thou wilt see, Reader, by the Progress of the Work, what this secret Envoy of the *Ottoman Port*, thought of the other Princes of *Italy*, and those of the *North*; and I have drawn his Picture, because thou maist understand better what I give thee of him.[12]

This *Arabian* (for he declares himself in his Writings, to have been of that Nation) having been taken and made a Slave by the *Christians*, was brought into *Sicily*, where he applied himself to Learning.[13] He studied *Logick* in his Captivity, and applied himself much to *History*; he overcame them by suffering with Patience the Blows of his Master, who often beat him for endeavouring to acquire those Lights, which this Brute had not. And finally, after much Labour, great Assiduity, and long Watchings, he came, as he writes himself, to understand *Greek* and *Latin* Authors; he had Commerce afterwards with the best Masters; and during his sojourning in the *French* Court, he joined Experience to the Knowledge he had acquired.

He explains himself neatly, and speaks of Things with great Frankness. His Style shews a great Liberty of Spirit, and never Passion; and if it appear that he accommodates himself to the Fashion of the Court, one may see that it is not out of a design to please, but that he wisely conforms himself sometimes to the *Geniuses* of Nations.

[11] Letter 21, bk. 1, vol. i gives an account of conspiracies by the Italian nobility (especially of Naples and Milan) to impose Spanish rule on the republic of Genoa in 1638. Gio Paolo Balbi led an initiative to transfer rule of Genoa to France in the 1630s to escape Spanish influence. After 1647 he was living in Amsterdam, Venice, and Bergamo, always pursued by the Genoese authorities. From the 1630s, waves of plague were troubling Italian cities. It struck Genoa with particular ferocity between 1656 and 1657, wiping out up to half its population. Mahmut has a Jewish informant in Genoa named Adonai. The reference to the Genoese as 'perfect chemists' is a metaphor; like alchemists, the Genoese turn base metal into gold, that is, they turn a profit from their trading enterprises.

[12] The first volume of the *Letters* provides an engraving of a bearded Mahmut in his ecclesiastical robe, with a globe by his feet, his bookshelves above his head, the spines of three of which read 'Alcoran', 'Tacitus', and 'St. Austin', with an image on the wall of Massianello holding his net. He is surrounded by papers and measuring instruments; there is an hourglass on his desk, and he holds a pen poised to write.

[13] Arabia is the home of Muhammad who introduced Islam to the tribes of the region in the 7th c. BC. By making Mahmut an Arabian whose name is a variant of Muhammad, Marana is suggesting he is a 'pure' Arab rather than an Ottoman Sunni, although he serves the Ottoman court.

Thou wilt find in his Letters *Wit* and *Learning*. If sometimes he appears tart, 'tis to shew his Vivacity, not disoblige; and he appears all over fully instructed in *Ancient* and *Modern* History. He is very reserved when he blames, and seems perswaded when he praises. When he speaks to the great Men of the *Port*, his Style is very grave; and he changes when he writes to meaner Persons. He never tells News that he is not assured of, nor thinks of divining Things that seem obscure to him.

He gives rare Lessons when he writes of the Revolutions of *Catalonia*, the Kingdoms of *Naples, Portugal* and *England*, which happened in our Days; with strange Circumstances, terrible Murders, and the Death of a Potent King, martyr'd by his own Subjects upon a Scaffold before his own Door.[14]

He weighs much the Duke of *Guise*'s hardy Resolution of going to *Naples*, to succour the Revolution there;[15] and he reasons not as a *Barbarian*, but like an able Statesman, and wise Philosopher, on the Rise and Ruin of States. He always discourses with Liberty, and what he says, is filled with solid and agreeable Thoughts. He speaks sometimes of the Cruelty and Tyranny of the *Turks*, of the Violence of the Ministers of the *Port*, and upon the precipitated Death which many of the *Sultans, Bassas* and *Viziers* are forced to suffer. But this Language is only to his Friends and Confidents.

However, though these Letters be neither *Greek* nor *Latin*, nor written by a *Christian*, they contain nothing of Barbarous; and though the Ignorant be in great Numbers amongst the *Turks*, there are yet Men of great Understanding, that write the *Annals* of the *Ottoman* Empire, though they are not easily come by; for, their Books not being printed, they scarce every reach us. We may notwithstanding believe,

---

[14] Catalonia, in north-eastern Spain, revolted against Spain in 1640 and placed itself under the protection of Louis XIII of France, but the revolt was quelled in the 1650s. The Naples revolt of 1647 is discussed under n. 3 above. Margaret of Savoy, duchess of Mantua, and her secretary of state, Miguel de Vasconcelos, led a nationalist revolution in Portugal against Spanish government on 1 December 1640. The English civil war begun in 1642 resulted in the execution of Charles I on a scaffold erected outside the banqueting hall of Whitehall on the morning of Tuesday, 30 January 1649.

[15] Henri II de Lorraine, fifth duke of Guise (1614–64), was chosen by the Neapolitans as their chief during the 1647 rebellion led by Aniello (see n. 3 above), where he was defeated and carried to Madrid, freed only by the intervention of the duke of Condé. A second attempt on Naples was a failure and he returned to the French court.

From *Letters Writ by a Turkish Spy*

That amongst this Nation, that we term Barbarous, there are great and wise Captains, good Men, and learned Authors; as we have amongst us Generals without Conduct, hypocritical *Votaries*, and ignorant Fellows that pretend to be Masters.

To justifie what I affirm of the *Turks*, let us but consider their Victories, which have gained them so many Kingdoms, their Power at Sea, their Exactness to punish Crimes, and to reward Merit. As for Printing, they would never endure it amongst them. A *Grand Vizier*'s Judgment of it was remarkable, which shews rather their Prudence than any effect of their Ignorance. A famous Printer of *Holland*, by Religion a *Jew*, came to *Constantinople*, bringing Presses with him, with Characters of all Sorts of *Idioms*, particularly *Arabick, Turk, Greek*, and *Persian* Letters, with design to introduce the use of Printing into that great City. As soon as the *Vizier* was informed of it, he caused the *Jew* to be Hanged, and broke all his Engines, and Millions of Characters which he had brought; declaring, it would be a great Cruelty, that One Man should, to enrich himself, take the Bread out of the Mouths of Eleven Thousand Scribes, who gained their Livings at *Constantinople* by their Pens.[16]

Peruse, Gentle Reader, what I offer, without fear of tiring thy self, or being deceived. As *Christian* Authors think of nothing ordinarily,

[16] Resistance to print in the Ottoman empire was strong partly because of the reverence held by the religious establishment for the handwritten word and partly because of the scribal industry's protection of its interests. The Ottoman Sultans Bayezid II and Selim I issued edicts in 1485 and 1515 forbidding Muslims to print texts in Arabic characters, although Jews and eventually other minorities were permitted to print texts in Hebrew and other languages. The first press in Istanbul was established by Jewish immigrants following their expulsion from Spain in 1492. Armenians began printing in Istanbul in 1567. The Bolognese scholar Luigi Ferdinando Marsigli, redeemed from Ottoman slavery in 1682, estimated that eighty thousand copyists were working in Istanbul. The first Muslim-owned press in Istanbul was not opened until the third decade of the 18th c. See Jonathan M. Bloom, *Paper before Print: The History and Impact of Paper in the Islamic World* (New Haven and London: Yale University Press, 2002), 220–2. European commentators were quick to misunderstand and criticize the Ottoman resistance to print. In his 1668 *The Present State of the Ottoman Empire*, Paul Rycaut states: 'The Art of Printing (a matter disputable, whether it hath brought more of benefit or mischief to the world) is absolutely prohibited amongst them, because it may give a beginning to that subtlety of Learning which is inconsistent with, as well as dangerous to the grosseness of their Government, and a means to deprive many of their livelihood, who gain their bread only by their Pen, and occasion the loss of that singular Art of fair Writing, wherein they excel or equal most Nations: the effect of which is evident amongst the Western people where Printing hat taken footing' (32).

but of writing Panegyricks in hopes of Reward, we have reason to believe not to find all the Truth in their Works. Interest and Passion do often make good Princes pass for Tyrants, and unjust and cruel Princes, are sometimes transferred to Posterity for Models of Justice and Clemency. This occasions Histories which issue from so corrupt a Source, to serve like a pitch'd Field for *Modern* Writers, where the one and the other combat for the destruction of Truth; the one falsly reporting what they have heard; and the other, by as badly representing the things they seem to witness. Most Princes will have their Altars, and then 'tis no wonder if there are Priests found to sacrifice to Falshood, and Idolaters to deface the Statue of Truth.

There is no *General* that will not always seem Conqueror, and Princes never confess their Losses, which occasions a Confusion, and the Actions of Men do thereby become doubtful.

How many times have we seen both the Victors and Vanquished make Bonfires for their Successes? And, in our Days, we have known the *French* rejoyce, and the *Spaniards* and *Germans* sing their *Te Deum* for the same thing.[17]

As we are perhaps now less just than in Ages past it is difficult to write things as they are, particularly the Lives of Princes; whose History cannot be writ without Fear, nor the Truth said without Danger. For these *Reasons*, we ought not to question the Credit of our *Arabian*, who reports with Liberty what came to his Knowledge. Besides, he being an Universal Enemy to *Christianity*, and a concealed one, neither disobliged or gained by any, and religiously true to his *Prince*, whom he adores as a *Divinity*; it cannot be imagined, that he says any thing for Fear or Favour.

As these Relations have been read with Attention and diligently examined, we may be assured of an exact History, abounding in considerable Events; and this History being separated into Letters as the Author writ them, the reader may read them without repining. If he will not acknowledge the *Translator's* Pains, let him at least receive the Labours of a dead Man with Civility, one that never dreamt his *Memorials* would be printed, and that served his Master faithfully.

[17] The 'Te Deum laudamus' (We praise thee, O God) is a canticle sung at matins in both the Roman Catholic and Anglican Churches.

From *Letters Writ by a Turkish Spy*

These Sentiments made him exactly follow the Sentence of St. *Austin*, found in the Front of his works:

> *Where Love is, there is no Labour, and if there*
> *be Labour, the Labour is loved.*

The *Translator* hath thought fit to retrench some Ceremonies, and proud Titles of the *Eastern* People. What is represented here, is in a familiar Style, such as the Ancient *Latins* used in their Writings to their *Consuls, Dictators*, and *Emperors* themselves. And if the Translation be not Elegant as the *Arabick*, do not accuse the Author, seeing it is not possible to reach the Force and Beauty of the Original.

Have moreover some Respect for the Memory of this *Mahometan*; for, living unknown, he was safe from the Insults of the Great Ones, so that he might write Truth without Danger, which ordinarily is disguised by Fear or Avarice, having first reported the Transactions of *Christians*, with no less Truth than Eloquence.

If what I have said cannot satisfie the Curious, expect the rest of these Letters, which will be found full of great *Actions*, Profitable *Instructions*, and good *Morals*. Thank God however, who raises Men that employ themselves in vanquishing Ignorance and Idleness. And in rendering Justice to *Mahmut*, a passionate *Slave* for the Interest of his *Master* and the Truth, have some Goodness for the *Translator*; who being born free, acknowledges no Master but *God*, his *King* and his *Reason*.

VOLUME i, BOOK 1, LETTER 1

Mahmut *the* Arabian, *and* Vilest *of the* Grand Signior's *Slaves, To* Hasnardarbassy, *Chief Treasurer to his Highness at* Constantinople.[18]

I have at length finish'd my Journey, after One Hundred and Forty Days March, arriving at *Paris* the 4th of this present *Moon*, according

---

[18] The reigning Ottoman sultan when Mahmut's letters begin was Murat IV (ruled 1623-40), his grand vizier (whom Mahmut refers to as the 'vizir azem'), Hafiz Ahmet Pasa. Murat was a traditionalist reformer of the Ottoman system, guided by an adviser named Koci Bey, an Albanian convert.

to the *Christians Style*.[19] I made no stay in *Hungary*, yet sojourn'd One and Forty Days at *Vienna*, where I observ'd all the Motions of that Court, according as I was order'd; of which I shall not now speak, having given a full Account to the ever-Invincible *Vizir Azem*. Being but newly arriv'd, I scarce know any Body, and am as little known my self. I have suffer'd my Hair to grow a little below my Ears; and as to my Lodging, 'tis in the House of an old *Flemming*, where my Room is so small, that Jealousie it self can scarce enter. And because I will have no Enemy near me, I will therefore admit of no Servant.

Being of low Stature, of an ill-favour'd Countenance, ill-shap'd, and by Nature not given to Talkativeness, I shall the better conceal my self. Instead of my Name, *Mahmut the Arabian*, I have taken on me that of *Titus the Moldavian*; and with a little Cassock of black Serge, which is the Habit I have chosen, I make two Figures; being in Heart what I ought to be; but Outwardly and in Appearance, what I never intend.

Carcoa at *Vienna*[20] furnishes me with Bread and Water, supplying me with just enough to live, and I desire no more. The Eggs here are dearer than Pullets[21] with you. It is to him that I will address my Letters.

Eliachim the *Jew* came to see me, who seems to be sufficiently inform'd of what passes in the World, and will be a useful Man to me: Yet I will never trust him more than I need.[22] Although I have a Dispensation from the *Mufti* for Lying and false Oaths, which I shall be obliged to make, yet I have still some Qualms on my Mind. However, our Sovereign must be serv'd, and I can commit no Sin, as long as this is my sole End. As for the Intelligence which I shall send, none shall come from me but what is true, unless I be first deceived my self.

---

[19] Marana is 'referring to the custom of the Chinese and other Orientals who divide the year by the moon instead of the calendar' according to his modern editor Weitzman. At the end of each letter he gives the number of the moon. In this letter it corresponds to our ninth month, or 11 September 1637.

[20] Carcoa is a fellow Ottoman spy based at Vienna (the Habsburgs were the chief rivals of the Ottomans in 17th-c. Europe). In Letter 4, bk. 1, vol. ii (dated the year 1642), Carcoa has disappeared from his post and is replaced by a Jew named Nathan Ben Saddi.

[21] Pullets i.e. the eggs of a young fowl.

[22] European Christian commentators were apt to see Jews in Europe as potential conspirators with Muslim forces, especially the Ottomans. Istanbul in the 16th and 17th c. was tolerant of its large Jewish population and 'Relations between Christians and Jews . . . were worse than between Christians and Muslims' (Philip Mansel, *Constantinople: City of the World's Desire 1453–1924* (London: John Murray, 1995), 122).

From *Letters Writ by a Turkish Spy*

It will be hard for me to mention any Thing considerable of a City which is not to be view'd in one Day, I having been there but Seven. 'Tis peopled like the Borders of the Sea with Sand, the Inhabitants lodging to the very Cock-lofts;[23] and Houses are built on the Bridges.

This great City is divided by a River, and both Parts of it are joined by a great Bridge of Stone, well built and very stately. In the midst of it is seen an Horse of Brass, with the Statue of *Henry* IV, which bestrides it; whose Heroick Actions have justly sirnamed him *The Great*, and he seems still to command this Capital of the Kingdom.[24] The other Bridges being full of Houses are not seen, appearing as if they had been made for the City, not the River.

The King's Palace is an ancient Building, yet retains a certain majesty, which denotes the Grandeur of its Master:[25] Within it appears a Desert; for the Court is always abroad, or in the Army.

A Church man, term'd at *Rome* a *Cardinal*, is the principal minister of State; his Name is *Armand du Plessis, Cardinal* of *Richlieu*. He is esteem'd a great Politician, a Man of Wit and Action, and every way fitted for the Place he holds.

All the People make Vows to Heaven, that their King may become a Father; for, the Queen has been barren these many Years.

I go into the Churches as a *Christian*; and when I seem attentive to their Mysteries, I hold our Sacred *Alcoran* in my hands, addressing my Prayers to our holy *Prophet*; and thus behaving my self, I give no Offence. I avoid Disputes, mind my own Concerns, and do nothing which may endanger my Salvation.

Preserve thy Health, and expect to hear from me as oft as the Interest of our Great and Mighty Monarch requires, who is the Master of my Life and Affections.

---

[23] Cock-loft: a small upper loft under the ridge of a roof (*OED*).

[24] Henri IV, first Bourbon king of France who reigned 1589–1610. He converted from Protestantism to Catholicism in 1593 in order to reunify France and win Paris at the end of the Wars of Religion. He completed the Tuilleries, built the great gallery of the Louvre, the Pont-Neuf, and the Place Royale in Paris.

[25] The royal residence at this point was at the Tuilleries Palace adjacent to the Louvre and begun in 1564. The building burnt down in 1871. Francis I (reigned 1515–47) had held his court at Fontainebleu. Louis XIV (reigned 1643–1715) set about completing the city-palace at the Louvre, but in the 1670s turned to more ambitious plans at Versailles.

I make thee no Present of my Services; for they be devoted to that *Lord*, whose Slave thou art,[26] as well as I. The Letters I write for the future, shall be directed to the Ministers of the *Divan*.

Live with the Piety of a good *Mussulman*, and the Prudence of an able Minister, and preserve the *Treasure* as thine own Heart, which, thou knowest, is the last expiring.

Paris, 11th *of the* 9th *Moon, of the Year* 1637, *according to the* Christian *Style*.

VOLUME iii, BOOK 1, LETTER 12

To the Magnificent *and* Redoubtable Vizir Azem.

It appears that the *Queen* of *France* is very Indulgent to her *Generals*, having call'd Home the *Duke* of *Enguien* from the Toils of War. This *Prince* neglecting the Wounds he receiv'd in the Battle of *Allersheim*, not many Days after, fell into a violent Fever: So that he was carried in a Horse-Litter to *Philipsburgh*, with no small Danger of his Life. As soon as he recovered his Health, he was commanded to return to France, and the Charge of the whole Army committed to *Mareschal Turenne*.[27]

Such tenderness is never shew'd to the Invincible *Ottoman General*, neither would they esteem it a Favour, but a Disgrace. When they go to the Wars, they make no underhand Leagues with the Elements to spare their Bodies; but, are resolved to Combat with Cold, Heat, Hunger, Thirst, and all the Hardships to which Soldiers are liable, as well as with the Swords of their Enemies. They take no other Armour against the Rigorous Frosts of a *Russian* Winter, or the Scorching Sands of a *Persian* Summer, but an Unshaken Resolution,

---

[26] All Ottoman courtiers were technically slaves. The only free man in the court, although according to his western descriptors a prisoner of the army, was the sultan.

[27] Henri de La Tour d'Auvergne, viscount de Turenne (1611–75), appointed Marshal of France in 1643 by Anne of Austria as Regent in Louis XIV's minority. In 1644, when the Bavarians seized Freiburg im Breisgau in the Thirty Years War, Turenne appealed for help and was joined by the small army of the duke d'Enghien, Louis II de Bourbon, prince de Condé, who took command of both armies. The Bavarians were forced to leave the Rhine river valley after several conflicts, including a battle at Allarsheim, and Enghien and Turenne took Philippsburg in September 1644.

From *Letters Writ by a Turkish Spy*

an Invincible Patience, and a Mind incapable of bowing under the worst Misfortunes. They are not angry with the Weapons of their Adversaries, when they carve in their Limbs the marks of an Honour, which will far out-last the Pain of their Wounds; and, in their Flesh hew deep Characters, or an Immortal Fame, and a Renown that shall know no Period. They are not parsimonious of their Blood, but court their Enemies to spill it on the Ground, from whence it will spring up in Laurels and Wreaths, to Crown them with Triumphs and Glories whilst they live, and to sweeten their Memory with the Praise of Future Generations.

Thus, Magnanimous *Vizir*, do the *Mussulman Heroes*, the *Props* of the *First Empire*, manifest their Courage, in defying of Dangers and Wounds, and scorning to capitulate with Fortune for Ease and Exemption from Death. They know, that when they march against the *Infidels*, 'tis in Vindication of the *Eternal Unity*: And therefore, instead of endeavouring to shun, they Court a Death so glorious, as that which will immediately Transport them to the *Bosom* of our *Holy Prophet*, and to the *Inexpressible Delights* of the *Gardens* of *Eden*. Where this Truth is firmly rooted, there is no room for Fear to plant it self. But the Case is otherwise with *Infidels*, who blaspheme that purest *Undivided Essence*. They assert and believe a *Plurality of Gods*, and therefore in time of Danger, amongst so many *Deities*, they know not whom to address, or whom to confide in.[28] The Apprehension of Death, is terrible to them, whose Hope is only in this Life; whose Consciences are stained with a thousand Pollutions, and yet renounce the very Method of being Clean. Who not only err themselves, but by their evil Example and Influence (for I speak of the *Princes* and *Great Ones*) draw Innumerable after them, to taste of the *Tree Zacon*, which grows in the *Middle* of *Hell*.[29]

[28] Mahmut is here making reference to the doctrine of jihad, an active struggle against armed force wherever necessary, in Islam. Those who die in jihad are thought to go straight to paradise. Mahmut also here voices the Islamic claim that Christianity, because of the concept of the Trinity, is not a monotheism.

[29] 'The Life and Actions of Mahomet', included in an anonymous book called *Four Treatises concerning the Doctrine, Discipline, and Worship of the Mahometans* (1712), complained of Muhammad that 'the main Arguments he made use of to delude Men into this Imposture, were his Promises and Threats, as being those which easiest work on the Passions of the Vulgar' (32). The anonymous author goes on to say that Muhammad made his concepts of paradise and hell 'agreeable to the Notions the Country had of the greatest

People speak variously of the *Duke* of *Enguin*'s Conduct in the Battle of *Allersheim*. His Creatures extol his Valour and Experience with *Hyperboles*: Whilst his Enemies endeavour to lessen his Reputation. Some say he owes his Revocation to the *Queen*'s dislike; others attribute it to the extraordinary Concern she has for his health. But, such as would be esteem'd the Wiser Sort, say his Return is voluntary and sought by himself, scorning to hold his *Commission* any longer at the Pleasure of *Cardinal Mazarin*; who, 'tis thought, first procured him this Employment, only to have him out of the Way, and take off his Application from the *Domestick* Affairs of *France*. These are the Discourses of the People at present, who yet perhaps may change their Opinion before the Sun goes down. They will always be Censuring and Descanting on the Actions of their *Superiors*; few being willing to think their Tongues were given 'em to lie Idle. It is but a Little Member, but often does Great Mischief by its Activity. One of the *Ancients* gave no good Character of it when he call'd it a *Dæmon*.[30] Yet we are not bound to believe all that the *Philosophers* said. *Æsop* gave the most impartial Account of this Member, when he said., '*Twas the* Best *and the* Worst.[31] Sometimes I sit silent many Hours together; not for want of Company; (for here's a Glut of that in this Populous City) nor, because I know not what to say, (for I could

Happiness and the greatest Misery' (33). Thus, for the nomadic tribes of Arabia, drinking boiling water, experiencing hot winds, and having nothing to eat but briars, thorns, and Zacon fruits constitutes hell, and gardens with much water, lots of precious metals and stones and beautiful amorous women on command would suggest paradise. Marana's specific source may have been ch. 29, 'Of the Religion of the Turks', in Jean de Thévenot's *The Travels of Monsieur de Thevenot into the Levant in Three Parts* (1687), in which he says that in the Muslim hell sinners drink scalding water and eat of the fruit of the tree of Zacon which grows out of the bottom of hell. The Zacon is a west Asian tree of the myrtle family which features in the Old Testament and its fruit is an unpalatable nut.

[30] James 3: 5 of the King James Bible (1611) says that 'the tongue is a little member, and boasteth great things'. James 3: 8 also says that 'the tongue can no man tame; it is an unruly evil, full of deadly poison'. I have not been able to locate the classical author who characterizes the tongue as a demon.

[31] Sir Roger L'Estrange's popular *Fables of Æsop, and other other eminent mythologists: with morals and reflections*, first published in 1669, gives in chs. 8 and 9 of 'The Life of Aesop' a story about Aesop preparing a splendid meal for his master Xanthus and his philosopher friends of four courses of ox tongues. The disgruntled guests ask for a better preparation on the morrow only to be served up with the same meal. Xanthus asks Aesop 'what's the Meaning of This, That *Tongues* should be the Best of Meats *One Day*, and the *Worst the Other*?' to which Aesop replies that the tongue can both build and pull down reputations (5th edn. corr. (1708), 11–12).

From *Letters Writ by a Turkish Spy*

speak a great Deal more than 'tis fit for others to hear) but, that I may study with less Interruption, how to serve my *Great Master*. For much talking enervates the Judgment, and evaporates the Mind into Air. Besides, by thus practising Silence in Private, I Learn the Art of restraining my Words in Publick, when it is requisite to promote the Ends at which I aim. 'Tis not for a Man in my Station, to be open and talkative; but to distinguish Persons and Seasons; to understand the due Stops and Advances of my Tongue; sometimes to say Much in a Little, at other Times to say Little or Nothing at all; but ever so to speak, as not to lay my self naked to the Hearers; yet to seem a very frank, open-hearted Man, in what I Discourse of.

I would not have thee conclude from what I have said, that *Mahmut* uses any Reserve to the *Ministers* of the *Divan*, who are *Mines* of *Science* and *Wisdom*, and can easily discern the Heart through the most artificial Veil of Words. But it is absolutely necessary for me to use Dissimulation in this *Court*; seeming many times ignorant of what I really know, that I may not be thought to know more than they would have me. I was never yet so indiscreet, as to publish any Secret that was committed to my Charge; whereby I have gained great Confidence, with Men who delight to unbosome their Intelligence. They esteem me a Man of Integrity, and fit to be trusted. Thus am I made privy to many Intrigues of the *Grandees*, and a Repository of the *Court*-News: Whilst they Whisper in *Mahmut*'s Ear what is Transacted in the Royal Bed Chambers, and private Apartments.

By this means, I came Acquainted with an Amour of *Cardinal Mazarini*, which is known but to a few. This *Minister* has none of the Worst Faces, and a proportionate Elegance in his Shape: Much addicted also to the Love of Women; yet he manages his Intrigues with that of Caution and Privacy, as not to expose the Honour of his *Function*. Among the rest, he had frequent Access to the Chamber of a certain *Countess-Dowager*, her Husband being lately deceas'd. This was not carried so privately, but 'twas Whisper'd about that a man was seen often to come out of this Ladies Chamber a little before Day; but no Body knew who it was (for the *Cardinal* went disguiz'd.) At last it came to the *Queen*'s Ear, who was resolv'd to unravel the Intrigue. She caused *Spies* to be plac'd at a convenient Distance from the Lady's Chamber-Door, which opened in a Gallery of the *Royal-Palace*, with

Orders to trace him Home. That Night the designed *Watch* was first set, it fortun'd, that the *Cardinal* being in the *Countesses* Chamber, her Maid (who was privy to this Amour) overheard these *Spies* talking to each other concerning her Lady; which made her more attentive (being in a Place where she could not be seen) till at length she plainly discovered, That they lay in wait to find out who it was that had been seen coming out of the Chamber. She consults the *Cardinal* what was best to be done to avoid Discovery. In fine, it was agreed between 'em, That the *Countess* should put on the *Cardinal's* Disguise, and he a Suit of her Cloaths; That she should go out at the usual Hour of his Retreat, and walk in the Gardens; That, if examin'd, she should pretend, this Disguise was to guard her from the rude Attempts of Men, who if they found a Lady alone in the Night-Time, would not fail to offer some Incivilities; that soon after her Departure, the *Cardinal* should go forth in her Dress, and shift for himself. This was perform'd accordingly. The Countess walk'd into the Gardens in the *Cardinal's* Disguise, followed by the *Spies*, whilst he goes to an Intimate Friend's House, (an *Italian*, whose Fortune depended on this *Minister*) and changes his Female Accoutrements, for the proper Apparel of his Sex. The *Countess*, having walk'd about half an Hour in the Garden, was seiz'd by one of the *Guards*, under suspicion of some ill Design. She was carried before the *Queen*, and examin'd. She then discover'd her self, begging the *Queen*'s Pardon, and telling her, That a particular Devotion, had oblig'd her to take that Course for several Mornings; But, if it offended Her *Majesty*, she would hold her self dispensed with, and would forbear. The *Queen* seeming satisfied with this Answer, dismissed her. Thus the Amours of the *Cardinal* and the *Countess*, remain'd a Secret; and there are but Three Persons (besides themselves) that know any thing of it; among which *Mahmut* is one.

Thou seest, *Illustrious Minister*, that the Reputation of my Secrecy, has gain'd me the Confidence of one of the *Cardinal's Privados*;[32] for I had this Relation from the *Italian*, whom I mention'd, at whose House the *Cardinal* chang'd his Disguise. I am not without Hopes, by the Prudent Management of this Discovery, to penetrate further into

---

[32] Privado: an intimate private friend, a confident; the favourite of a ruler (*OED*). Mazarin was a good-looking man, with persuasive charm; his enemies accused him of conducting a secret affair with Anne of Austria.

From *Letters Writ by a Turkish Spy*

the *Court* Intrigues. For he that told me this Story, consider'd not that he made me thereby Master of his Fortune; and that it is no longer safe for him, to deny me any Intelligence I require of him. He has put a Key into my Hand, which will open his Breast at my Pleasure.

Yet I need not magisterially claim Discoveries from him, as the only Conditions, on which he is to expect my Concealing what he has already disclos'd. There is a more dextrous and serviceable way to become his *Confessor*, without such an ungrateful Insult; whilst with a well acted Candour, I feign a Relation of such things, as I suspect, yet cannot be certain are true, till attested by himself; professing at the same time, not to believe those pretended Reports I heard. If I shall be so happy as to do any effectual Service to the *Grand Signior* by this Engagement, it will answer my Ends, and I shall not repent of my Craft.

Mahmut Salutes thee, *Sovereign Bassa*, in the humblest Posture of Adoration, lying prostrate on the Ground, in Contemplation of thy Grandeur. Beseeching *God*, That he would grant this Favour to thee, to live happily, and to die in thy Bed.

Paris, 20*th* of the 11*th* *Moon of the Year* 1645.

VOLUME iii, BOOK 2, LETTER 21

To Pestelihali, *his Brother*[33]

I thought my self forgotten by the *Son of* my *Mother*, who has suffer'd so many *Decades* of *Moons* to measure out the Term of his unkind Silence, and of my Melancholy. 'Tis now Three Years since I heard from thee; But, I will not complain of a Fault so ingenuously expiated, though late. Thou hast made me ample Amends, in sending me such an Elaborate and Succinct *History* of thy *Travels*: In reading of which, I know not whether my Pleasure or Profit is greater. Thou hast so interwoven Delightful Adventures of thy own, and pleasant Passages of others, with Curious and Solid Observations, that a Man Improves himself Insensibly; whilst the Charming Language and

[33] Pestelihali is Mahmut's only surviving relative, who sets off on his travels in the East in 1639. Mahmut's most confidential letters critical of the Ottoman regime are often addressed to him.

227

Letter Fictions

Miscellany serve as a Spur, at once to rowze and fasten his Attention, to Points of most useful Knowledge.

The *Christians* are apt to despise the *True Believers*, as a Company of Ignorant People, Unacquainted with the World, Unpolish'd both in their Understandings and Manners, not vers'd in the *Liberal Sciences*, nor addicted to the Study of any Thing, but Riches and Honour, and how to augment the *Musselman Empire*. They consider not at the same time, that *God* has made us *Rational* Creatures, as well as them; has indued us with the same *Natural* Faculties; and that in all *Nations*, he has Inspir'd some with a Thirst of Knowledge, furnishing them also with the Abilities and Means to attain it. They consider not, that if *Printing* be prohibited among us, 'tis to suppress the Multitude of Unprofitable *Books*, with which *Europe* too much abounds: And, that in their Stead we have many Thousands of Industrious *Scribes*, whose Employment is, to insinuate the most Excellent and Learned *Treasures* of the *Ancients*. And that consequently a studious *Mahometan* cannot be destitute of such *Books*, as may instruct him in *True Philosophy*, sound *Morals*, and the *History* of the most Memorable Transactions in the World. Assuredly, our *Arabia* may boast of its *Avicen's*, *Mesne's*, *Averroe's*, *Hali's* and *Albumazar's*;[34] and that she

[34] These are Islamic philosophers who were known to the West from the medieval period onward and who were instrumental in incorporating classical with Islamic traditions. Avicenna (Ibn Sina, 980–1037) was an Iranian physician, most famed for his contributions to Aristotelian medicine and philosophy especially in the *Kitab ash-shifa*, a huge work of logic, science, metaphysics, mathematics, and psychology. Averroes (Ibn Rashd, 1126–96) was a Cordoban-born philosopher-jurist who integrated Islamic traditions with ancient Greek thought. He wrote summaries and commentaries on Aristotle and on Plato's 'Republic'. In Islamic thought his major contribution was to argue that theology should be subject to the scrutiny of philosophy in order to assure happiness in the whole Islamic community. Mesue is Joannes Mesue, or Yuhanna Ibn Masawayh (d. 857–8), a physician famous in the West for his writings on antidotes, under whose name a number of pseudonymous Italian publications in Latin appeared in the Renaissance such as *In Antidotarium Ioannis Fillii Mesuae, censura* (1546) and Bassanio Complano's *Bassani Complani medici Laudensis disputatio de agrimonie* (1611). Albumasor is Albumsar, Abu Ma'shar Ja'far al-Balkhi, an Arabic astronomer whose *Greater Introduction to Astronomy* was translated by Adelard of Bath about 1133. Albumsar adjusted the Aristotelian prime mover to the Koranic doctrine of the omnipotence and transcendence of God's will. For the medieval appropriation of Arabic philosophy and science, see Dorothee Metlizki, *The Matter of Araby in Medieval England* (New Haven: Yale University Press, 1977). Hali is the common name used in European writing of the period to refer to Ali, Muhammad's cousin and son-in-law, fourth caliph and the saint of Shi'ite Islam, who was accounted very learned. Another contender, however, is Ali b. sahl b. Rabban al-Tabari (d. 855), a Nestorian Christian who, at the age of 70, converted to Islam and wrote a refutation of Christianity.

From *Letters Writ by a Turkish Spy*

has brought forth many others who need not in any Point of *Humane or Divine Learning*, yield the *Palms* to the most Eminent *Divines*, *Philsophers*, *Orators* and *Poets* among the *Christians*.

Add to this the equal Benefit some of our *Belief* reap, by Travelling into Foreign Countries, which crowns all their Studies with Experimental Knowledge and Wisdom: Reading them as familiar, with the different *Natures of Man*, and the various *Constitutions of Government*, as before they were with *Books*.

This appears evident in thy Letter, which is replenished with so many solid Remarks and sage Comments, on the *Laws* and *Customs* of the *Regions*, through which thou hast pass'd, their *Religions*, *Strength* and *Riches*, and whatsoever else was worthy a *Traveller*'s Notice; That were this *Narrative* publish'd in *Christendom*, the *Nazarenes*[35] would forbear to speak so contemptibly of the *True Believers*.

But they flatter themselves with a false Notion, That the *Ottomans* never travel beyond the Limits of their own *Empire*, except the *Publick Chiauses*, who are sent by the *Grand Signior*. They are ignorant, that the *August Port* maintains *Private Agents* in all Nations; and, that there is hardly any *Prince*'s Court in *Christendom* without a *Mussulman* in it one Time or other. 'Tis true, we appear not in the *Garb* peculiar to the *East*. Our Mission requires a *Conformity* to the *Fashions* of the *People* where we Reside. But, we still retain the Interiour Vestment of *Mahometan Purity*, being in a double Sense *Circumcised*.[36] Thus we become Masters of the *Christians*' Secrets, whilst they account us Stupid, Ignorant, and Men void of Common Sense.

Besides, had we not this Advantage, in these *Western* Parts, yet the Universal Privilege of Travelling and maintaining free Commerce over all the *East*, must needs afford great opportunities of Accomplishment, to see among the *Caravans* of so many Thousands as visit *Persia*, *India*, *China*, *Tartary*, and all Places where the *Faith* of the *Missioner* of *God* is professed.

I am extreamly pleased with thy fortunate Escapes from *Robbers* on the Road, whose Malice rarely extends farther, than to deprive a

---

[35] Nazarenes. In Acts 24: 5, Jesus ('of Nazareth') is referred to as a 'Nazarene' and it was later applied to those who followed his teachings.

[36] The fact that Mahmut is circumcised might reveal that he is not a Christian, but he is 'doubly' circumcised because he has been 'cut off' from his original self by living in disguise amongst Christians.

Man of those *Outward Goods*, which, if he be *wise*, he will not call *his Own*. Much more am I delighted, with thy Deliverance from those *Female* Thieves, who steal from Men their Hearts and Reason; which last is our Noblest, and only proper Inheritance. All *Persia* and the *Indies*, abound with *Courtezans*; and he had need of *Osman*'s Chastity,[37] who would withstand so many and strong Temptations.

Thou needest not wonder at the Effeminacy of the present Mogul, who suffers himself and his *State*, to be govern'd by *Women*. That Subtle and Aspiring Sex, have always sought to undermine or overreach our *Race*. They keep behind the *Scenes*, yet act their Parts, in all the *Tragedies* and *Revolutions* of the *World*. The Father of the present *Indian* King,[38] made an Absolute Resignation of his *Sovereignty* to his Queen, for Four and Twenty Hours.[39] This *Prince*, by a strange Affectation, called himself, *King of the World*. His Wife was the Daughter of an *Arabian* Captain, who had served him in the Wars. But, having forfeited his Head by some Notorious *Treason*, his Daughter went and threw her self at the *Mogul*'s Feet, to beg his Life. He fell passionately in Love with her (for she had not her Equal for Beauty in all the *East*) granted her *Petition*, and married her. Afterwards, she got such an *Empire* over him, that he would do Nothing without her Advice and Consent. At her Instigation, he made *War* or *Peace*: And to please her cruel Humour, he put out the Eyes of his Eldest Son.[40] But, not satisfied with these Discoveries of his Love, and resolving to make herself Famous by some Extraordinary Action,

[37] Along with Omar and Ali, Osman is counted as one of the prophet Muhammad's closest friends. In vol. vii, bk. 1, Letter 16, Mahmut defends Islam to a Jewish correspondent by listing the virtues of Ali, Omar, and 'the Chaste, and generous *Osman*'. The Ottoman empire takes its name from its first emperor, Osman, the namesake of this figure.

[38] Shah Jahan is the ruling emperor of Mughal empire to whom Mahmut refers (reigned 1627–57). His father is Jahangir (reigned 1605–27). All the Mughal emperors took names on their accession that indicated their authority and Jahangir does indeed mean 'World-Conqueror'.

[39] The story Mahmut delivers of Nourmahal's twenty-four-hour reign is taken from the 'Account of the Money of Asia' that opens the second part of the Huguenot jeweller Jean-Baptiste Tavernier's *The Six Voyages of John Baptista Tavernier . . . Through Turkey into Persia and the East-Indies* (1677). The closeness of the details given, down to the images used on the coins minted over this short period suggest that this was Marana's source. Jahangir married in 1611 the widow of one of his Afghan captains. She became known as Nur Jahan ('Light of the World') or Nur Mahal ('Light of the Seraglio').

[40] Jahangir had Khusrau, his eldest son who led a revolt shortly after his accession in 1605, blinded and kept in prison until he died in 1622.

From *Letters Writ by a Turkish Spy*

she never ceas'd solliciting the King, with all the Arts of Female Policy, till she had prevailed on him, to surrender up his Authority to her for the Space of a Day. In which Time (having prepared all things before hand ready for her Purpose) she caused Ten Millions of *Roupies*, in Silver and Gold, to be coin'd, and stamp'd with the *Twelve Signs* of the *Zodiack*; contrary to the *Fundamental Laws* of the *Empire*, the *Express Prohibition* of our *Holy Prophet*, and the *Universal Practice* of the *Mussulmans* throughout the *World*, who admit not the *Representations* of any *Creatures* that have *Life*.[41] This Relation I had from my Uncle *Useph*, who resided in the *Indian Court* Eleven Years. He added moreover, that during this short *Female Reign*, she cut off the Heads of seven *Grandees*, the most zealous for the *Mussulman Faith* among all the *Indian Princes*, and established as many *Idolaters* in their *Places*: And, that if her Orders had been fully executed, she had quite changed the *Government*, Consecrated the most beautiful *Mosques* to the *Service of Idols*, Exterminated the *True Faithful*, and restored the *Ancient Abominations* of the *Infidels*. Which thou wilt not think Impracticable, when thou considerest That the Number of the *Uncircumcised* in the *Indies*, far exceeds that of the *Mussulmans*, there being Ten thousand of those, to a Hundred of such as profess the *Unity* of the *Divine Nature*.[42] But however, there was *Loyalty* found even among those *Pagans*; and, they would not suffer a *Blind Zeal* for the *Worship* of their *Gods*, to supplant the *Duty* they ow'd their *King*.

The Description thou hast made of *Candahar*, and the Method thou hast projected to take that *Impregnable City*, discover at once thy Conduct and Diligence, in procuring Liberty to survey so narrowly, the most Important Place of the *Indies*;[43] and thy Skill in Fortifications, with the Quickness of thy Invention, which has suggested to thee, that which all the *Engineers* of *Asia* have never so much as dreamt of. This is the right Use of Travelling, when a Man returns from Foreign

---

[41] See Jean-Baptiste Tavernier, *Six Voyages*, pt. 2, p. 11: 'you must take notice, that all the Coins of those Kings have only the Characters of the Countrey upon each side of the Piece. But this Queen caus'd one of the twelve Signs to be stamp'd upon each side of Hers, which is contrary to the Law of *Mahomet*, that forbids all manner of representations' (11).

[42] Hinduism was not recognized as a monotheism until late in the 18th c.

[43] Kandahar, capital of southern Afghanistan, was the frontier to Persia and Usbek and thus of strategic importance in any advance from other eastern territories into Mughal India. It was lost and regained by Mughal emperors at a number of points in their history.

Nations, cultivated with Experimental Knowledge, and stock'd with Improvements, that may render him serviceable to his Country.

Thou condemnest the Injustice and Avarice of the *Indian Moguls*; who, as soon as any of the *Omrahs*, or *Great Men* die, cause all his Estate and Goods to be seiz'd, to their own proper Use.[44] Whereby it comes to pass, that the Widow and Children of the Deceased, are reduced to the lowest Conditions of Poverty, being many Times forced to beg for a Subsistence. 'Tis true, this is an Oppression not to be justified, especially in those who profess to Believe in *One God Creator* of *All Things*, the *Incorrupt Judge* of the *Universe*. What thinkest thou then of our *Sultans*, who not having Patience to wait, till a *Naval* Death shall make them *Heirs* to the *Wealth* of a *Bassa*, generally secure their *Title*, and hasten their Possession by a *Bow-string*?[45] These are *Royals'* Violences: Though the Resignation of *Subjects*, must not tax them with any Crime, who are accountable to none but God.

It was, however a notable Piece of Raillery, with which the Widow of a Rich *Merchant*, reproved this Unreasonable Custom in the present *Mogul*. Her Husband was an *Idolater*, who had heaped together an Immense Treasure by Trading and Usury; and, when he died, left her worth Two Hundred Thousand *Roupies*. Her Son, some Years after coming of Age, demanded of her a Stock to set up with as a *Merchant*. Which she, either out of Avarice, or for other Ends, refused him; furnishing him only with such small Sums, as served to nourish his Discontent, and tempt him to a lewd, careless Life. But, at length, not being able to prevail on his Mother, to part with so much as would answer his Expectations, he complained to the *Mogul*, disclosing also what Estate his Father had left. The *Mogul* being informed of so much Riches, sent for the Young Man's Mother, and commanded her, to send him Half her Money; ordering, that the

[44] European travellers failed to comprehend the system of taxation privileges on agricultural production administered by the Mughal emperors. François Bernier, in a letter to Louis XIV's financial adviser, Colbert, given in the first volume of his memoirs (*History of the Late Revolution of the Empire of the Great Mogol*, 1671), simply sees Mughal government as a system whereby no one except the monarch has control over property: 'All the Lands of that Empire being the *Mogol's* propriety, it follows, that there are neither Dutchies, nor Marquisats, nor any family rich in Land, and subsisting of its own income and patrimony'; he adds that a son may find himself destitute after his father dies although often the Great Mogul gives the widow and her family a pension (30–1).

[45] See n. 13 to Eliza Haywood, 'The History of the Christian Eunuch' in Part 2.

other Half, should be divided between her Self and her Son. The Widow not being at all surprised, or cast down at this unjust Proposal, made the *Mogul* this short Reply: *'O King, may the Gods make thee Happy. My Son has some Reason to require his Share of his Father's Estate, being his Blood running in his Veins; but I desire to know, what Relation Thou art to my Husband or Me, that Thou claimest a Share in his Inheritance'.* The *Prince* abash'd at so smart and bold an Address, commanded her to give Half her Estate to her Son, and dismissed her.

I have heard some of our *Chiauses* praise the *Magnificence* of the *Mogul's Court*, the Infinite Number of his Attendants: But above all they extoll the Inimitable Grandeur of his *Throne*, which is adorn'd with so many Topazes, Rubies, Emeralds, Pearls and Diamonds, as amount to Thirty Millions of *Roupies*.[46] But, were it not much better, if in stead of all this Needless Glory, he could boast, That his *Empire* is founded in the Hearts of his *Subjects*? He does not consider, That such prodigious Heaps of envied Treasure are but so many glittering *Snares*, Golden *Manacles*, which serve for no other Life, but to chain him up from that Freedom, and those more Innocent Delights, that the Meanest of his Subjects enjoy.

Thou hast, I perceived, discoursed with the *Indian Bramins*: Dost not thou discover, even in these *Idolaters*, a Contempt of Riches? What mean Thoughts have they of the Splendor and Gayeties of the *Court*? What a low Esteem, of the Long and Proud *Series* of *Titles*, with which the *Moguls* endeavour to exalt themselves? Whilst they are call'd the *Light of the World*, and *Companions of the Sun*,[47] these poor *Philosophers* know, That in a little Time they shall be laid in *Darkness*, and have no better *Society* than that of *Worms*. What signifies their *Pedigree*; or, that the present *Mogul*, is but the *Tenth Descendant* from the *Mighty Temurlen*, who made all *Asia* tremble; he has lost the

---

[46] In 'An Historical and Political Description of the Empire of the Great Mogol', ch. 8, bk. 2, pt. 2 of Tavernier's *Six Voyages*, the jeweller reports counting 108 pale rubies and 160 emeralds on the largest throne, embroidered in pearls and in the shape of peacocks, with parasols covered in diamonds on either side of it. Tavernier claims it was begun by Tamerlane and completed by Shah Jahan (122). See also n. 11 to 'The History of Commladeve' from *Tales, from the Inatulla of Delhi* in Part 1 of this anthology.

[47] Nur Jahan, meaning Light of the World, is the title taken by Nur Mahal when she rose to power and Companion of the Sun may be a reference to Akbar (reigned 1556–1605), known as the 'nursling of Divine light'.

Vertue of his *Glorious Ancestor.*[48] 'Tis that alone, makes all Men truly *Noble.*

Thou tellest me, That the *Empire* of the *Mogul* affords him more *Revenues*, than the *Dominions* of any Two the most Potent *Monarchs* on Earth. I have heard as much from Others;[49] which convinces me, That thou hast inform'd thy self rightly of the *Present State* of the *Indies*. But dost thou therefore esteem this *Monarch* the Richer? Consider the vast Extent of his *Dominions*, which are said to contain more than Six Hundred Leagues in Length, and thou wilt find, that to maintain so great a Tract of Ground, both against his *Foreign* and *Domestick* Enemies, he is oblig'd to keep in Constant Pay, some Millions of his Subjects and Strangers: For he is in the Midst of Enemies, even among his own *Subjects*. There are above an Hundred *Sovereigns* in his *Empire*, who perpetually by Turns molest his *Government*, refusing to pay *Tribute*, and raising Armies against him:[50] Whereby it comes to pass, That he is at an Infinite Expence to defend himself, and carry on those Endless Wars. Thou thy self having observ'd, That one in two *Moons*, there is an Indispensible Necessity of paying these prodigious Armies: Not a Soldier throughout his *Empire*, having any thing to live on, save the Wages he receives of the King.

Consider also, that this *Monarch*, always keeps some Thousands of the finest Horses in the World, near his Person, such as cost him Thousands of *Roupies* apiece; Besides a Thousand Elephants; with an Incredible Number of Mules, Camels, and other Beasts of Burden, to carry his Wives, his Goods and Provisions, when he takes the Field: That whole Cities, even as large as *Constantinople*, are obliged to follow the King's Camp for Subsistence, their Livelihood altogether

---

[48] The term 'Mughal' or 'Mogol' derives from the Mongol forces led by Timur which, fresh from conquests in Persia, entered Delhi in 1398, sacked the city, enslaved or massacred the Hindu population, and then withdrew. His descendant Babur founded the Mughal state between 1526 and 1530.

[49] François Bernier comments that the Mughal emperor has more wealth than the Ottoman and Persian emperors' fortunes combined, but adds the proviso that he has many more expenses (letter to Colbert in *History*, 57).

[50] The Mughal emperors constantly struggled to unify their Indian territories under Muslim rule. Bernier lists some of the key challenges to Mughal authority as the Patans and the kings of Golconda and Visapour. The story of 'Padmani' given in Catrou is just one indicator of the continuing resistance of Rajasthan (see Part 3).

depending on the Army.[51] Add to this, the Immense Charges of his *Seraglio*, his Castles and Sea-Port Towns, with all the other Necessary Expences of the *State*, and thou wilt conclude, That when this *Potentate* comes to cast up his Accounts, he will find himself a Poor Man.

But, I shall cloy thee with a Rehearsal of such Things, as thou can'st not be a Stranger to.

Only tell me, Whether one of the *Rains* or *Princes* subject to the *Mogul* be the real *Descendent* of *Porus*, the Ancient King of *India*, in the Time of *Alexander the Great*?[52] I have been told by several Travellers, that there is such a One, that his Name is *Rana*, and that an Hundred of the *Idolatrous Priests* pay Homage to him, as to their *Natural Sovereign*.[53]

Thou confirmest the Truth, of what has been so often reported in these Parts, that the *Prince* of *Java* has Six Fingers on each Hand, and as many Toes on his Feet.[54]

But, that seems very strange, which thou relates, of a certain *Language* among the *Indians*, which is not Vulgarly spoken; but, that all their *Books* of *Theology*, the *Pandects* of their *Laws*, the *Records* of their *Nation*, and the *Treatises* of *Human Arts* and *Sciences* are written in it. And, that this *Language* is taught in their *Schools*, *Colleges*, and *Academies*, even as *Latin* is among the *Christians*. I cannot enough admire at this: For, where and when was this *Language* spoken? How came it to be disus'd? There seems to be a Mystery in it, that none of their *Brachmans* can give any other Account of this, save, That it is the *Language*, wherein *God* gave to the *First Creature* he made, the *Four Books* of the *Law*; which, according to their

---

[51] See Bernier's description of the opulence of Aurangzeb's court on the move to Kashmir in Part 3 of this anthology.

[52] Porus: see n. 3 in *The General History of the Mogol Empire* in Part 3 of this anthology.

[53] On Rana (or Rana Pratap), see introduction and n. 2 to *General History of the Mogol Empire* in Part 3 of this anthology.

[54] This information also comes from Tavernier. In ch. 20 'Of the Princes who follow the *Mahumetan* Religion in *Europe, Asia* and *Africa* ' of 'A Relation of the Grand Seignor's Seraglio' appended to the *Six Voyages* (1677), Tavernier comments 'Since I have mentioned the Emperour of Java, I shall, by the way, insert here an observation, which I made at the time of my being in that Island, which was, That the eldest Son of that Emperour, who reign'd in the year 1648 had six fingers on each of his hands, and six toes on each foot, and all of equal length' (95).

Chronology, was above Thirty Millions of Years ago.[55] I tell thee, my Dear Brother, this News has started some odd Notions in my Mind: For, when I consider, that this *Language*, as thou sayest, has nothing in it Common with the *Indian* that is now spoken, nor with any other *Language* of *Asia*, or of the World; and yet, that it is a Copious and Regular *Language*, learn'd by *Grammar*, like the other *Maternal Languages*; and that in this *Obsolete Language, Books* are written, wherein it is asserted, that the *World* is so many Millions of Years old; I could almost turn *Pythagorean*, and believe the *World* to be within a *Minute* of *Eternal*.[56] And, where would be the Absurdity? Since *God* had equally the same Infinite Power, Wisdom and Goodness from all *Eternity*, as he had Five or Six Thousand Years ago, what should hinder him then from exercising these *Divine Attributes* sooner? What should retard him, from drawing forth this Glorious *Fabrick* earlier, from the *Womb* of *Nothing*? Suffer thy Imagination to start backwards as far as thou canst, even to Millions of Ages, and yet thou canst not conceive a Time, wherein this Fair Unmeasurable *Expanse*, was not stretch'd out. As if *Nature* her self had engraven on our Intellects, this *Record* of the *World's* Untraceable *Antiquity*; in that our strongest, swiftest Thoughts, are far too weak and slow, to follow Time back to its Endless Origin.

[55] The reference is to Sanskrit, an old Indo-Aryan language similar in grammar to Latin or Greek, and the classical literary language of the Hindus of India. Vedic Sanskrit, based on a dialect of north-western India, dates from as early as 1800 BC. It was described and standardized in the important grammar book by Panini, dating from about the 5th c. BC. Literary activity in so-called classical Sanskrit, which is close to but not identical with the language described by Panini, flourished from c.500 BC to AD 1000. The four Books of the Law are the four Vedas (sacred hymns and verses in ancient Sanskrit which make up the Hindu scripture): Rigveda, Yajurveda, Samaveda, and Atharvaveda. The whole of Vedic literature was preserved orally, although there are some manuscripts. Since Hindu Brahmans had no remit to proselytize, European scholars such as François Bernier and Alexander Dow, who became proficient in the Persian used in Mughal administration, found it difficult to acquire competence in Sanskrit and to understand Hindu religion, despite their best efforts.

[56] The Greek philosopher Pythagoras (580–500 BC) established an academy in southern Italy in 532 BC from which much of the thinking ascribed to him derives. None of his writings survive but the Pythagorean school influenced Plato and Aristotle. Mahmut most often refers to him admiringly as the founder of the belief in transmigration (that the soul passes from one body to another on the death of the body). At the heart of Pythagoreanism is a belief in the unity of the cosmos, the belief that reality is mathematical in nature, the heavenly destiny of the soul and the use of philosophy as a means of spiritual purification.

From *Letters Writ by a Turkish Spy*

The *Revolution* in *China*, surpasses the *Common Changes* in *Kingdoms* and *Empires*. There is Something Excessively *Tragical*, in the *Catastrophe* of that *Royal* House.[57]

Brother, in beholding that, thou hast seen *Humane Nature* in a *Trance*: And, thou art so thy self, if, after this, thou canst be fond of any Thing on Earth. *Traveller*, adieu.

Paris, 25th *of the* 1st *Moon, of the Year* 1647.

VOLUME viii, BOOK 4, LETTER 18

To Dgnet Oglou[58]

This comes to thy Hands by the same Post with one to the *Kaimacham*; therefore I pray thee be quick in executing the Contents of it. I have not One Friend in the *Seraill*, whom I dare trust with such a Secret: Thou art my only Refuge at a Juncture which requires Fidelity, Prudence, and a dexterous Conduct in diving and searching into a certain Mystery, which, for ought I know, may concern my Life.

To tell thee in short, *Nathan Ben Saddi*, the *Sultan*'s Agent Incognito at *Vienna*, a Jew by Descent and Religion,[59] is, I fear, privately murder'd by some Order from the *Divan*. But for what

---

[57] In April 1644, a post-station attendant from a rural family in China, Li Zicheng, led an attack on the Ming capital of Peking. The Ming emperor, Chongzhen, hanged himself on a tree at the foot of a hill in the imperial garden just outside the walls of the Forbidden City when he heard that Li's hundreds of thousands of troops had entered the city. The depredations of Li Zicheng and another rebel leader, Zhang Xianzhong, in northern and central China—combined with the decadence and isolation of the Ming court in the preceding years—left the way open for Manchu forces who eliminated Li and Zhang in 1645 and 1647 respectively, and hunted down and suppressed the remnants of resistance rallying around the Ming ruling house. By 1662 they had killed the last Ming claimants. In 1644 the Manchu boy emperor Shunzhi took the throne as the first Qing emperor under the Regency of Dorgon.

[58] Dgnet Oglou is the recipient of Mahmut's most confidential letters about his feelings and his most incendiary musings about the Ottoman Porte. Dgnet Oglou, we learn, was his fellow slave in their youth and rival for the affections of the lovely Greek woman, Daria. At one point he retires to Damascus to be a farmer, but he soon returns to the Ottoman court to resume an unspecified post there.

[59] In vol. ii, bk. 1, Letter 11, Mahmut writes his first letter to the Jew Nathan Ben Saddi who has replaced his first contact Carcoa as a spy for the Ottomans in Vienna. He requests his correspondent to send him a copy of Carcoa's journal. Many of his letters to Nathan Ben Saddi are concerned with the attempt to convert him to Islam.

Reasons I know not, unless it were in Complyance with the Old Maxims of the Sublime Port, which seldom suffers any Slave to go to his Sepulchre in Peace, who has serv'd the Grand Signior many Years in any eminent Station. He has been miss'd at *Vienna* these Eight Weeks, and within a Day or two after his First Absence the Body of a Dead Man was found floating on the *Danube*, but so disfigur'd with Wounds, as it could not possibly be known who he was; which gives me the greater Suspicion that it was he. And if so, I may expect to be serv'd so my self in a little Time. For my Turn is next.

Therefore, if thou hast any Love or Friendship for me, be watchful on my Behalf: Attend the Whispers of the Court, and observe the Language of those who discourse with their Fingers Ends.[60] The Cast of the Eye many Times discovers the secret Sentiments of the Heart: So does a Shrug of the Shoulder, a Pout of the Lip, or any other Artificial Gesture. They are all Significant and Expressive of what Affections and Thoughts we harbour within. Thou know'st how to act the Mute upon Occasion, as well as any in the *Serrail*. I conjure thee to use great Dexterity, and no less Expedition in unravelling this Secret. Feign to know something more than thou dost, that so thou may'st really learn what I would have thee know concerning *Nathan*'s Fate, and mine too, if possible. Let no cold Indifference make thee neglect this due Care of thy Friend's Interest and Life. We were born to serve one another with mutual Zeal and Fidelity. The good Offices thou dost me, are but lent to be repayd again with others, whenever Opportunity presents it self. But these Arguments are superfluous. I know thou lovest me, and wilt be Active at this Juncture on my Account.

In full and entire Confidence of this, I take my Repose under the Shadow of the Divine Mercy; begging of God, to afford thee a Shelter in Time of Peril; and that when thou and I have weather'd all the Tempests of this Mortal Life, we may Triumphantly enter the Port of Paradise, and enjoy one another in Eternal Felicity.

Paris, 6*th* of the 11*th* Moon, of the Year 1682.

---

[60] See 'The History of the Christian Eunuch', n. 7 in Part 2, on the mutes who served in the Ottoman court.

Persian Letters (1722)

Charles de Secondat, Baron de Montesquieu

Copy-text: vol. ii of the 1st edition of the 1st English translation
by John Ozell (London, 1722)

After the solemn, frequently misogynist, tone of the Turkish
spy, the collection of letters published in French under the
title *Lettres Persanes* of 1721 must have come as a welcome
relief. There are 150 letters (expanded to 161 in later editions)
written to and from two Persian travellers in Europe between
1711 and 1720, addressing the period of the Regency of
Philippe d'Orléans from 1715 to 1723 in France after the death
of Louis XIV. They owe much to the *Letters Writ by a
Turkish Spy*. Like them, they offer a comprehensive comparison of different political systems and social mores, but
they do so in a far more accessible and open manner, not least
because they introduce a variety of correspondents (eunuchs
in a Persian harem, the women of the harem, as well as the
two cosmopolitan travellers), but also because the claustro-
phobic life of the disguised spy is replaced by the curious
enquiry of the travellers, Rica and Usbek, who often take
pleasure in being the object of European scrutiny as well as
scrutinizing the cultures they encounter.

The *Lettres Persanes* are the first publication of Charles-
Louis de Secondat de Montesquieu (1689–1755), better
known now as a political theorist of the Enlightenment. Born
in Bordeaux, he completed a law degree in that city and lived
in Paris between 1708 and 1713. In 1714 he became a

councillor of the Bordeaux Parlement and made a financially advantageous marriage to a Huguenot lady, Jeanne de Lartigue. In 1715 he inherited the barony of Montesquieu and the post of *président à mortier* at the Bordeaux Parlement. The *Lettres Persanes* were published anonymously in Holland (a common ploy to avoid reprisals in France for incendiary material) and ran into ten editions in the year following. They were translated, to almost equal enthusiasm, into English in 1722 by John Ozell (d. 1743), a prolific translator and auditor-general of the city of London. By 1773, this translation had gone into its sixth edition.

Montesquieu's publication was the earliest of a succession of Enlightenment texts from *philosophes* such as Voltaire and Diderot which used imaginary travels and oriental literature as a medium for the critique of traditional European values. Their key preoccupation is with intellectual, religious, and social 'freedoms' and the freedom of the style—studiedly conversational, often sexually explicit (as in the letter from Rica given below)—is part of that preoccupation. Montesquieu went on to produce in 1748 his most famous work, *L'Esprit des Lois*, which articulated in theoretical terms many of the premises outlined in this fictional text: the critique of despotism, the advocacy of the separation of powers in government, the idea that all human association should be founded on mutual gratitude rather than fear or exploitation.

Yet the *Persian Letters* do not constitute a unified and coherent satire. The text works more like a series of periodical essays although there is a narrative thread that holds the whole together. Usbek, the older traveller, has left his harem in the care of his chief eunuch; in his absence, a revolt occurs resulting in the death by suicide of his favourite and apparently most virtuous wife, Roxana, discovered to be in fact sexually unfaithful and desperate for her liberty. Montesquieu splits the central role of narrating 'traveller' between two figures, Usbek, the powerful and educated elder statesmen who struggles to keep his eye on his affairs in his Persian harem, and Rica, the young, single, and curious cosmopolitan who becomes increasingly 'westernized'. Montesquieu also apportions them different roles as informant writers, associating Usbek with acts of visual authority and Rica with acts of verbal dexterity.

Montesquieu's satirical targets are various. The most obvious is the European commonplace that oriental cultures and people are uncivilized and barbaric. The letter from Rica to Usbek can serve as an example here. Rica narrates a story to a French court lady which illustrates the learning and intelligence of individual harem women and challenges her assumption that polygamy and purdah are necessarily oppressive to women. However, the fact that he sends a copy of the story to his fellow-traveller, Usbek, who operates a system of strict retirement and enclosure amongst his harem, also indicates a second strand of satire in Montesquieu's writing, the argument that authority can only be exercised through winning gratitude and consent rather than through fear and tyranny. So, Persian culture is an example of despotism that the Parisian culture (and the choice of Persia as the country of origin of the travellers may well have been made simply on the basis of the phonetic similarities between 'Perse' and 'Paris') must recognize as wrong and avoid in its own experience of the Regency. See Lisa Lowe, 'Travel Narratives and Orientalism: Montagu and Montesquieu', *Critical Terrains: French and British Orientalisms* (Ithaca, NY, and London: Cornell University Press, 1991), 30–74.

Montesquieu also satirizes social vices among the upper classes such as folly, vanity, triviality, egotism, effeminacy, all of which are identified and mocked by his two Persian correspondents. The complexity of the text lies in the fact that Persian culture acts both as a contrast and analogy to the Parisian one. As contrast, the revolt of the harem women against the slavery they endure is a warning to the French aristocracy, that despotism cannot win love and duty from those it oppresses. French absolutism must avoid becoming like oriental despotism. But the harem serves not only as a contrast to French monarchy, but also a parallel to it; Usbek's eunuchs are, like the Regency, an inadequate substitute for genuine monarchical rule and, as a result, the seraglio revolts. Montesquieu admired Philippe d'Orléans but disliked his administration and a similar ambiguity is registered in his treatment of Usbek and his eunuch ministry.

The hybridity of the *Persian Letters* as satire is also apparent on the level of form. Montesquieu exploits another familiar and popular tradition in the epistolary form, what was known as the Portuguese style, alongside his obvious debt to the *Letters Writ by a Turkish Spy*. The *Lettres Portugaises* (1669) or *Five Love-Letters from a Nun to a Cavalier*, translated into English from French by Sir Roger L'Estrange in 1678, were written in the voice of a French nun, Mariana Ana Alcaforada, to the Portuguese soldier who has first seduced and then abandoned her. They were probably in fact authored by Gabriel Joseph de Laverne de Guilleragues (1628–85). The prose fictional variant of a tradition that stretches back to Ovid's *Heroides*, the letters had considerable influence in the development of a 'free' style of amatory expression that broke from the formal and formulaic classicism of prose romance. The letters from Zachi and from Roxane given below are orientalized manifestations of the 'Portuguese' style of passionate epistolary expression, stressing bodily trauma and hysterical loss. The harem and the nunnery were twin places of fascination for Enlightenment authors such as Montesquieu and Denis Diderot (1713–84)—who composed *La Religieuse* (1760), set in a convent, and *Les Bijoux Indiscrets* (1748), set in an oriental court—as examples of sites where 'natural' desire is repressed and/or perverted under artificial legislation and tyrannous authority. See Ruth Bernard Yeazell, *Harems of the Mind: Passages of Western Art and Literature* (New Haven and London: Yale University Press, 2000).

The choice of Persia as the location for much of the *Persian Letters* is an unusual one. Of all the oriental courts, Persia was the least accessible to European informants and oriental literature rarely sited its action there. The region was best known as the home of Zoroastrianism and literary representations of Persian culture most often concerned themselves with ancient pre-Islamic history. British contact was largely mediated through France. Louis XIV's ministers negotiated a treaty signed at Isfahan in 1708 which temporarily alleviated the growing persecution of missionaries in Persia. The British maintained an embassy there from 1627, and their Christian missionary activity was carried out under the auspices of the French East India Company (Shah Abbas I (reigned 1587–1618) was famously tolerant of Christians). Information about Persia came from those engaged in independent trading ventures such as Sir John Chardin, the French Huguenot jeweller, whose 1686 *Journal du Voiage . . . en Perse & aux Indes orientales* (translated into English in the same year as *The Travels of Sir John Chardin into Persia and the East-Indies*) was the primary source for most information about Persia in the later seventeenth century. His contemporary, the doctor John Fryer, provided an English description of Persia from his travels there in the 1670s, *A New Account of the East Indies and Persia*, in 1698. The French traveller Jean de Thévenot, who first visited Sunni Turkey and then Shi'ite Persia, represents the latter in his *The Travels of Monsieur De Thevenot into the Levant in Three Parts* (1687) as more despotic, more vain, and more cruel, but more tolerant in matters of religion, than its Ottoman rival.

I shall write no Epistle Dedicatory, nor demand Protection for this Book. It will be read, if it is good; if bad, I care not whether it be read or no.

I have begun with these Letters, to try the Taste of the Publick. I have many more in my Cabinet, which may be publish'd in time.

But it is upon Condition that I am not found out; for as soon as my Name is known, I am silent for ever. I know a Lady who walks very well, and yet limps if any one looks on her.[1] The faults of the Work may satisfy the Critics, without exposing those of my Person to them. Besides; were it told who I am, every one would cry,' 'Tis like him: His Book is his true Character: He might have employ'd his Time better: It does not become a Man of Gravity.' The Criticks never

---

[1] Thought to be Montesquieu's wife, a Huguenot named Jeanne de Lartigue, who bore him three children. He married her for her money and they spent much of the marriage living apart as he travelled.

miss these Reflections, because little or no Wit is required in hitting upon them.

The *Persians* who wrote these Letters, lodg'd at my House. We liv'd together; and as they look'd upon me as one of another World, they conceal'd nothing from me. Indeed 'twas hardly possible for men at such a distance from Home to have Secrets that could affect me, and accordingly they communicated to me the greatest Part of their Letters. I took Copies of 'em, and laid my Hands on some they wou'd willingly have kept from me, as exposing a little too much the *Persian* Vanity and Jealousie.

Thus I am a Translator only. My greatest Trouble was to make this Work as conformable as I cou'd to our Manners. I have endavour'd to ease the Reader as much as possible with respect to the *Asiatick* Stile, and have left out abundance of sublime Expressions, which would have carry'd him into the Clouds, and tir'd him with their Sublimity.

This however is not all I have done for him. I have curtail'd the long Compliments, of which the Orientals are more prodigal than even we our selves; and have left out most of those minute Passages, which cannot well bear the Light, and ought always to be buried between Friends.

If most of those that have publish'd Collections of Letters had done the same thing, there would scarce have been enough left to trouble the Press with.

I can't help observing, that I have been often surpriz'd to find these *Persians* as well inform'd as my self of the Manners and Customs of our Nation. Even the nicest Circumstances have not escap'd them; as they have done many *Germans* who have travell'd thro' *France.* I impute it to their long Abode among us, without reckoning that it is easier for an *Asiatic* to learn the *French* Manners in one Year, than for a *French* Man to learn those of *Asia* in four; because the former discover as much as the latter conceal themselves.

Custom permits every Translator, nay every barbarous Commentator, to adorn the Head of his Version, or his Glossary, with the Panegyrick of the Original, and to set forth its Utility, Merit and Excellence. I have done no such thing. The Reasons are easily guess'd at. One of the best is, that it would be very tedious, in a Place of it self generally very insipid; I mean, a Preface.

From Persian Letters

LETTER 1

Usbek *to his friend* Rustan, *at* Ispahan.

We stay'd but one Day at *Com*: when we had paid our Devotions at the Tomb of the Virgin who brought forth twelve Prophets,[2] we proceeded on our Journey, and arriv'd yesterday at *Tauris*, being the twenty fifth of our Departure from *Ispahan*.

Rica and I are perhaps the two first *Persians* that ever left their own Country out of a desire of Knowledge; and renounc'd the sweets of Tranquility, for the laborious search of Wisdom.

We were born in a flourishing Kingdom; but we did not believe there was nothing to be learnt out of its Limits; or that there was no Light but the Oriental, by which we could be illuminated.

Tell me what they say of our Travels. Don't flatter me. I do not expect many Approbators. Direct to me at *Erzeron*, where I shall stay some time. Adieu, dear *Rustan*; and be assur'd that wherever I am, thou wilt always have a faithful Friend.

Tauris, *15th of the Moon* Saphar, 1711.[3]

LETTER 2.

Usbek *to the Chief Black Eunuch[4] at his Serail in* Ispahan.

Thou art the faithful Guardian of the fairest Women in *Persia*. I have trusted with thee the dearest things in the World. Thou hast in thy

---

[2] Fatimah (605–33), daughter of Mahomet, gave birth to twelve caliphs of the Shi'ite tradition. Montesquieu is here confusing her with the Fatimah venerated at Kum (see Glossary), the daughter of Mousa al Kacim, the seventh caliph. The name means in Arabic 'shining one'.

[3] The Muslim months follow the lunar months and do not have a fixed number of days so the Gregorian year gradually comes forward with respect to the Muslim calendar. Montesquieu ignored this problem making the months of any one year experience the same climate; and he makes the Muslim year begin in Dulkaada (January) instead of Muharram (March). The month of Saphar is April. The next letter also falls in Saphar, the following two in Muharram, rendered as Maharram (March) and the first moon of Jomada, rendered as Gemmadi (July). The last letter extracted here falls in Rajab, rendered as Rebiab (March).

[4] On black eunuchs, see n. 6 to Galland, *Arabian Nights Entertainments* in Part 1, and n. 7 to Eliza Haywood, 'The History of the Christian Eunuch' in Part 2.

Hands the Keys of those fatal Doors, that are never open'd but to me. Whilst thou watchest over the Treasure of my Heart, it is at rest, and in an entire Security. Thou art upon Guard in the Silence of the Night, and the Tumult of the Day. Thy indefatigable Cares support thy Virtue when it staggers. If the Women thou guardest wou'd go away, thou depriv'st them of all hope of doing it. Thou art the Flail of Vice, and the Pillar of Fidelity.

Thou command'st them, and thou art obey'd. Thou dost whatever they will of thee, and they do implicitely whatever thou wills for them, according to the Laws of the Serail. Thou makest it thy Glory to render them the meanest Services, and with Respect and Fear submittest to their lawful Orders. Thou servest them as the Slave of their Slaves; and as Master in thy turn, commandest them as sovereignly as I do my self, when thou art apprehensive of any Transgression of the Laws of Chastity and Modesty.

Remember that I rais'd thee from nothing; and, from the lowest of my Slaves, lifted thee to the Office thou art now possess'd of; the Charge of the Delights of my Soul. Behave thy self with the most profound Submission towards those that divide my Love: but at the same time make 'em sensible of their extreme Dependance. Provide for them all innocent Pleasures. Deceive their Disquiets; amuse them with Musick, Dances, and delicious Liquors. Perswade them to meet often. If they would go into the Country, carry them thither; But take care no Man comes near them. Exhort them to Cleanliness, the Image of the Purity of the Soul. Talk frequently of me to them. I long to see them in that charming Place of which themselves are the greatest Ornament.

Tauris, 18th *of the Moon* Saphar, 1711.

LETTER 3

Zachi *to* Usbek, *at* Tauris.

We order'd the chief Eunuch to carry us into the Country. He will tell thee that no Accident befell us. When we were to cross the River, and

quit our Litters; we, according to Custom, put our selves into Cases:
Two Slaves carry'd us on their Shoulders, and we escap'd the Eyes of
all Men.[5]

How can I live, dear *Usbek*, in thy Serrail at *Ispahan*; in those
Places where I eternally call to mind my past Pleasures; where my
Desires every Day suffer fresh Violence? I wander from one Apartment to another, always searching, but I never find thee. Instead of
thee, I meet a cruel Remembrance of my lost Happiness. Sometimes
I'm in the Place, where I first receiv'd thee in my Arms: sometimes in
that where thou decidedst the famous Dispute among thy Wives. Each
of us pretended to be superior to the other in Beauty. We presented
our selves before thee, after having put our Inventions to the Rack, to
dress our selves out to the best Advantage. With Pleasure didst thou
behold the Wonders of our Art. Thou admiredst the Ardency of our
Passion, and the Extent of our Imagination to please thee; but soon
didst thou give up all those borrow'd Charms, and fix thy Eyes on the
Graces of Nature. Thou destroy'dst all our Work. We must strip our
selves of those Ornaments that incommoded rather than serv'd us.
We must appear before thee in our native Simplicity. What car'd I for
Modesty! I was inspir'd with an Ambition to conquer. O happy *Usbek*,
what Worlds of Charms were then in thy View? We saw thy Eyes a
long while roving from Enchantment to Enchantment. A long while
thy Soul remain'd in doubt, where to fix. Every new Grace demanded
a Tribute. We were in an Instant cover'd with thy Kisses. Thy curious
Glances reach'd the most secret Places. A thousand different Postures
are presented to thy View. Thou command'st us with Pleasure, and
with Transport we obey. I own, *Usbek*, a Passion stronger than
Ambition inspir'd me with the Hopes of pleasing thee. I insensibly
perceiv'd that thy Heart was mine. Thou took'st me. Thou left'st me.
Again thou took'st me, and I knew how to keep thee. Mine was the
Triumph, and Despair my Rivals. It seem'd as if there were only we

[5] Numerous informants about Persia, notably John Chardin, refer to these measures
taken to prevent harem women from being seen by men other than the eunuchs when they
were travelling. In Letter 45, Zachi describes another journey in which the eunuchs refuse
to open the boxes despite the cries of the women when they experience a storm on the
water and the eunuchs' execution of two men who try to catch a glimpse of the women
when they are moved from their curtained sedans on camels into the boxes to be transported over water.

two in the World, and nothing else in it worth our Care. Wou'd to Heaven my Rivals had had the Courage to stay and see what Tokens of Love I receiv'd from thee. Had they been Witness of my Raptures, they wou'd have seen the Difference between my Love and theirs; they wou'd have seen, that though they might dispute Charms with me, they cou'd never pretend to be so sensible of the Joy as I was—But where am I? whither does this vain Relation lead me? 'Tis a Misfortune not to have been belov'd; but 'tis an Affront to be belov'd no more. Thou leav'st us, *Usbek*, to go rambling in barbarous Climates. How then! Dost thou think 'tis nothing to be belov'd? Ah *Usbek*, thou dost not know what thou losest. I sigh, but my Sighs are not heard; I weep, and thou dost not see my Tears. Love seems to live in this Serail, and thou art so insensible as to fly from it. Ah my dear *Usbek*, how happy wou'dst thou be, didst thou know thy own Happiness!

From the Serail at Fatme, *the* 21st *of the Moon* Maharram, 1711.

LETTER 135

Rica to Usbek

Toward the end of the week I will come and see thee. O how agreeably will the hours slide away in thy conversation!

Not long ago I was introduc'd to a Court-Lady, who had a mind to see my outlandish figure. I found her beautiful, worthy of the Regards of our Monarch, and of holding an August Rank in the sacred place where his Heart reposeth.

She ask'd me a thousand questions about *Persia*, and what manner of life the *Persian* Women led: I found that the Seraglio was not what she liked, and that she disapprov'd of one man's being divided between ten or twelve Women. She could not without envy behold the happiness of the one, nor without pity the condition of the others. As she lov'd reading, especially the Poets and Romances,[6] she desir'd me to give her some Account of ours: what I said of them redoubled

---

[6] Presumably 17th-c. romances such as those by Madeleine de Scudéry and Costes de la Calprenède in which history, including oriental history, is driven by the admiration of male heroes for lovely chaste heroines.

her curiosity: she begg'd I would translate for her a fragment of some of those which I had brought along with me. I did so, and some days after sent her a *Persian* Tale: perhaps thou wilt not be displeas'd to see it in this disguise.

In the Days of *Cheik-Ali-Can*,[7] there liv'd a Woman in *Persia*, whose Name was *Zulema*, she could repeat the whole Alcoran from one end to the other: there was not a Dervise that better understood the traditions of the Holy Prophets: there was nothing mysterious in the *Arabian* Doctors,[8] which she did not fully comprehend the meaning of: and to this knowledge was added a sprightliness of wit which made it difficult to guess whether she meant to amuse or instruct those she convers'd with.

One day being with her companions, in an apartment of the Seraglio; one of 'em ask'd her what she thought of a future state? and whether she believ'd that ancient Tradition of our Doctors, that Paradise is for none but Men.

'It is the vulgar Opinion', says she to them; 'there has been no stone unturn'd to degrade our sex: nay there's a nation, scattered throughout all *Asia*, call'd the *Jewish* Nation, who assert from the Authority of their sacred Books, that we Women have no Souls.[9]

'These injurious opinions have no other foundation, but the pride of the men, who are far extending their Superiority, even beyond the limits of Life; never considering that, in the Great Day, all Creatures shall appear before God, and seem as nothing: nor will there be among them any other distinction or prerogative, but what shall arise from Virtue.[10]

---

[7] Cheik-Ali-Can: the grand vizier of Safavid Shah Suleiman III (1666–94), Ali Khan, who took office in 1668.

[8] For Arabian doctors, see n. 34 to Marana, 'Letters Writ by a Turkish Spy', above.

[9] Jean de Thévenot comments in ch. 42 'Of the beauty, manners, and apparrel of the Turkish Women' in his *Travels of Monsieur de Thevenot into the Levant* (1687) that 'The Turks do not believe that Women go to Heaven, and hardly account them Rational Creatures; the truth is, they take them only for their service as they would a Horse: but seeing they have many of them, and that they often spend their love upon their own Sex' (57). This was a common misconception of European writers about Islam—in fact the Qur'an says that women go to a different paradise from men—along with the claim that Islam did not ascribe souls to women (I have not located the same charge here made about Judaism). Delarivier Manley's 1707 play *Almyna; or the Arabian Vow* has a Muslim heroine persuade her misogynist husband that women have souls through philosophical and historical argument.

[10] According to medieval Islamic philosophy, the Day of Judgement will be the Last Day of terrestrial time heralded by a trumpet blast and preceded by apocalyptic signs

'God will not be limited in his rewards: and as the men that have liv'd well, and have made right use of the power they have over us here below, will in Paradise be replenish'd with celestial and ravishing Beauties, and such as if a Mortal had beheld 'em, he would have given himself immediately death to come at 'em:[11] so in like manner shall virtuous women go into a place of Delights, where they shall be inebriated with full draughts of Pleasure, in company of those divine men, who shall be subjected unto them: each woman shall have a Seraglio, wherein the men shall be shut up, and Eunuchs far more trusty than ours to look after them.

'I have read', added she, 'in an *Arabian* Book, of a certain man nam'd *Ibrahim*, who was insupportably Jealous; he had twelve wives, all exceeding beautiful, whom he us'd after a very severe manner: he almost always kept them under Lock and Key in their Chamber, where they could neither see nor speak to one another; for he was even jealous of an innocent friendship:[12] all his actions had a taint of his natural brutality: no kind word ever issu'd out of his mouth; and never did he make the least sign with his hand, or the least nod with his head, which did not add something to the rigour of their slavery.

'One day, that they were all together in the Hall of the Seraglio, one of 'em, bolder than the rest, upbraided him for his Ill-nature. Says she to him, "When people study so much to make themselves dreaded, 'tis a sure sign that they have done something for which they know they're hated: we live so very unhappy, that we can't help desiring a change: others, in my place, would wish your death; I only wish my own." This Speech, which ought to have soften'd him, put him into a violent rage; he drew his Dagger, and bury'd it in her Bosom. "My dear companions," said she with a dying voice, "if Heaven has pity of my

which reverse the natural and moral order of things. Each person is handed a book of his or her deeds to read and the deeds are weighed in a scale. The saved traverse a bridge and enter the gardens of paradise whereas the damned fall from it into hell. The 'Day' will last hundreds or thousands of years.

[11] The 'beauties' are 'houris' (black-eyed ones), the 15-year-old courtesans in the Islamic Paradise whose virginity is constantly renewed, described by Thévenot as 'exceedingly beautiful, as white as new-lay'd Eggs, with great black Eyes, and the complexion of the Body extremely white' (*Travels*, ch. 29, 39).

[12] The *Persian Letters* make frequent reference to lesbianism within the harem. Another of Usbek's wives, Zephis, is separated from her deft-handed maid, Zelid, by the black eunuch who suspects them of lesbian familiarities.

Virtue, you will be reveng'd": saying thus, she left this worthless world, to go to the Mansions of Delight, where such women as have past a well-spent life enjoy a Bliss which is continually renewing.

'The first thing she saw was a smiling meadow, whose verdure was enamel'd with variety of the liveliest and most fragrant flowers: a brook, whose stream, more transparent than Crystal, made its way thro' infinite turnings and windings: afterwards she enter'd into those charming bowers, whose silence was only interrupted with the melodious warbling of birds: then spacious gardens presented themselves to her view: Nature had adorn'd them with her simplicity, and the utmost magnificence: then she proceeded to a stately Palace prepar'd for her, crowded with heavenly men, that were destined for her delight.

'Two of these immediately began to undress her: others put her into the Bath, and perfum'd her all over with the most delicious essences: then they presented her with a habit infinitely richer than her own: afterwards they led her into a spacious Hall, where she found a fire made with Aromatic Woods, and a table spread with the most exquisite dainties. Every thing seem'd to conspire to transport her senses: on the one hand was heard Music, so much the more divine, as it was soft: on the other, she beheld nothing but the dances of those divine men, whose sole business was to pleasure Her. Yet as those Pleasures were only in order to lead her insensibly to others far greater, she was conducted into a Chamber, and after once more uncloathing her, she was laid on a rich Bed, where two men, inexpressibly handsome, receiv'd her in their arms. Here she was intoxicated, and her ecstasies exceeded even her desires. "I am quite besides my self," says she to them; "I believe I should die, were I not assur'd of my immortality; 'tis too much; let me go; I am convulst with the violent delight. So; 'tis done; you now restore a little Calm to my senses; I begin to breathe, and come again to my self—why have they taken away the Lights? why may I not survey your divine beauty? Why may I not see—but to what purpose? You again throw me back into my first transports. O ye Gods, how amiable is this Darkness! what, shall I be immortal? and with you too? I shall—no—I ask your pardon, Gentlemen; for I plainly see you will not ask mine."

'After many reiterated commands, she was obey'd: but not till she was seriously resolv'd to be: she repos'd her self in a languishing manner, and slumber'd in their arms. Two moments Rest repair'd her Faintness: she receiv'd two kisses which of a sudden re-inflam'd her, and caus'd her to open her eyes. "I am uneasy," says she; "I'm afraid you cease to love me." This was a Doubt wherein she resolv'd not long to continue: whereupon they gave her all the satisfaction she could wish: "I am undeceiv'd," said she; "I cry ye mercy: I can depend upon you: you speak not one word to me; but your actions I like better than any thing you could say. Yes, yes, I frankly own, never was love like yours: but how! you both contend for the honour of persuading me? ah! if you thus contend, if you join ambition to the pleasure of my overthrow, I am undone: you'll both remain Conquerors, and only I be conquered: but you shall purchase the Victory very dear."

'This Scene was interrupted by nothing but the Day-light: her faithful lovely Domestics came into her Chamber, and rais'd these two young men, who were led by two old ones to the respective places where they were kept for Pleasure. She afterwards got up, and at first shew'd herself to that idolatrous Court, in all the Charms of a plain Undress, and afterwards cloath'd in the most sumptuous Ornaments. This Night had burnish'd her Beauty: it had given life to her Complexion, and expression to her Graces. All the day was spent in Dances, Consorts, Banquets, Gaming, and the like: and 'twas observ'd, that *Anäis* stole away from time to time, and flew to her two young Heroes; after some precious moments of converse, she return'd to the company she had quitted, always with a serener countenance than before. To cut short, towards the evening they lost her for good and all; she went and shut her self up in the Seraglio, whither she told them she would go and contract Acquaintance with those immortal Captives, who were to live for ever with her; she therefore visited the most retir'd, and the most charming apartments of the place, where she reckon'd up fifty Slaves miraculously beautiful: she stray'd all night from Chamber to Chamber, every where receiving their homage, always different, and always the same.

Thus you see how the immortal *Anäis* pass'd her life; sometimes amidst the splendid pleasures, sometimes amidst the solitary: either admir'd by a shining company, or else caress'd by a Lover distractedly fond of her: oftentimes she would forsake the enchanted Palace, and remove into a Sylvan Grotto: the flowers seem'd to grow from every step she took; and the Loves and Sports presented themselves in crowds to meet her on the way.[13] More than eight days she continu'd in this happy abode; and all that while, being continually beside her self, she had not made the least reflexion: she had enjoy'd her happiness without knowing it, or without having had so much as one of those quiet moments wherein the Soul does as it were call her self to account, and gives it self audience amidst the silence of the Passions.

'The Blest have Pleasures so strong, that they rarely can enjoy this liberty of the mind: hence it is, that being irreclaimably attacht to present objects, they intirely lose the memory of things past; and retain no longer any regard to what they knew or lov'd in the other world.

'But *Anaïs*, whose mind was truly philosophical, had pass'd almost her whole Life in meditation: she had carry'd her reflexions much further, than one would have expected from a woman left to her self. The austere retreat which her husband had confin'd her to, had procur'd her no other advantage but this: 'twas this force and strength of mind, which had made her slight the fear her Companions were struck with; and despise Death, which was to end her Sufferings, and being her Felicity.

'Thus by little and little she waded out of the ebriety[14] of Pleasure, and lockt her self up, alone, in an apartment of her Palace. She gave a loose to pleasing reflections upon her past condition, and her present happiness: she could not forbear pitying the misfortune of her Companions: 'tis natural to compassionate the pains we our selves have pass'd through. *Anaïs* kept not within the bare bounds of Compassion; being mov'd with Tenderness towards those unhappy Creatures, she found her self inclin'd to relieve them.

'She order'd one of those young Men that were about her, to assume the shape of her Husband; she bad him go to the Seraglio, seize it, turn him out of it, and continue there in his Place till such time as she recall'd him.

'The execution was speedy; he cut the Air; arriv'd at the Gate of the Seraglio, but *Ibrahim* was not there. He knocks; the Doors fly open; the Eunuchs prostrate themselves at his Feet; he hurries to the

---

[13] C. J. Betts, in a modern translation, renders this phrase as 'amusements thronged about her' (*Persian Letters* (London: Penguin Books, 1993), 251).

[14] ebriety: the state or habit of being intoxicated (*OED*).

Apartments where *Ibrahim's* women were shut up: he had before taken the Keys out of the Pocket of that jealous-pated wretch, to whom he had made himself invisible. He goes in; he much surprizes 'em with his mild and affable Air, and yet more with his Fondness, and the rapidity of his Caresses: they were all equally astonish'd at his performances, and would have taken it for a Dream, had there been less of reality in it.

'Whilst these new scenes were playing in the Seraglio, *Ibrahim* knocks, names himself to them, storms and makes a Clamour: after he had gone through a world of difficulties, he enters, and puts the Eunuchs into a terrible disorder: he fetches large strides: but starts back, and falls as from the clouds when he sees the false *Ibrahim*, his real Image, injoying all the liberties of a Master. He calls out for help: he bids the Eunuchs assist him in killing that Impostor; but he is not obey'd: there's nothing now remains but one remedy, and that a very poor one, which is, to refer it to the Judgment of his women.

'In the space of an Hour the false *Ibrahim* had corrupted all his Judges: the other is driven away, and ignominiously dragg'd out of the Seraglio; and had receiv'd a thousand Deaths, had not his Rival order'd his Life to be spar'd: at length the new *Ibrahim*, remaining Master of the Field of Battle, shew'd himself more and more worthy of the choice they had made, and signaliz'd himself by miracles till then unknown. "You are not like *Ibrahim*," said the women. "He is not like me, you mean", cries the triumphant *Ibrahim*. "What must a man do to prove himself yours, if what I do suffices not?"

' "Far be it from us to doubt it," say the women. "If you are not *Ibrahim*, we are satisfy'd you have well deserv'd to be him: you are more our Spouse in one Day, than he has been in the course of ten Years." "Then you'll give me your word", cry'd he, "that you'll declare your selves in my favour, against that Impostor." "We do, we do," said they, with one voice; "we'll take an Oath of everlasting fidelity to you: we have been but too long abus'd: the old Rogue did not at all suspect our virtue; he only suspected his own inability; we plainly see, that Men are otherguess Creatures than he: no, no, 'tis you they are like: O, could you but know how much you make us hate him".—"Well, I'll give you cause more and more to hate him," reply'd the false *Ibrahim*: "you don't yet know how much he has wrong'd you." "We judge of his injustice by the greatness of our revenge," cry'd they. "Yes," says the Divine Man, "you're in the right; I proportion'd the expiation to the crime; I'm mighty glad my way of punishing has pleas'd you." "But," said they, "suppose this Impostor should return; what shall we do then?" "I believe", answer'd he, "'twou'd be a hard matter for him to deceive you in the part I have acted: 'tis a Place hardly to be supply'd by artifice; and besides, I'll send him packing so far, you shall never more hear of him: then will I take your happiness into my care; you shall not find Me jealous, I shall know how to be secure of you without confining you; I have too good an opinon of my own merit, to think you will prove false to me: if you are not virtuous with me, whom will you be so?" This conversation lasted some time between him and those women, who being more pleas'd with the difference of the two *Ibrahims* that the resemblance, did not concern themselves so much about having these mysteries cleared up to them. At length the Husband at his wit's end returns once more upon them, to interrupt their pleasures: he found the whole House swimming with joy, and the women more incredulous than ever. 'Twas no place for a jealous Man: out he goes in a rage, and a moment after the false *Ibrahim* follows him, lays hold on him, transports him through the Air, and leaves him four hundred Leagues from the Place.

'O Gods, in what affliction were these women by the absence of their dear *Ibrahim*! Already had their Eunuchs reassum'd their natural Severity: the whole House was in tears: sometimes they imagin'd, all that had happen'd to 'em was nothing a Dream: they look'd at each other: and recall'd to mind the minutest circumstances of these wonderful Adventures. At last *Ibrahim* returns to 'em more amiable than before: it seem'd to them as if his Voyage had not been in the least laborious: the new Master behav'd so different from the other, he surpriz'd the whole Neighbourhood. He turn'd away all the Eunuchs; made his House free to every body; he wou'd not suffer his women so much as to be veil'd; 'twas a thing entirely new to see them at public Entertainments amongst the men, and as free as they. *Ibrahim* believ'd, with reason, that the customs of the Country were not for such Citizens as he. Mean while he spar'd for no expence, he made the Estate fly; insomuch that the jealous *Ibrahim* returning three

Years afterwards from foreign Countries, whither he had been carry'd, found nothing left but his Wives, and six and thirty Children.

Paris, *the* 26*th of the Moon* Gemmadi 1, 1720.

LETTER 150

Roxana[15] *to* Usbek, *at* Paris.

Yes, I have deceived thee, I have corrupted thy Eunuchs: I made a sport of thy Jealousy; and found means to turn thy hated Seraglio into a place of pleasure and delight.

I feel the near approaches of Death; the poison is working in my veins. For, what should I do here, since the only man that made life agreeable is no more?[16] I am dying: my Ghost is upon the wing, but takes its flight in good company: I have just sent away those sacrilegious Guardians that have shed the purest blood in the world.

How could'st thou think me so credulous, as to fancy my self sent into the world for no other purpose than to adore thy Caprices? that at the same time thou allowed'st thy self all manner of liberties, thou hadst a right to confine all my desire? No: I liv'd indeed in servitude, but still I was free: I reformed thy Laws by those of Nature, and my Mind still kept it self independent.

Thou oughtest even to thank me for the Sacrifice I made thee, in humbling my self so much as to seem faithful to thee; in poorly

---

[15] Roxana is Usbek's favourite wife. In Letter 26 he describes how she resisted his advances after their marriage for two months and could not look at him without blushing for three. He takes these actions as a sign of her chastity and only discovers in this letter that they rather indicated her resistance and loathing. The choice of name for this wife is not insignificant. It came in Europe to indicate a woman of loose morals or courtesan. Montesquieu may have had in mind in particular Jean Racine's tragedy *Bajazet* of 1672, relating to events of 1635 to 1638 in the Ottoman court: here, Roxane, favoured courtesan of Sultan Amurat (Murad IV 1623–40), who has been left to govern the seraglio in his absence at war, pursues the sultan's handsome brother, Bajazet. Bajazet's affections are engaged by the lovely and noble-born Ottoman Princess Atalide, but he is persuaded by the treacherous vizier Acomat to play Roxane along. When she discovers the cheat, enraged with jealousy, Roxane orders Bajazet's death, before herself being killed by the sultan's emissary, and the play concludes with the suicide of Atalide.

[16] Letter 149 from the chief eunuch Solim informs Usbek that Roxana's unnamed lover was killed by the eunuchs who broke into her chamber and discovered them together.

confining within my heart what I ought to have made conspicuous to the whole world: lastly, in prophaning of Vertue, by suffering to go by that name, my submission to thy whims.

Thou wast amaz'd at not finding in me the transports of Love: hadst thou thoroughly known me, thou hadst found nothing in my heart but the most violent hatred.

But thou hast had a long time the advantage of believing, that a heart like mine was a slave to thee: we were both of us happy: you fancy'd you cheated me, and I all the while actually cheated you.

Doubtless this Language seems new to thee: is it possible, after I have overwhelm'd thee with grief, I should likewise force thee to admire my courage? but it is done: the Poison consumes me: my strength forsakes me: my pen drops out of my hand: I feel even my very Hatred decay; I am Dying.

From the Seraglio at Ispahan, *the* 8*th* *of the Moon* Rebiab, 1720.

The Citizen of the World; or Letters from a Chinese Philosopher, residing in London, to his Friends in the East (1762)

Oliver Goldsmith

Copy-text: vols. i and ii of the 1st edition (London, 1762)

A periodical called the *Public Ledger, or Daily Register of Commerce and Intelligence* began publication on 12 January 1760. Oliver Goldsmith (1730–74) had an agreement with one of the proprietors, John Newberry, to provide papers of an amusing character twice a week for salary of £100 per annum. He produced a series of 119 Chinese letters which were published complete in two volumes in 1762 under the title *The Citizen of the World*. It was this publication that drew Goldsmith to public attention, although he had published a minor essay, *An Enquiry into the Present State of Learning in Europe*, in 1659 and a number of periodical essays, particularly in *The Bee*.

Goldsmith was the son of an Anglo-Irish clergyman; he was educated at Trinity College, Dublin, and left Ireland in 1752 to study at the medical school in Edinburgh. He did not

From The Citizen of the World

complete his degree and arrived in London penniless in 1756. Here, despite his uncouthness in society, his eccentricity and extravagance (exacerbated by an addiction to gambling), his talent and charm as a writer made him a central figure in literary circles. He became in 1764 one of the five founder members of a club which met weekly for supper and talk and included the painter Joshua Reynolds, and the writers Edmund Burke and Samuel Johnson. He was also an accomplished poet and a prolific essayist, always in need of funds from his publications but nevertheless dying in poverty. Although politically conservative, his writings are always marked by a comic and humane sympathy.

The letters of Lien Chi Altangi, a Confucian sage who travels from China to live in England, that constitute *The Citizen of the World* are evidently in the tradition of the *Letters Writ by a Turkish Spy* and the *Persian Letters*, but they avoid the former's fascination with state intrigue and the latter's eroticism. Their focus is rather on a gentle satire of fashionable life and pretension. Their author's direct debt (and Goldsmith was an inveterate borrower of others' writings) was to a work by Jean Baptiste de Boyer, Marquis d'Argens (1704–71), a French soldier who moved to Holland to gain intellectual freedom; Argen's *Lettres Juives, Chinoises et Cabalistiques* (1736, 1738) were published as separate works entitled *Jewish Letters* and *Chinese Letters* in English translation, the latter in 1741. For information about China, Goldsmith drew on the Jesuit compiler Jean-Baptiste Du Halde, whose collection he used in an English translation entitled *A Description of the Empire of China* (2 vols., 1738, 1741) and Louis Le Comte's *Nouveaux Mémoires sur l'état présent de la Chine* (Goldsmith referred to the third French edition of 1697), the latter also written in the form of a series of letters. The notes below use an earlier translation of Du Halde's text (4 vols. in 1736), almost the same in terms of content, because this version of the text was also a source for Horace Walpole's tale given in this anthology, *Mi Li*. For his letter writer, Goldsmith snatched the name of the addressee in Horace Walpole's satirical pamphlet of 1757, *A Letter from Xo Ho, a Chinese Philosopher at London, to his Friend Lien Chi at Peking* (see *Hieroglyphic Tales* in Part 2 of this collection).

Letter Fictions

And the name of Lien Chi's addressee, Fum Hoam, is taken from a popular oriental tale by the French lawyer turned novelist, Thomas-Simon Gueullette, known in English translation as *Chinese Tales: or, the Wonderful Adventures of the Mandarine Fum-Hoam* (1725).

Lien Chi Altangi writes to Fum-Hoam, first president of the ceremonial academy at Peking, and provides him with accounts of the manners, social institutions, and domestic arrangements of the English in London. Interwoven with satirical accounts of newspapers, the graves of poets at Westminster Abbey, the theatre, gaming, horse racing, are letters which give sage pseudo-Confucian advice about accepting life's misfortunes, not falling prey to superstition, the importance of relative judgement, and a plot borrowed from oriental romances in which Lien Chi's son, who has set out to follow him, is enslaved in Persia, encounters and falls in love with a beautiful fellow captive, escapes to England, and rediscovers his beloved in the person of the niece of his father's dearest friend and guide, the man in black.

I give two letters here. The first is a textbook example of the 'reverse ethnography' of the oriental letter in which Lien Chi mocks the prejudices and preconceptions of Europeans about his native culture. Oliver Goldsmith was a persistent critic of the cult of Chinoiserie, the European imitation of Chinese imports such as porcelain, lacquerware, furniture, silks, and wall hangings. See 'Chinoiserie and the Aesthetics of Legitimacy', in David Porter, *Ideographia: The Chinese Cypher in Early Modern Europe* (Stanford, Calif.: Stanford University Press, 2001), 133–92. Reviewing a play adapted from Voltaire by Arthur Murphy entitled *The Orphan of China*, Goldsmith complained:

> We have seen gardens laid out in the Eastern manner; houses ornamented in front by zig-zag lines, and rooms stuck round with Chinese vases, and Indian pagods. If such whimsies prevail among those who conduct the pleasures of the times, and consequently lead the fashion, is it to be wondered, if even poetry itself should conform, and the public be presented with a piece formed upon Chinese manners? manners which, tho' the poet should happen to mistake, he has this consolation left, that few readers are able

From The Citizen of the World

to detect the imposture. (*The Critical Review* (May 1759),
in *Collected Works of Oliver Goldsmith*, ed. Arthur Friedman
(Oxford: Clarendon Press, 1966), i. 170–2)

The irony of course lies in the fact that Lien Chi, as the
product of Oliver Goldsmith's pen, might be seen as just
another whimsical product of the taste for things Chinese, an
object displayed by his author in pursuit of public reputation
and to demonstrate his virtuosity. The second letter given
here illustrates Goldsmith's hostility to travel as a commercial
venture. Lien Chi argues that travel should be performed by
philosophers such as himself, driven not by conflict or profit,
but by intellectual curiosity.

LETTER 14[1]

I was some days ago agreeably surprised by a message from a lady of
distinction, who sent me word, that she most passionately desired the
pleasure of my acquaintance; and, with the utmost impatience,
expected an interview. I will not deny, my dear Fum Hoam, but that
my vanity was raised at such an invitation, I flattered myself that she
had seen me in some public place, and had conceived an affection for
my person, which thus induced her to deviate from the usual decorums
of the sex. My imagination painted her in all the bloom of youth and
beauty. I fancied her attended by the loves and graces, and I set out with
the most pleasing expectations of seeing the conquest I had made.

When I was introduced into her apartment, my expectations were
quickly at an end; I perceived a little shrivelled figure indolently
reclined on a sofa, who nodded by way of approbation at my
approach.[2] This, as I was afterwards informed, was the lady herself,

---

[1] The letter first appeared in *The Public Ledger* for Thursday, 28 February 1760.

[2] Goldsmith borrows this scenario from a work in imitation of the Persian Letters by
the Whig politician George Lyttelton (1709–73), *Letters from a Persian in England, to his
Friend at Ispahan*: 'The other Morning, a Friend of mine came to me, and told me, with
the Air of one who brings an agreeable Piece of News, that there was a Lady who most

a woman equally distinguished for rank, politeness, taste and understanding. As I was dressed after the fashion of Europe, she had taken me for an Englishman, and consequently saluted me in her ordinary manner; but when the footman informed her grace that I was the gentleman from China, she instantly lifted herself from the couch, while her eyes sparkled with unusual vivacity. 'Bless me! can this be the gentleman that was born so far from home? What an unusual share of *somethingness* in his whole appearance. Lord how I am charmed with the outlandish cut of his face; how bewitching the exotic breadth of his forehead.[3] I would give the world to see him in his country dress. Pray turn about, Sir, and let me see you behind. There! there's a travell'd air for you. You that attend there, bring up a plate of beef cut into small pieces; I have a violent passion to see him eat. Pray, Sir, have you got your chop-sticks about you? It will be pretty to see the meat carried to the mouth with a jerk. Pray speak a little Chinese: I have learned something of the language myself.[4] Lord, have you nothing pretty from China about you; something that one does not know what to do with? I have got twenty things from China that are no use in the world. Look at those jars, they are of the right pea-green:[5] these are the

passionately desir'd the Pleasure of my Acquaintance, and had commission'd him to carry me to see her.—I will not deny to thee, that my Vanity was a little flatter'd with this Message . . . I painted her in my own Imagination very young, and very handsome, and set out with most pleasing Expectations, to see the Conquest I had made. But when I arriv'd at the Place of Assignation, I found a little old Woman very dirty' (Letter LXXI, 2nd edn. (1735), 215-16). The lady, who has pretensions to theological learning, rejects with disgust his offer to furnish her with a Persian tale in place of her desire for him to explain Islam.

[3] Louis Le Comte tells us that the Chinese 'would have a man big, tall, and gross; they would have him have a broad forehead, eyes little and fat, a short nose, great ears, a mouth of a middle size, a long beard, and black hair' (*A Compleat History of the Empire of China*, 2nd edn. corr. (1739), 124).

[4] Despite 17th-c. interest in the Chinese language as a possible remnant of a universal pre-lapsarian tongue, it was not until the 19th c. that Europe saw genuine scholarship in this field. Shen Fo Tsung, protégé of the Jesuit Father Couplet, visited England in 1686 and taught the orientalist Thomas Hyde some Chinese. The Bodleian Library had a collection of Chinese books from English nobles and merchantmen, but no one capable of reading them. See ch. 2, 'A Confusion of Tongues', in William Appleton, *A Cycle of Cathay. The Chinese Vogue in England during the Seventeenth and Eighteenth Centuries* (New York: Columbia University Press, 1951).

[5] Jean-Baptiste Du Halde refers to a 'counterfeit' sort of China-ware made to simulate the most ancient vases 'in which there is nothing particular in the Make unless with respect to the Varnish, which is made of a yellow Stone, and being mixed with the commons sort gives the Vessels the Colour of Sea-green' (*The General History of China* (1736), ii. 353). The lady is revealing her ignorance by taking her pea-green vessels as antiques.

From The Citizen of the World

furniture.' *'Dear madam'*, said I, *'those, though they may appear fine in your eyes, are but paltry to a Chinese; but, as they are useful utensils, it is proper they should have a place in every apartment.'* 'Useful! Sir,' replied the lady; 'sure you mistake, they are of no use in the world.' *'What! are they not filled with an infusion of tea as in China?'* replied I. 'Quite empty and useless upon my honour, Sir.' *'Then they are the most cumbrous and clumsy furniture in the world, as nothing is truly elegant but what unites use with beauty.'* [6] 'I protest,' says the lady, 'I shall begin to suspect thee of being an actual barbarian. I suppose also you hold my two beautiful pagods in contempt.' *'What!'* cried I, *'has Fohi spread his gross superstitions here also? Pagods of all kinds are my aversion.'*[7] 'A Chinese, a traveller, and want taste! It surprises me. Pray, sir, examine the beauties of the Chinese temple which you see at the end of the garden. Is there any thing in China more beautiful?'[8] *'Where I stand I see nothing, madam, at the end of the garden that may not as well be called an Egyptian pyramid as a Chinese temple; for that little building in view is as like the one as t'other.'* 'What! Sir, is not that a Chinese temple? you must surely be mistaken. Mr. Freeze, who designed it, calls it one, and nobody disputes his pretensions to taste.' I now found it vain to contradict the lady in any thing she thought fit to advance: so was resolved rather to act the disciple than the instructor. She took me through several rooms all furnished, as she told me, in the Chinese manner; sprawling dragons, squatting pagods, and clumsy mandarines,

[6] Le Comte summarizes, 'As for porcelain, it is such an ordinary moveable, that it is the ornament of every house; the tables, the side-boards, nay, the kitchen is cumber'd with it, for they eat and drink out of it, it is their ordinary vessel' (*Compleat History*, 150).

[7] The term 'pagod' can refer to an idol temple, an idol or image of a deity, or a person who is reverenced as a deity. Here, the reference is to the Buddha (Gautama or Siddhartha Buddha), commonly referred to as 'Fo' or 'Fo-Hi' by European commentators. Du Halde gives the story of the Buddha and says that 'at Thirty he was wholly inspired by the Divinity, and became Fo or Pagod, as the *Indians* call him, looking upon himself as a God' (*General History of China*, iii. 36). Jesuit missionaries and informants such as Du Halde and Le Comte were deeply antagonistic to Buddhism in China and sought to promote Confucianism as a secular morality compatible with Christianity. As a Confucian character, Lien Chi is assumed to have nothing but contempt for Buddhism. Buddhism came to China in the first centuries AD and was recognized officially in the 6th c. AD.

[8] On the vogue for Chinese gardens and mock temples, see introduction to Horace Walpole, 'Mi Li', in Part 2. See also Goldsmith's attack on Chinoiserie and especially the Chinese garden in his review of Arthur Murphy's play, *The Orphan of China*, discussed in the introduction above.

were stuck upon every shelf: In turning round one must have used caution not to demolish a part of the precarious furniture.

In a house like this, thought I, one must live continually upon the watch; the inhabitant must resemble a knight in an enchanted castle, who expects to meet an adventure at every turning. *'But, Madam'*, said I, *'do no accidents every happen to all this finery?'* 'Man, Sir,' replied the lady, 'is born to misfortunes, and it is but fit I should have a share. Three weeks ago, a careless servant snapp'd off the head of a favourite mandarine: I had scarce done grieving for that, when a monkey broke a beautiful jar; this I took the more to heart, as the injury was done me by a friend: however, I survived the calamity; when yesterday crash went half a dozen dragons upon the marble hearth stone; and yet I live; I survive it all: you can't conceive what comfort I find under afflictions from philosophy. There is Seneca, and Bolingbroke, and some others, who guide me through life, and teach me to support its calamities'[9]— I could not but smile at a woman who makes her own misfortunes, and then deplores the miseries of her situation. Wherefore, tired of acting with dissimulation, and willing to indulge my meditations in solitude, I took leave just as the servant was bringing in a plate of beef, pursuant to the directions of his mistress. Adieu.

LETTER 105[10]

I have frequently been amazed at the ignorance of almost all the European travellers, who have penetrated any considerable way eastward into Asia. They have been influenced either by motives of commerce or piety, and their accounts are such as might reasonably be

---

[9] Lucius Annaeus Seneca (d. 65) was exiled by the Emperor Claudius to Corsica in 41. He spent eight years on the island where he wrote his major philosophical works advocating a marriage of pragmatic ethics with stoicism, the belief that the universe is rational and guided by fate. He returned to Rome in 54 when Nero became emperor and was one of the latter's chief advisers. Henry St John, 1st viscount Bolingbroke (1678–1751), after a brilliant career as a Tory politician and secretary of state in 1710, was dismissed on the accession of the pro-Whig George I, impeached, and attainted. He fled to Paris where he served James Stuart as private secretary but was pardoned after disavowing the Jacobite cause in 1723 and returned to England. In exile, he wrote *Reflections upon Exile and Reflections Concerning Innate Moral Principles* under the influence of Voltaire as attempts to come to terms with his disappointments.

[10] The letter first appeared in the *Public Ledger*, Monday, 26 January 1761.

expected from men of very narrow or very prejudiced education, the dictates of superstition or the result of ignorance. Is it not surprizing, that in such a variety of adventurers not one single philosopher should be found; for as to the travels of Gemelli, the learned are long agreed that the whole is but an imposture.[11]

There is scarce any country how rude or incultivated soever, where the inhabitants are not possessed of some peculiar secrets, either in nature or art, which might be transplanted with success; in Siberian Tartary, for instance, the natives extract a strong spirit from milk, which is a secret probably unknown to the chymists of Europe. In the most savage parts of India, they are possessed of the secret of dying vegetable substances scarlet; and of refining lead into a metal which, for hardness and colour, is little inferior to silver; not one of which secrets but would in Europe make a man's fortune. The power of the Asiatics in producing winds, or bringing down rain, the Europeans are apt to treat as fabulous, because they have no instances of the like nature among themselves; but they would have treated the secrets of gunpowder, and the mariner's compass, in the same manner, had they been told the Chinese used such arts before the invention was common with themselves at home.[12]

Of all the English philosophers I most reverence *Bacon*, that great and hardy genius;[13] he it is who allows of secrets yet unknown; who,

---

[11] Gemelli: the reference is found in the version of the Preface by Du Halde given in the first volume of a translation of the Jesuit's text published by Edward Cave in 1738 (the earlier 1736 translation has a different version of the Preface). It was Cave's text which Goldsmith used. There, Du Halde refers to 'a certain *Italian* Traveller who in a Book printed at *Naples* in 1720, entitled *Giro del Mondo* . . . has given a particular Description of the Emperor of *China's* Palace; of which he cou'd have no Idea, but what his Fancy suggested.' A footnote identifies the Italian traveller as 'Dr. *I. Francis Gemelli Careri*' (*A Description of the Empire of China* (1738), i, p. i).

[12] Gunpowder was discovered in 11th-c. China and not until the 14th in Europe. The mariner's compass was in use in China in the 10th c. but not invented in Europe until *c.*1180. The first use of movable type in China was between 1041 and 1048 and in Europe 1430–60.

[13] Francis Bacon (1561–26), lord chancellor of England 1618–21, is consistently praised by fictional oriental informants for his method of inductive reasoning as a means of analysing and classifying the material world, especially in the *Novum Organum; Historia Naturalis et Experimentalis ad Condendam Philosophiam: Sive Phaenomena Universi* (1622). Bacon promotes a technique of 'gradual ascent', that is, the patient accumulation of well-founded generalizations of steadily increasing degrees of generality. This method is expected to dislodge the vague and unfounded concepts of everyday life and identify in their place important differences and similarities in the experienced world. Bacon may

undaunted by the seeming difficulties that oppose, prompts human curiosity to examine every part of nature, and even exhorts man to try whether he cannot subject the tempest, the thunder, and even earthquakes to human control: O did a man of his daring spirit, of his genius, penetration, and learning travel to those countries which have been visited only by the superstitious and mercenary, what might not mankind expect: how would he enlighten the regions to which he travelled! And what a variety of knowledge and useful improvement would he not bring back in exchange!

There is probably no country so barbarous, that would not disclose all it knew, if it received from the traveller equivalent information; and I am apt to think, that a person, who was ready to give more knowledge than he received, would be welcome wherever he came. All his care in travelling should only be to suit his intellectual banquet to the people with whom he conversed; he should not attempt to teach the unlettered Tartar astronomy, nor yet instruct the polite Chinese in the ruder arts of subsistence; he should endeavour to improve the Barbarian in the secrets of living comfortably; and the inhabitant of a more refined country in the speculative pleasures of science. How much more nobly would a philosopher thus employed spend his time, than by sitting at home earnestly intent upon adding one more star to his catalogue; or one monster more to his collection; or still, if possible, more triflingly sedulous in the incatenation[14] of fleas, or the sculpture of a cherry-stone.

I never consider this subject, without being surprized how none of those societies so laudably established in England for the promotion of arts and learning, have never thought of sending one of their members into the most eastern parts of Asia, to make what discoveries he was able. To be convinced of the utility of such an undertaking, let them but read the relations of their own travellers. It will be there found, that they are as often deceived themselves, as they attempt to deceive others. The merchant tells us perhaps the price of different

also have appealed to Goldsmith as a reference here because his *Advancement of Learning* (1606) makes several remarks on the Chinese writing system in an attempt to incorporate the Chinese example into a more general argument on the theory of language.

[14] incatenation: putting in or fastening with chains; harnessing; a linking or being linked together (*OED*).

commodities, the methods of baling them up, and the properest manner for an European to preserve his health in the country. The missioner, on the other hand, informs us, with what pleasure the country to which he was sent embraced christianity, and the numbers he converted; what methods he took to keep Lent in a region where there was no fish, or the shifts he made to celebrate the rites of his religion, in places where there was neither bread not wine; such accounts, with the usual appendage of marriages and funerals, inscriptions, rivers, and mountains, make up the whole of an European traveller's diary;[15] but as to all the secrets of which the inhabitants are possessed, those are universally atttributed to magic; and when the traveller can give no other account of the wonders he sees performed, he very contentedly ascribes them to the power of the devil.

It was an usual observation of *Boyle*, the English chymist, that if every artist would but discover what new observations occurred to him in the exercise of his trade, philosophy would thence gain innumerable improvements.[16] It may be observed, with still greater justice, that if the useful knowledge of every country, howsoever barbarous, was gleaned by a judicious observer, the advantages would be inestimable. Are there not even in Europe, many useful inventions known or practised, but in one place? The instrument, as an example, for cutting down corn in Germany, is much more handy and expeditious, in my opinion, than the sickle used in England. The cheap and expeditious manner of making vinegar without previous fermentation, is known only in a part of France. If such discoveries therefore, remain still to be known at home; what funds of knowledge might not be

---

[15] Missionaries and merchants were indeed the only European travellers to gain access to China in the 17th and 18th c. and then on very restricted terms. Merchants were confined to the region of Canton and obliged to deal only with the Cohong monopoly there. Jesuit missionaries achieved some toleration through their knowledge of mathematics and astronomy which in some cases gave them access to the emperor himself. See Jonathan Spence, *The Chan's Great Continent: China in Western Minds* (London: Allen Lane Penguin Press, 1999).

[16] Robert Boyle (1627–91) formed the 'Experimental Philosophy Club' in Oxford in the 1650s and 1660s with Christopher Wren, John Locke, John Wilkins, and others. A chemist and physicist from a wealthy family as the son of the earl of Cork, he was well informed about Continental scientific developments and played a major role in the foundation of the Royal Society (1660). His best-known works are *The Sceptical Chemist* (1660) and the *Origin of Forms and Qualities* (1666). He argued strongly for the need of applying the principles and methods of chemistry to the study of the natural world and to medicine.

collected, in countries yet unexplored, or only passed through by ignorant travellers in hasty caravans.

The caution with which foreigners are received in Asia, may be alledged as an objection to such a design. But how readily have several European merchants found admission into regions the most suspecting, under the character of *Sanjapius*, or northern pilgrims; to such not even China itself denies access.

To send out a traveller, properly qualified for these purposes, might be an object of national concern; it would in some measure repair the breaches made by ambition; and might shew that there are still some who boasted a greater name than that of patriots, who professed themselves lovers of men. The only difficulty would remain in chusing a proper person, for so arduous an enterprize. He should be a man of a philosophical turn, one apt to deduce consequences of general utility from particular occurrences, neither swollen with pride, nor hardened by prejudice, neither wedded to one particular system, nor instructed only in one particular science; neither wholly a botanist, nor quite an antiquarian; his mind should be tinctured with miscellaneous knowledge, and his manners humanized by an intercourse with men. He should be, in some measure, an enthusiast to the design; fond of travelling, from a rapid imagination, and an innate love of change; furnished with a body capable sustaining every fatigue, and an heart not easily terrified at danger.

Adieu.

GLOSSARY

1. Oriental terms

agah   aga, leader, superior, commander, the term literally means 'gentleman' or 'master'

aguacy-dié   the *akàsdiah* from *akas* (sky) and *diah* (lamp), a tall light, used to make the royal Mughal camp conspicuous from a distance

alcoran   most common rendering in English of *Qur'an*, the holy book of Islam

am/amba   from the Sanskrit *amra*, the North Indian name for the mangoe. The term mango is derived from the Portuguese *manga* from the Tamil name *mankay*

ananas   European term derived from Brazilian nane for the pineapple

anis   aniseed

antimony   fine metallic powder still commonly used to stain eyelids black

ashmak   yashmak, turkish veil or cloak

bagnios   Turkish baths with rooms for steaming etc. Men and women had separate establishments for bathing

banianes   trading class among the Hindu

bassa/bassaw/great bassa   bashaw, earlier form of the Turkish title *pasha*, formerly borne in Turkey by officers of high rank, as military commanders, and governors of provinces

bazar   bazaar, a marketplace or permanent market

bonze   a term applied by Europeans to Buddhist priests

boule-ponges   a kind of punch

brahmins   Brahmans, the priestly caste of Hindus. Vedic society was divided into four classes, with Brahmans of the highest class. Brahmans are the guardians of the Veda, learning and reciting it during rituals. Their duties are to teach the Veda and to sacrifice for others

Glossary

cadi a civil judge among the Turks, Arabs, and Persian, usually the judge of a town or village

caravansera a kind of inn where caravans put up, being a large quadrangular building with a spacious court in the middle

chiause chiaus, a Turkish messenger or ambassador

chojaserai chief eunuch in the Mughal seraglio

cimeter scimitar, a short, curved, single-edged sword

cotoual cutwal, the commandant of a fort or simply a superintendent, one in a position of authority

dervise dervish, a Muslim friar or member of a Sufi order dedicated to reach a higher plane of spirituality, who has taken vows of poverty and austere life, sometimes used to refer simply to a priest of Islam

dewan various applications in India. The term can refer to (*a*) the head financial minister or treasurer of a state under Muslim governments (*b*) the prime minister of a native state, or (*c*) in Bengal, a native servant in charge of the affairs of a house of business or a large domestic establishment, a steward

divan a council of state, and in the Ottoman empire, the privy council of the Porte, presided over by the Sultan, or in his absence by the grand vizier

dooly same as a palanquin, a covered chair carried on men's shoulders

durbah durbar, a public audience or levee held by a native Indian prince or Mughal ruler, sometimes used to apply to any Indian court

embarys a mode of covered transport for women in Mughal India

feloucca felucca, a small vessel propelled by oars or sails, or both

ferace feridgi, the long coat, often of calico, worn by Turkish women outside the house

Gentile heathen, or pagan, commonly used to discriminate Hindu populations from Muslim in India

gourze-berdars mace-bearers, from *gurz*, a Persian word signifying a mace or war-club

Grand Signior chief ruler, usually applied to the Ottoman emperor

hanze open seat for travel on an elephant in India

hing the drug asafetida, a concreted resinous gum, with a strong alliaceous odour, procured in central Asia

Glossary

houris   the ever-virginal and ever-willing women promised by Muhammad to his followers in the Muslim paradise. Dark-eyed and dark-haired

janizaries   janissaries, Turkish infantry, constituting the sultan's guard and the main part of the standing army. The body was first organized in the 14th c., and was composed mainly of tributary children of Christians. The term is also used to refer to seraglio guards in Muslim kingdoms in general

kaimacham   kaimakam, an officer or minister of the Ottoman court. In the sultan's absence from Istanbul, a kaimakam would be appointed to rule in his place

kanates/kanats   screens that go round tents in the Mughal camp

karguais   khargahs from the Hindi term for folding tents, some with one, others with two doors

kichery   rice, Indian term from which the British derived the dish 'kedgeree'

manseb-dars   mansabdars, those with a ranking in the Mughal hierarchy, i.e. minor lords

mikdembar   a form of covered transport in India put on top of an elephant to carry a woman in purdah

Mokam   morning meeting attended by the Mughal emperor

Mufti   the official head of religion within the state in the Ottoman empire is known as the 'Grand Mufti'. A Mufti is a Muslim cleric or expert in Islamic law empowered to give rulings on religious matters

nagar-kane   Indian tent holding the *Nakárah khánah*, a monster kettledrum sometimes as tall as four feet played by one man. The tent would hold about twenty pairs of these drums, as well as trumpets, horns, and cymbals

navab/nawab   a Muslim official who acted as a deputy ruler or viceroy of a province or district under the Mughal empire, hence also used to refer to the governor or a town or district, or person of high status

nayb   naib, lieutenant or deputy to the cadi (judge) in a district or town

nilgau   from the Hindu for 'blue cow', a large antelope common over northern India

omrahs   nobility of the class of *amirs* (Muslim princes) in the Mughal court

palakeys   *see* palanquin

palanquin   a covered litter, usually for one person, consisting of a large box with wooden shutters, carried by four or six (rarely two) men by means of poles projecting before and behind

Glossary

pandects a complete body of the laws of any country (originally used for a compendium in fifty books of Roman civil law made by order of the Emperor Justinian in the 6th c.). The term 'pundit' is also used to refer to a learned Hindu, versed in Sanskrit and in the philosophy, religion, and jurisprudence of India

peiche-kanes from the Hindu *Paish-khanah*, advance house or camp, the double set of tents used to progress the Mughal court when travelling in India

pismire ant

purdo or **purda** a curtain or screen, used to refer also to the condition of women in the harem who are kept hidden from sight behind screens

Ragepute Rajput, the warrior caste in Hinduism. From the Sanskrit *raja-putra* for 'son of a king', the term refers to landowners organized in patrilineal clans and located mainly in central and northern India, especially in former Rajputana ('Land of the Rajputs'). The Rajputs regard themselves as descendants or members of the Kshattriya (warrior ruling) class

Rain a variant of the word *Rana*, a Hindu prince

Raja originally the title given in India to a king or prince, conferred as a title of nobility on Hindu, and adopted as the usual designation of Javanese rulers

Sanjapin variant of Sannyasi or Sunnyasin, a Brahman in the fourth stage of his life; a wandering fakir or religious mendicant

serrail seraglio, the Ottoman palace, sometimes used to refer to the women's quarters, the harem, alone. The Turko-Persian word *saray* for palace was here by a false etymology confused with the Italian word *serrare*. to shut up or enclose

souray serai, a long-necked earthenware flagon for water

subaltern a subordinate or inferior

sultana the wife or concubine or mother of a sultan, the sovereign or chief ruler of a Muslim country

tact-raven *Takht-i rawàn*, from *takht*, a seat or throne and *rawàn*, the present participle of the verb *raftan*, to go or proceed. It was carried on men's shoulders and used only by royalty

tary palm wine

tchadoule chaudol, a covered palanquin

Glossary

tchauky-kane *Chauki-khánah*, prison-tent in the Mughal camp. The first part has passed into English as a slang word for prison

timbals instrument like a drum

2. Oriental locations

Agra (in Catrou) city, west-central Uttar Pradesh state, north-central India, on the Yamuna (Jumna) river. Founded by Sikandar Lodi in the early 16th c.

Amasia Amasya il, province of northern Turkey, on the Yesil river. The capital city, Amasya, became a major centre of learning in Anatolia after being incorporated into the Ottoman empire by Sultan Bayezid I (reigned 1389–1402)

Arabia south-western Asia, the Arabian Peninsula, usually divided in 17th-c. accounts into three: desert, Petra, and 'felix' (Arabia the Happy)

Armenia Christian Indo-European region in north-west Asia, from the early 16th c. under Ottoman rule

Babelmandel Bab-el-Mandeb, strait between north-east Arabia and south-west Africa that connects the Red Sea with the Gulf of Aden and the Indian Ocean. The Arabic name means 'gate of tears' because of the perilousness of the strait

Bember Bhimbar, where there were rest-houses built for the camps of the Mughal emperors as they approached Kashmir

Bengal and the **strait of Bengal** region in the north-east of the Indian subcontinent

Candahar/Kandahar city now located in south-central Afghanistan. On main routes via Herat to central Asia, to Kabul, and to India, it was of strategic importance and thus subject to recurrent conquests

Caramania now the area of Lycia in Turkey, previously Anatolia. Under Ottoman control from the late 14th c.

Cathay the name by which North China was known in medieval Europe. The word is derived from Khitay (or Khitan), the name of a semi-nomadic people who left south-eastern Mongolia in the 10th c. to conquer part of Manchuria and northern China, which they held for about 200 years

Chach-limar the Shalimar gardens are to the east of Lahore; covering 17 hectares, they were laid out in 1641 by Shah Jahan

Glossary

Chanbalich variant of the name 'Cambalu' or 'Kambaluk' given by Marco Polo to Kublai Khan's (1215–94) new capital in the Mongolian conquest of China (now known as Beijing)

China in Galland more often used to designate a vast empire extending eastward beyond Persia, rather than the territory now referred to as China

Chitor hill fort capital of Mewar, southern Rajasthan, princely state established in the 8th c. by Sisodia Rajputs (warrior rulers of the historic region of Rajputana)

Circassia stretched from the Sea of Azov to Mingrelia, north-east of the Black Sea and was a tributary of the Ottomans. The term 'Caucasian' derives from this area populated by white peoples and the women of Circassia had a reputation for great beauty

Com Kum, a town north of Ispahan, where Fatima, daughter of the seventh caliph Mousa al Kacim is venerated

Coromandel broad coastal plain in eastern Tamil Nadu state, southern India. Famous for its ancient temples such as Mahabalipuram and Mamallapuram

Danube the second longest river in Europe, which flows through seven countries and the capital cities Vienna, Belgrade, and Budapest

Dely Delhi, city in north-central India, which has served as the capital to a number of powerful empires. Delhi lost importance when the Mughal Emperors Akbar (1556–1605) and Jahangir (1605–27) moved their head-quarters, respectively, to Fatehpur Sikri and Agra, but in 1638 Shah Jahan laid the foundations of the seventh city of Delhi, Shahjahanabad, which has come to be known as Old Delhi

Epirus coastal region of north-western Greece and southern Albania

Erzeron Erzurum, a city in eastern Turkey, capital of Turkish Armenia. On a caravan route from Anatolia to Iran, Erzurum has been a major commercial and military centre since antiquity

Eskerdou Skardu, town in Pakistan in the Karakoram Range. Passes for foot traffic across the mountains led northward from Skardu and Leh and from the Vale of Kashmir into China

Ganges great river of the plains of northern India. The Gangetic Plain, across which it flows, is the centre of the territory of Hindustan and has seen the foundation of the great civilizations of the East from the kingdom of Asoka in the 3rd c. BC, down to the Mughal empire

Glossary

Genna Yamuna, or Jumna, Indian river of Uttar Pradesh, northern India. It passes Delhi and Agra and joins the Ganges near Allahabad

Golconda fortress and ruined city lying west of Hyderabad in north-central Andhra Pradesh state, southern India. From 1512 to 1687 it was the capital of the Qutb Shahi kingdom, one of five Muslim sultanates of the Deccan

Ispahan Isfahan or Esfahan, major city of western Iran. The Safavid emperor, Abbas I (the Great), who reigned 1588–1629, made it his capital in 1598 and built there the remarkable palace of Maydan-e Shah, and the famous mosque, Masjed-e Shah ('Royal Mosque'; now Masjed-e Emam), begun in 1611/12 but not finished until after Abbas's death

Java Indonesian island south-east of Sumatra and Malaysia. The independent Majapahit empire fell to Muslim forces in the early 16 c. Dutch ships first visited Java in 1596, and from the 1670s, the Dutch East India Company began to assert its control over Java's various Muslim kingdoms

Kachemire region of north-western Indian subcontinent. Named after an ascetic, Kashyapa, who, according to myth, reclaimed the land from a vast lake. From the 9th to the 12th c. the region was a centre of Hindu culture. A succession of Hindu dynasties ruled Kashmir until 1346, when it came under Muslim rule

Lahor Lahore was the capital of the Punjab for more than 900 years. The Mughals captured the city in 1524. In the 16th and 17th c., Lahore was often the place of royal residence. The city was under British rule from 1849 to 1947, when the Indian subcontinent gained independence. In 1955 Lahore was selected as the capital of the newly created province of West Pakistan. After West Pakistan was divided into four provinces in 1970, Lahore became the capital of the new Punjab province

Liperda an unidentified location in Persia. Possibly the port of Lingeh (Bandar-i-Lingeh) on the south-eastern coast of Iran not far from Bandar Abbas, an important port for Euro-Iranian trade in the 17th and 18th c.

Maslipatam Masulipatam, an eastern Andhra Pradesh state famous for carpet-weaving, the first British trading settlement on the Bay of Bengal (1611)

Moka Al-mukha, Mokha, a town in south-western Yemen on the Red Sea. Founded in the 14th c., from the 15th c. its major export was coffee to Europe and the Middle East. The Ottoman's surrendered Mocha to the Yemeni imam (leader) Muhammad al-Mu'ayyad I in 1636.

Glossary

Moldavia   in the north-eastern corner of the Balkan region, the Moldavian principality was taken by the Turks in the late 15th c. and organized into two districts of the Ottoman empire

Muscovy   grand principality of Moscow dating from the second half of the 13th c. The princes of Muscovy collected the Russian tribute for the Tartar Khan which gave them economic power in the region. By the late 15th c., the prince of Muscovy was in effect the ruler of Russia

Nug   unidentified Indian river near Chitor

Oguzio   section of the Mediterranean coast occupied by the Oghouz Turks, original founders of the Ottoman empire

Pegu   port city, southern Myanmar (Burma), on the Pegu river, 57 miles north-east of Yangôn (Rangoon)

Pekin   Peking, now known as Beijing, capital of China and home of the forbidden city of the Chinese emperors

Penje-ab   the Punjab, a large alluvial plain in north-western India. It is bounded by the Yamuna river on the east, the Shiwalik hills on the north, the arid zone of Rajasthan on the south, and the Ravi and Sutlej rivers on the north-west and south-west, respectively. Of strategic importance as it is now situated on the India/Pakistan border

Pera   on the other side of the Bosphorus from the walled city of Istanbul, this is the area where ambassadors and other foreign nationals not citizens of Turkey lived

Persia   kingdom of south-west Asia, now Iran, sometimes used to refer to the whole of the Iranian plateau

Port   the government of the Ottoman empire. The name is a French translation of Turkish *Bâbiâli* ('High Gate', or 'Gate of the Eminent'), which was the official name of the gate giving access to the buildings of the principal state departments in Istanbul

St Helena   island in the South Atlantic ocean

Samarcande   Samarkand, now a city in Uzbekistan

Scymdi   probably Sind, where the mouth of the Indus is situated

Serendib   Sri Lanka

Sewalic   Siwalik hills, sub-Himalayan range which extends for more than 1,000 miles from the Tista river, Sikkim (India), through Nepal, across north-western India, and into northern Pakistan

Glossary

Siberian Tartary   vast, underpopulated region in the north-east of Eurasia. Siberia takes its name from the Tatar khanate of Sibir ('sleeping land'), which was conquered in 1583 by a brigand named Yermak. Russian cossacks took control of the region in the mid-17th c. Mongol peoples maintained separate territories in the east and west

Surat   city in Gujurat, west-central India. The British established their first trading post here in 1612. Until the late 18th c. it was the emporium of India. Surat exported cloth and gold and manufactured textiles as well as being a centre for shipbuilding

Tartary, or **Great Tartary**   vaguely defined territory in central Asia

Tauris   Tabriz, the fourth largest city in Iran (Persia), in the extreme north-west of the country, now the capital of the Iranian province of Azerbaijan

Tchenau   the Chináb, nearly 72 miles from Lahore by Bernier's route

Tigris   Asian river flowing south-eastward from what is now Turkey for 1,180 miles towards the Persian gulf; it meets, at the Shatt al-Arab, with the Euphrates

Usbeck   Uzbek, central Asian region now known as Uzbekistan. Its people were the result of a mixing of Iranian settled populations with nomadic Mongols or Turkic tribes that invaded the region between the 11th and 15th c.